Lecture Notes in Computer Science 1826

Edited by G. Goos, J. Hartmanis and J. van Leeuwen

Springer
Berlin
Heidelberg
New York
Barcelona
Hong Kong
London
Milan
Paris
Singapore
Tokyo

Walter Cazzola Robert J. Stroud
Francesco Tisato (Eds.)

Reflection
and Software Engineering

Springer

Series Editors

Gerhard Goos, Karlsruhe University, Germany
Juris Hartmanis, Cornell University, NY, USA
Jan van Leeuwen, Utrecht University, The Netherlands

Volume Editors

Walter Cazzola
Università degli Studi di Milano Bicocca
Dipartimento di Informatica, Sistemistica e Comunicazione
and
Università di Genova - DISI
Via Dodecaneso 35, 16146 Genova, Italy
E-mail: cazzola@disi.unige.it

Robert J. Stroud
University of Newcastle upon Tyne, Department of Computer Science
Newcastle upon Tyne NE1 7RU, UK
E-mail: R.J.Stroud@ncl.ac.uk

Francesco Tisato
Università degli Studi di Milano Bicocca
Dipartimento di Informatica, Sistemistica e Comunicazione
Via Bicocca degli Arcimboldi 8, 20126 Milano, Italy
E-mail: tisato@disco.unimib.it

Cataloging-in-Publication Data applied for

Die Deutsche Bibliothek - CIP-Einheitsaufnahme

Reflection and software engineering / Walter Cazzola ... (ed.). -
Berlin ; Heidelberg ; New York ; Barcelona ; Hong Kong ; London ;
Milan ; Paris ; Singapore ; Tokyo : Springer, 2000
  (Lecture notes in computer science ; Vol. 1826)
  ISBN 3-540-67761-5

CR Subject Classification (1998): D.2, D.1.5, F.3, D.3

ISSN 0302-9743
ISBN 3-540-67761-5 Springer-Verlag Berlin Heidelberg New York

Springer-Verlag is a company in the BertelsmannSpringer publishing group.
© Springer-Verlag Berlin Heidelberg 2000
Printed in Germany

Typesetting: Camera-ready by author, data conversion by PTP-Berlin, Stefan Sossna
Printed on acid-free paper   SPIN: 10721153   06/3142   5 4 3 2 1 0

Preface

This volume represents a first attempt to bring together ideas from two previously unrelated research areas, namely *Software Engineering* and *Computational Reflection*, and to evaluate the benefits that each can bring to the other.

Computational reflection, or for short reflection, is quite a young discipline that is steadily attracting attention within the community of object-oriented researchers and practitioners. The properties of transparency, separation of concerns, and extensibility supported by reflection have largely been accepted as useful for software development and design. Reflective features have been included in successful software development technologies such as the Java™ language. Reflection has proved to be useful in some of the most challenging areas of software engineering, including component-based software development, as demonstrated by extensive use of the reflective concept of introspection in the Enterprise JavaBeans™ component technology. Nevertheless, there are still cognitive barriers separating reflection from the discipline of software engineering, and, more specifically, object-oriented reflection from object-oriented software engineering. Only a few authors have begun to explore the opportunities offered by the inter-disciplinary application of concepts from reflection and software engineering, that is, from the novel research area of reflective software engineering.

It is our belief that current trends in ongoing research in object-oriented reflection and software engineering clearly indicate that an inter-disciplinary approach would be of utmost relevance for both. The overall goal of this volume is to support the circulation of ideas between these disciplines. Several interactions can be expected to take place between software engineering and object-oriented reflection, some of which we cannot even foresee. Both the application of reflective techniques and concepts to software engineering and, vice versa, the application to object-oriented reflection of software engineering techniques, methodologies, and concepts, are likely to support improvement and deeper understanding of these areas.

Software engineering may benefit from a cross-fertilization with object-oriented reflection in several ways. Reflective features such as transparency, separation of concerns, and extensibility are likely to be of increasing relevance in the modern software engineering scenario, where the trend is towards systems that exhibit sophisticated functional and non-functional requirements; that are built from independently developed and evolved COTS components; that support plug-and-play, end-user directed reconfigurability; that make extensive use of networking and internetworking; that can be automatically upgraded through the Internet; that are open; and so on. Several of these issues highlight the need for a system to manage itself to some extent, to inspect components interfaces dynamically, to augment its application-specific functionality with additional properties, and so on. From a pragmatic point of view, several object-oriented reflection techniques and technologies lend themselves to be employed in addressing these issues. On a more conceptual level, several key object-oriented reflection principles could play an interesting role as general software design principles. Even more fundamentally, object-oriented reflection may provide a cleaner conceptual framework than that underlying the rather ad-hoc solutions embedded in most commercial platforms and technologies, including component-based software development technologies, system management technologies, and so on. The transparent nature of reflection makes it well suited to address problems such as evolution of legacy systems, customizable software, product families, and more. The scope of application of object-oriented reflection concepts in software engineering conceptually spans activities related to all the phases of the software life-cycle, from analysis and architectural design to development, reuse, maintenance, and evolution.

The reverse also holds. In the last two decades, object-oriented reflection has generated a rich offspring in terms of reflective programming languages and reflective systems. The background of most researchers in the field is in disciplines that were traditionally insulated from software engineering (e.g., artificial intelligence). It is thus likely that several applications of software design and development concepts, principles, techniques, and methodologies from software engineering to object-oriented reflection are still to be clearly detected and investigated.

It should be highlighted that the purpose of supporting a dialogue among software engineering and object-oriented reflection researchers and practitioners is more than simply stimulating a (useful) cross-discipline application of established results. We believe that both disciplines have reached a point where each needs concepts from the other in order to achieve significant improvements in several areas.

During OOPSLA 99, the editors of this volume organized and held a workshop (OORaSE 99 - 1st OOPSLA Workshop on Reflection and Software Engineering) with the aim of focusing interest on this emerging area and providing a meeting-point for researchers working on ideas straddling the research topics. The event proved a success both for the interest aroused and for the quality of the contributions presented. This volume is a natural follow-up to the workshop. It contains the best contributions presented at the workshop, improved both by the exchange of opinions that the authors had with the others attendees, and by the advice given to them by the reviewers of the volume. The volume also contains some contributions from experts in this field of research.

We would like to thank all the researchers who submitted papers to our workshop, both for their interest in our proposal and for their eﬀorts in the emerging area of re ection and software engineering. We would also like to thank the members of our program committee:

Shigeru Chiba,   University of Tsukuba, Japan
Stéphane Ducasse, University of Geneva, Switzerland
Serge Demeyer,   University of Berne, Switzerland
                    University of Antwerp, Belgium
John Lamping,   Xerox Parc, USA
Satoshi Matsuoka, Tokyo Institute of Technology, Japan
Dave Thomas,   Founder OTI Inc. and President, Bedarra Corp., Canada

and the external reviewers:

Franz Achermann   University of Geneva, Switzerland
Massimo Ancona   University of Genoa, Italy
Gregor Kiczales   Xerox Parc, USA
Cristina Videira Lopes Xerox Parc, USA

who helped us in judging and selecting the submitted works for presentation at the workshop and then helped to improve the best papers in order for them to be published in this book. We would also like to thank the invited authors who accepted our invitation to contribute to this volume, and last but not least the Department of Informatics, Systems and Communication of the University of Milano Bicocca for its ﬁnancial support.

April   W. Cazzola, R. J. Stroud, and F. Tisato

Contents

Engineering Java-Based Reflective Languages

Dynamic Recon guration through Reflection

Shifting Up Reflection from the Implementation to the Analysis Level

Walter Cazzola, Andrea Sosio, and Francesco Tisato

DISCo - Department of Informatics, Systems, and Communication,
University of Milano Bicocca, Milano, Italy
cazzola | sosio | tisato @disco.unimib.it

Abstract Traditional methods for object-oriented analysis and modeling focus on the functional speci cation of software systems, i.e., application domain modeling. Non-functional requirements such as fault-
tolerance, distribution, integration with legacy systems, and so on, have
no clear collocation within the analysis process, since they are related
to the architecture and workings of the system itself rather than the application domain. They are thus addressed in the system's design, based
on the partitioning of the system's functionality into classes resulting
from analysis. As a consequence, the *smooth transition from analysis
to design* that is usually celebrated as one of the main advantages of
the object-oriented paradigm does not actually hold for what concerns
non-functional issues. A side e ect is that functional and non-functional
concerns tend to be mixed at the implementation level. We argue that
the reflective approach whereby non-functional properties are ascribed to
a meta-level of the software system may be extended back to analysis.
Adopting a reflective approach in object-oriented analysis may support
the precise speci cation of non-functional requirements in analysis and,
if used in conjunction with a reflective approach to design, recover the
smooth transition from analysis to design in the case of non-functional
system's properties.

1 Introduction

Traditional methods for object-oriented analysis and modeling focus on the
functional speci2cation of software systems. The relevant concepts from the
application domain are modeled using concepts (classes, object, operation, attributes, associations between classes, and so on) whose scope hardly includes
non-functional requirements such as fault-tolerance, distribution, performance,
persistence, security, and so on. These are not related to properties of the entities in the *real world*, but rather to *properties of the software objects that
represent those entities.* Such non-functional requirements play a major role in
the contract between customer and developer, and are usually included in analysis documents, maybe in the form of labels or *stereotypes* attached to analysis
classes. Nevertheless, their treatment lacks a clear collocation in traditional object oriented processes. As a consequence, they tend to be less precisely speci2ed

W. Cazzola et al. (Eds.): Reflection and Software Engineering, LNCS 1826, pp. 1 20, 2000.
© Springer-Verlag Berlin Heidelberg 2000

in analysis, and they do not bene2t from the *smooth transition from analysis to design* which is usually regarded as one of the main advantages of the object oriented paradigm. As a consequence, non-functional requirements are only actually dealt with in the design phase. In traditional object-oriented methods, this phase re2nes the (functional) model produced during analysis. Since non-functional issues have no separate collocation in the decomposition produced by analysis, they tend to be addressed sparsely within the classes resulting from analysis and their re2nements. This is not satisfactory if one considers that non-functional requirements are often largely (if not completely) orthogonal to functional ones. It also has the consequence, that code related to non-functional issues is often intertwined with "functional" code, which makes it hard to later modify or adjust the non-functional properties of a system based on changed requirements, versions, and so on.

The main purpose of this paper is that of illustrating in some details the problem described above and proposing a solution. We argue that a *reflective* approach is well suited to address this problem. Re ection is pivoted on the idea of decomposing a system into a base-level and one or more meta-levels that perform computation *on the computation of the lower levels.* Thus, the domain of the meta-level is the base-level, just like the domain of the base-level is the application domain itself. Non-functional requirements, which relate to the workings of the system rather than the application domain, lend themselves to be described as *functional requirements of the meta-level.* In traditional literature on re ection, this approach is only adopted as a *design* or *implementation* solution. We believe that the same ideas can be usefully "shifted up" to the analysis stage. Just as the meta-level may be programmed in the same paradigm (and even language) of the base-level, traditional OO concepts, notations, meta-models, methods, and methodologies used for conventional OO analysis can be employed in the analysis of non-functional properties once these are recast as computation on computation. Finally, as a last advantage, if one also adopts a *reflective approach to design,* the smooth transition from analysis to design is recovered.

Although re ection has gained increasing attention within the last decade, and is now recognized as a relevant and useful feature in OO languages and programming systems, there is still a lack of research e2orts devoted to the de2nition of an OO *process* for re ective systems. As this paper proposes an integrated re ective approach to analysis and design, it can also be regarded as an attempt to shed some light on what such a process might look like.

The outline of the paper is as follows. Section 2 discusses the problems encountered in traditional object oriented analysis for what concerns the treatment of non-functional requirements. Section 3 lists some major concepts from the discipline of (OO) re ection, which provide a basis for solving those problems. Section 4 illustrates our proposal of a *reflective object-oriented analysis,* discussing how non-functional requirements 2t into such an approach to OO analysis. Section 5 brie y points at related works in the discipline of re ection, and section 6 draws some conclusions.

2 Non-functional Requirements and Traditional Object-Oriented Analysis

The fundamental step in traditional OO analysis is related to the modeling of the *application domain*, and results in the de2nition of the collection (hierarchy) of classes corresponding to the relevant concepts in the domain and of the relationships (associations) between those classes. Following a traditional, consolidated style of software engineering, the authors of those methods insist that implementation details (*how*) should be (as systematically as possible) ignored in analysis (which relates to *what* the system does). Once classes for the relevant entities in the domain are found, as well as their general behavior and relationships, the design begins based on the classes found in the analysis, that are re2ned and progressively enriched with details about *how* they are going to meet their spec-i2cation. In this process, new classes may be added (sometimes referred to as *architectural* as opposed to *application* or *business* classes) whose purpose is that of providing a concrete infrastructure for the analysis classes to work. One of the major bene2ts coming from object-orientation is the smooth transition from analysis to design; the classes that are found in the analysis phase often preserve their original interfaces and overall interrelationships when they are re2ned into more concrete design classes, although several details are usually added.

This general idea is of course valuable and could hardly be criticized *per se*. Nevertheless, we believe that there is a missing piece, namely, the treatment of non-functional requirements has no clear collocation in the process outlined above. While it is sensible to postpone the treatment of *how issues* such as the choice of algorithms and data structures, the same does not hold for many non-functional requirements. Issues related to fault-tolerance, distribution, performance, persistence, integration with legacy or pre-existing systems, networking, authentication and security, and so on, may be as relevant to the customer as functional ones. (Also relevant may be non-functional requirements on the process, such as limitations to budget or time to market, development resources, or the need to reuse COTS components, although we will not discuss this topic in this paper). These requirements are not captured in analysis if this is conceived as domain modeling alone, since non-functional requirements tend to be express-ible only in terms of properties of the *system* rather than real-world entities. Note that many traditional methods explicitly prescribe that, after a 2rst description of the system, the analyst should prune all those elements of the model that are extraneous to the real world [23]; this prescription often leads to suppressing non-functional requirements in analysis. Some object-oriented processes have also been proposed where analysis explicitly addresses some major system-related issues; an example is the *inception* phase of the Rational Object Process, where the overall architecture of a system is de2ned. Nevertheless, while object-oriented concepts obviously apply well to the description of a system s functionality, we lack a similar vocabulary of concepts for most non-functional issues (i.e., issues about the system s workings). In other words, the problem with non-functional requirements is that they are not easily captured by traditional OO concepts as employed by traditional OO modeling notations and meta-models.

To illustrate the problem, we shall consider a classical banking system example (of course narrowing our discussion to a very small subset of requirements). We shall refer to UML [3] as a modeling notation, and to a typical object-oriented process employing this notation. (Of course, several di2erent processes have been proposed in the literature; nevertheless, they are all similar with respect to how they deal with non-functional requirements).

The 2rst stage of the process is requirement analysis, which in UML is done with use cases describing the actors interacting with the system and typical uses of the system. For a banking system, for example, the basic actor is the customer, and use cases include obtaining an account and deposits/withdrawals. Use cases represent the primary contract between the software purchaser and developer. They are not related to the system s structure, and do not include detailed information on the application domain, although they are intended to drive, to a great extent, the subsequent stages of the process.

Fig. 1 describes some simple use cases for a banking system.

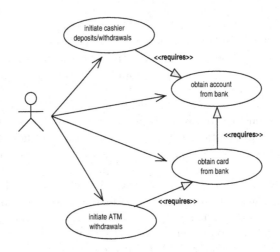

Fig. 1. Bank use case.

Requirement analysis is followed by domain analysis (sometimes simply referred to as *analysis*), where the basic real-world entities involved in the system are modeled within one or more classes and related diagrams. This activity is also referred to as *domain modeling*. Fig. 2 describes a class diagram for the banking system.

The classes provided in this diagram should provide the functionality described by use cases, although use-cases are at a higher abstraction level, i.e., a single use case may involve a complex interaction pattern involving a possibly large collection of objects. Sequence diagrams and other dynamic diagrams can aid in describing the bundle of interactions that correspond to a use case. In this case, obtaining an account is achieved via the `create_account` operation of class

`Bank`, and interactions with an ATM are modeled by the operations to prepare, cancel, or commit a transaction (we do not consider cashier transactions).

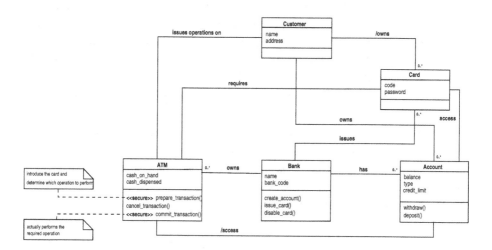

Fig. 2. Bank class diagram.

In domain modeling, non-functional issues have no clear collocation. Consider the problem of specifying that operations on the ATM should be secure. While saying that money may be drawn from a bank account may result, say, in the de2nition of a `withdraw` operation in class `Account`, saying that an operation is secure has no obvious counterpart in traditional object oriented concepts. Nonetheless, this obviously *is* a requirement (and a fundamental one), so that it should clearly mentioned *before* design. Current practice in UML modeling typically approaches this problem using free text speci2cations or stereotypes. Stereotypes are adopted in UML as a mechanism to extend the expressive power of the basic notation with new semantic concepts. In Fig. 2, the operations `prepare_transaction` and `commit_transaction` of the ATM are marked as «secure». Unfortunately, unless the concept of security is elsewhere formally speci2ed, a «secure» stereotype is hardly more than an informal, and vague, reminder for the designer/implementor. This non-precise speci2cation of (perhaps essential) system features is of course a non ideal situation, since, for example, it reduces the e2ectiveness of requirements analysis as a contract between customer and developer. Note that the primary role ascribed to use cases in UML, and the fact that use cases do not capture non-functional issues, may contribute to this situation.

Related problems occur in the *transition from analysis to design*. Functional requirements are relatively easily translated into design elements (concrete classes, methods, attributes); this is usually regarded as one of the major (if not the main) bene2t of the object-oriented paradigm itself. The classes that were found during analysis are usually kept through to the design stage. They

are possibly enriched with new operations and attributes, and their workings
may be augmented by "helper" or "ancillary" classes. Non-functional issues, of
course, are not tackled as easily. Of course, there is no unique and easy way
to map stereotypes (which, by de2nition, could have any meaning) or free text
notes into design. In some cases stereotypes are used to represent non-functional
properties which are well-known and have a *standard* design and implementation counterpart. This is the case of the «persistent» stereotype. In a typical
design, a Persistent_Object class is introduced, providing operations to store
an object, retrieve it from 2le, and so on. All classes that were labeled with the
«persistent» stereotype are then connected to the Persistent_Object via inheritance, so that their instances are now persistent objects, among other things.
Nevertheless, not all non-functional issues are as standard and well-known. The
fact that non-functional properties are tackled *based on the functional partitioning that resulted from analysis* may lead to bad design especially for those
non-functional requirements that are not naturally related to any speci2c object,
but rather require a system-wide infrastructure.

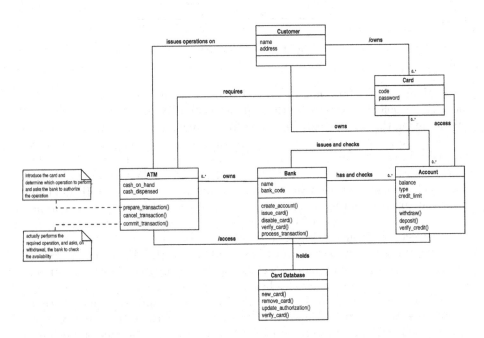

Fig. 3. Re ned bank class diagram.

A typical outcome of this state of facts is that code related to non-functional
issues is often intertwined with *functional* code in the implemented system, thus
reducing modi2ability and reusability. Consider the case of ATM transactions.
Functionally, an ATM transaction is just a movement of money. Nevertheless, it
requires a complex non-functional infrastructure including concurrency control,

fault-tolerance support, authentication, and possibly more. In a traditional OO process, the designer may receive, as an outcome of analysis, a class ATM providing one or more operations labeled by stereotypes such as «atomic», «secure», «reliable», and so on. The designer will probably cope with these additional properties re2ning the ATM operations into a very complex activities, including security checking and so on, and perhaps described by a state diagram with dozens of states and transitions. The resulting implementation is necessarily one where the basic semantics of withdraw is obscured and dispersed in the midst of a plethora of additional code that has little to do with the movement of money *per se*, thus making the ATM object harder to reuse and modify. The e2ects of this problem often span multiple classes. Fig. 3 describes an arrangement for dealing with security. An additional Card Database class has been added, managing a database of existing cards and their passwords. Whenever the bank issues a new card, it should notify this to the Card Database (via update_authorization); the same occurs, conversely, when a card expires. Also, each transaction should involve a call to an operation of Card Database (say, verify_card) to check whether the authorization may be granted. In the example, the ATM invokes the verify_card of Bank, which in turn will include a call to the Card Database to check the card against the authentication information held in the database itself.

Changes in the analysis documents (e.g., if the customer asks for a higher level of security, e.g., security in network communication between ATMs and banks) provide no hint as to how the system design and implementation should be changed (e.g., changes cannot be traced easily from analysis onto design and implementation). The lack of traceability of non-functional issues from analysis to design is a relevant problem as it is often the case that non-functional properties of a system should be tuned for di2erent versions, products in product families, ports, and so on.

As a 2nal note, we would like to note that many of the considerations above also apply for issues which are not usually considered as non-functional (the boundary between functional and non-functional is of course quite blurred). For example, the problem of blocking withdrawals from an account when the credit limit is reached could be cleanly dealt with in much the same way as authentication, as we shall see below.

3 Object Oriented Reflection

3.1 Basic Concepts

Computational re ection (or *reflection* for short) is de2ned as the activity performed by an agent when doing computations about itself [19]. The concept applies quite naturally to the OOP paradigm [9,11,19]. Just as objects in conventional OOP are representations of *real world* entities, they can themselves be represented by other objects, usually referred to as *meta-objects*, whose computation is intended to observe and modify their *referents* (the objects they represent). Meta-computation is often performed by meta-objects by *trapping* the normal computation of their referents; in other words, an action of the referent is trapped by the meta-object, which performs a meta-computation either substituting or encapsulating the referent s actions. Of course, meta-objects themselves can be represented, i.e., they may be the referents of meta-meta-objects, and so on. A re ective system is thus structured in multiple levels, constituting a *reflective tower*. The objects in the base level are termed *base-objects* and perform computation on the entities of the application domain. The objects in the other levels (termed *meta-levels*) perform computation on the objects residing in the lower levels.

There is no need for the association between base-objects and meta-objects to be 1-to-1: several meta-objects may share a single referent, and a single meta-object may have multiple referents. The interface between adjacent levels in the re ective tower is usually termed a *meta-object protocol* (MOP) [16]. Albeit several distinct re ection models have been proposed in the literature (e.g., where meta-objects are coincident with classes, or instances of a special class `MetaObject`, and so on), such a distinction is not relevant for this discussion and will be omitted.

In all re ective models and MOPs, an essential concept is that of *rei cation*. In order to compute on the lower levels computation, each level maintains a set of data structures representing (or, in re ection parlance, a *rei cation of*) such computation. Of course, the aspects of the lower levels system that are rei2ed depend on the re ective model (e.g., structure, state and behavior, communication). In any case, the data structure comprising a rei2cation are *causally connected* to the aspect(s) of the system being rei2ed; that is, any change to those aspects re ects in the rei2cation, and vice versa. It is a duty of the re ective framework to preserve the causal connection link between the levels (depending on the re ective model, this infrastructure may operate at compile- or at run-time): the designers and programmers of meta-objects are insulated from the details of how causal connection is achieved. Meta-objects can be programmed in exactly the same programming paradigm as conventional computation. It is in fact possible, and most usual, that all levels of the re ective tower be programmed in the same *programming language*. The fact that all the levels of the tower be implemented in a single language quali2es, for some authors, as one of the characterizing features of re ection proper [11].

Another key feature of all re ective models is that of *transparency* [24]. In the context of re ection, this term is used to indicate that the objects in each level are completely *unaware* of the presence and workings of those in the levels above. In other words, each meta-level is added to the base-level without modifying the referent level itself. The virtual machine of the re ective language, in other words, enforces causal connection between a meta-level and its referent level in a way that is transparent *both* to the programmer of the meta-level and to the programmer of the referent level.

3.2   Re ection and Non-functional Properties

An application of re ection, supported by the feature of *transparency*, is the (non-intrusive) *evolution* of a system: the behavior or structure of the objects in a system can be modi2ed, enriched, and/or substituted without modifying the original system s code. In principle, this may have interesting applications to the evolution of non-stopping systems or systems that are only available in black-box form. Depending on the speci2c support provided by the re ective language virtual machine, the evolution of a system through the addition of a meta-level may require recompilation or maybe done dynamically.

Another well-known application, which is the one that will be considered in this paper, is that of adopting a re ective approach to separate functional and (possibly several distinct) non-functional features in the *design* of a system (the issue of analysis will be considered in a later section). In a typical approach, the base-level objects may be entrusted to meet the application s functional requirements, while meta-levels augment the base-level functionality ensuring non-functional properties (e.g., fault tolerance, persistence, distribution, and so on). With reference to this partitioning of a system, in the following we will sometimes refer to the base-level objects as *functional objects* and to meta-level objects as *non-functional objects*. While functional objects model entities in the real world (such as `Account`), non-functional objects model properties of functional objects (to re ect this, non-functional classes may have names that correspond to properties, e.g., `Fault_Tolerant_Object`).

There are several reasons why a design could bene2t from such an approach. Of course, separation of concerns (in general, hence also in this case) enhances the system s modi2ability. Depending on whether a required modi2cation of the system involves functional or non-functional properties, functional objects alone or non-functional objects alone may be modi2ed. If the collection of data comprising an account changes, for example, the (functional) class `Account` will be modi2ed; if, say, a higher level of fault-tolerance is required, the (non-functional) class `Fault_Tolerant_Object` will be changed.

This approach also enhances reusability in two ways: 2rst, the very same functional object (e.g., a `Account` object) can be reused with or without the additional properties implemented by its associated meta-objects, depending on context. Any additional feature of an object (e.g., fault-tolerance, the capability to migrate across platforms, persistence, and so on) has an associated overhead. In a re ective approach, all such features are not hardwired into the code of the object itself but implemented by separated meta-objects; whenever the additional features are not required, the corresponding meta-objects are simply not instantiated. Note that there is a di2erence between the re ective approach to persistence and that mentioned in the previous section. In the re ective approach a functional object becomes persistent because there is a meta-object that *transparently* modi2es its behavior (e.g., intercepts its constructor/destructor and complements them as to load/store an image from/to 2le). On the other hand, in the non-re ective approach the non-functional object inherits methods related to persistency which appear in *its own* interface, with the same status of methods such as `withdraw` or `deposit`. These methods must be invoked (probably by the object itself) if the object is to be made persistent. The result is that, even if inheritance may promise some form of separation of concerns, there will necessarily be some intertwining of functional and non-functional code. For example, the reverse operation (giving up the persistency of the `Account` by suppressing the inheritance relation to `Persistent_Object`) is not usually possible. As a second form of reuse, many non-functional properties lend themselves to be implemented in a way that is essentially independent of the speci2c class of objects for which they are implemented. As an example, support for persistence is usually independent of the speci2c type of object being made persistent, as demonstrated by the adoption of `persistent` classes in Java and other mainstream OO programming languages. In our opinion, this is likely to hold for several typical non-functional properties; some examples are provided by the works on re ective approaches to fault-tolerance [1,10], persistence [17], atomicity [26], and authentication [2,22,25]. Based on this fact, it is reasonable to expect that the same meta-object can be reused to attach the same non-functional property to di2erent functional objects.

In this paper, we are interested in considering whether the idea of computation about computation can be a convenient point of view from which to tackle the analysis of a system s non-functional properties. As stated above, such properties can usually be described as properties of the objects comprising the system rather than real-world entities. It thus seems reasonable to expect that, just as we model properties of entities in the real-world by conventional objects, we could model properties of objects themselves by meta-objects. In a re ective system designed along the lines described above, non-functional properties of the system are actually treated as functionality of the meta-level, whose domain is the software system. This homogeneity of design would yield several bene2ts if *shifted up* to analysis. This is the subject of the following section.

4   Shifting Up Reflection to Analysis

4.1   General Concepts

Two main points from the considerations of the previous section can be highlighted:

1. the property of *transparency* of re ection allows for functional and non-functional concerns to be clearly separated in the design of a system, being respectively entrusted to the base-level and to the meta-levels;
2. the concept of *rei cation*, and the transparent application of causal connection by the virtual machine of a re ective programming language, allows for meta-levels to be programmed in the same paradigm as the base-level.

Based on these two points we envisioned a novel approach to the treatment of non-functional properties in OO analysis. As we discussed in section 2, non-functional properties have no clear collocation in traditional OO analysis because they have no counterpart in the vocabulary of OO concepts. Fault-tolerance cannot be represented as a class, an object, an operation, an attribute, an association between classes, and so on. Nevertheless, in a re ective approach, those non-functional properties are represented by meta-objects. Meta-objects are objects themselves, and lend themselves to be described in OO terms. The transition to the *meta*, in a sense, transforms something that is *about* an object (a property of an object) *into an object itself*; it *rei es* a property. As a consequence of this transformation, object properties themselves are absorbed into the scope of notations and meta-models for OO modeling and hence become natural subjects for OO analysis. This can be further illustrated by the following parallelism. Just like the concept of rei2cation allows for meta-levels (that implement *computation on computation*) to be programmed in the same language as used for the base-level (that implements *computation on the domain*), so it allows for the computation performed by the meta-level to be analyzed and modeled using the same concepts and techniques that are used to analyze and model the computation in the base level. When applied to base-level objects, these concepts are used to described properties of the real-world entities that those objects model (e.g., operations model the dynamics of real-world objects, such as drawing money from a bank account). When applied to meta-level objects, the same concepts model properties of the *software objects that represent real-world entities within the system* (e.g., operations model the dynamics of software objects, such as their ability to be saved onto, or restored from, 2les). This leads us to the main idea presented in this paper.

4.2   Re ective Object-Oriented Analysis

We argue that the considerations made insofar suggest a novel approach to OO analysis, that we shall term *reflective object-oriented analysis* (ROOA). In ROOA, the requirements of the system are partitioned, during the analysis phase, into concepts related to the domain and concepts related to the software system operating in that domain (i.e., into functional and non-functional). The concepts related to the software system may, themselves, be partitioned according to the properties they deal with (fault-tolerance, persistence, distribution, reliability, and so on). Observe that this partitioning is orthogonal to the traditional partitioning of the functional requirements of a system, namely that guided by OO concepts applied to the application domain. It is then natural to speak of additional "levels" of speci2cation, which complement the traditional (functional) level. Note that we are not proposing a *method*; it is not our assumption, as for now, that this partitioning into levels be a step that must be taken *before* or *after* traditional analysis. Our perception is simply that such a partitioning should *complement* the traditional functional partitioning as assumed, explicitly or implicitly, by current OO methods. Let us consider the banking system again. The ROOA approach may a2ect the very 2rst stage of the process, i.e., the de2nition of use cases. Non-functional or re ective use cases appear whenever there is some requirement which involves an actor performing an operation that relates to the system rather than the application domain. An example is a user con2guring or recon2guring the system, or adding an ATM.

ROOA anyway mostly a2ects class diagrams. These are also separated according to the principle stated above (analysis of the domain vs. analysis of the system). In doing this, we rely on the concept of meta-objects, although with that we simply refer to an object that *models a property of another object*. While we obviously refer to the same concept as found in re ection, please note that in this discipline the term is used in a design/implementation context and not an analysis context. Meta-objects as introduced in this paper may well be implemented with conventional (non-re ective) means. A meta-object provides a model of a software entity, just like an object is a model of a real-world entity. Of course, just as conventional objects only model some aspects of real-world entities (those that are relevant to the system s functionality), in the same way ROOA meta-objects model just some speci2c aspect of software entities (e.g., persistence, fault-tolerance, and so on). As for traditional use cases and class diagrams, non-functional use cases should be made to correspond to interactions of the external actors with meta-objects. As in re ection, we shall consider meta-objects as comprising a di2erent level of the system, which is largely independent of the base-level where conventional objects reside. We also allow for several independently speci2ed meta-levels to coexist, each describing some particular aspect of the functional objects properties.

Each system of this partitioning can be analyzed using standard OO analysis techniques, and speci2ed within a traditional OO meta-model (e.g., the UML meta-model). All the concepts from the standard OO vocabulary can be used when modeling meta-levels (class, inheritance, association, attribute, operation, and so on), albeit, as mentioned in the previous subsection, these levels are about properties of the system rather than the domain. Of course, the workings and semantics of the link that binds the meta-level(s) in the analysis diagrams to the analysis base should be de2ned, i.e., the problem should be solved of how the UML meta-model (or a similar model) can be enriched with a concept corresponding, in abstract terms, to the causal connection relationship between base- and meta-level objects in re ective designs and systems. Given the variety of re ective models, this topic is by itself worth a thorough research. In order to illustrate more of our approach and its consequences, in the next section we shall make a (somewhat simplistic) proposal about how this can done.

4.3   Causal Connection in Analysis

As suggested above, we model non-functional properties in terms of computation performed by meta-objects *on the computation of functional ones*. In general, non-functional objects may perform computation on the *state* and/or the *behavior* of base-level objects. In the following, we will adopt a simple convention, and use the same name for a base-level object and the meta-object that models its non-functional properties. In describing how meta-objects may interact with base-level objects, we will of course rely on the results from re ection, although let us note again that we are not necessarily considering a re ective implementation.

State is of course represented by attributes of objects. Meta-objects hence should be entrusted to observe and modify the attributes of (base-level) objects. Thus, the meta-model should be extended to include the possibility of specifying which attributes of an object are observed by the meta-object. For the purpose of

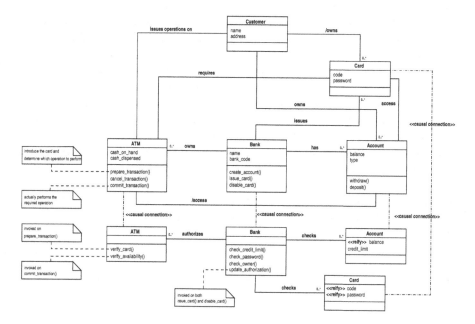

Fig. 4. Reflective bank class diagram.

this paper, we shall rely on name-matching, i.e., in the examples that follow the meta-object s attribute x will be intended to be an image of the corresponding attribute x in the referent. Also, we shall mark the rei2cation (i.e., the copy of the attribute held by the meta-object) with stereotype «reify». Of course, a more exible mechanism should be useful in practice, although we won t cover the syntactical problem of how to describe correspondences between attributes in di2erent levels.

Behavior in object systems is usually expressed in terms of invocations of operations (methods). Meta-objects provide operations that integrate and augment those of their functional counterparts by wrapping (i.e., either enriching or substituting) them. In our examples, we shall provide an external speci2cation of mappings between methods using text notes. These compensating operations are assumed to be invoked whenever the referent s operations are invoked, and will usually perform some activity before and/or after invoking the referent s method. That outline above is in fact the general strategy adopted in current re ective languages to augment the base-level computation. Note that there are open problems in the discipline of re ection about the workings of both state and behavior observation and modi2cation (e.g., the fact that re ection breaks encapsulation, and the problem of multiple meta-levels trapping a single base-level method call). We shall not consider these problems here and let the reader refer to solutions and discussions found in the re ection literature (e.g., [8,13,21]).

Given these premises, consider the statement that ATM transactions are secure and how this would be expressed in ROOA (Fig. 4). This represents the same classes as found in Fig. 3 (for functional objects), complemented by classes for meta-objects performing computation on the functional objects. We use a dotted and dashed line to represent the association between the classes of functional objects and those of the meta-objects (which may be introduced in UML as a «causal connection» stereotyped association), and adopt the convention of using the same name for functional classes and their corresponding meta-objects classes. Meta-objects are charged with managing security. A meta-object is introduced for each ATM, Account, Card, and for each Bank.

Whenever the Bank issues a new card, or an old card expires, this operation is trapped by the Bank meta-object, which adds the new card onto (removes the expired card from) its database of cards, together with the associated password. Next, whenever a transaction is prepared in the ATM (i.e., the card is inserted and the password introduced), the ATM s meta-object intercepts this operation and checks the card with the Bank meta-object. The overall functioning is close to that depicted in Fig. 3 (i.e., the Bank class of the meta-level works essentially in the same way as the Card Database), except that a re ective approach keeps the two levels clearly separated and avoids intermixing functional and non-functional concerns in the base-level. Note that we can also delegate to the meta-level issues that may be regarded as functional, for example managing the credit limit for accounts. In the example, operation commit_transaction is trapped by the ATM s meta-object which executes an operation of its own (verify_availability) to check whether the requested operation can be performed, again with the Bank meta-object. Since this check is in uenced by the current balance and the credit limit of the account, this information also has to be rei2ed at the meta-level (this is why an Account meta-object is needed). Note that, if management of credit is done at the meta-level, the credit limit itself becomes a meta-level information (there is no need for a credit_limit attribute at the base-level).

Of course, it is up to the analyst to decide what should be modeled in meta-level terms, evaluating pros and cons (just as successful mechanisms such as exception handling are used in di2erent ways by di2erent designers). Even if ROOA is strictly adopted for non-functional issues, it is rather obvious that different analysts and designers should disagree as to what is *functional*. It su2 ces, here, to point out at the e2ects: in the system of Fig. 4, it is very likely that many operations at the base-level have a straightforward implementation that directly corresponds to their abstract view as could be found in requirements as produced by the customer (e.g., a withdrawal removes money, and nothing else).

4.4   After ROOA: Design and Implementation

ROOA, as described above, is an *analysis* technique and does not include prescriptions about design and implementation. *Per se*, the approach should yield a more precise speci2cation of non-functional issues. After such requirements have been analyzed and modeled, it is up to the designer/implementor to decide to what extent should a re ective approach be followed in the subsequent stages of development. As mentioned in section 2, one of the drawbacks of the conventional approaches to analysis is a lack of separation of concerns, in the implementation, between functional and non-functional issues. To solve this problem, a re ective approach could be applied in design as well, that is, the system could actually be *designed* following a decomposition into levels in the reflective sense (i.e., be designed as to have a reflective architecture). If this is done, ROOA provides the additional benefit that *a smooth transition from analysis to design for non-functional requirements* is achieved. Meta-objects are implemented as instances of independent classes and are designed to rule over, and modify, the behavior and state of functional objects. Carrying a reflective approach to design allows the developer to take full advantage of ROOA, and ideally solves all the problems we mentioned in section 2 for what concerns the tackling of non-functional issues in system development.

If the system is designed as to have a reflective architecture, there is a further choice to be taken, namely whether a reflective language should or should not be used for the actual *implementation*. Although many popular languages (first of all Java) include some weak form of reflection, it does not seem reasonable to expect reflective languages to be widely adopted in (industry) development. Nevertheless, of course, the ROOA approach (complemented with reflective design) does not require that a reflective language be used. If a reflective language is used, the link between the non-functional and functional levels is implicitly provided by causal connection. The specific form of reflection we relied upon in this paper (reflection on state and behavior) was explicitly chosen because it is fully supported by many reflective languages, including OpenC++ [7], and OpenJava [29]. On the other hand, if a reflective language is *not* used in the implementation, support for causal connection should be explicitly implemented as a part of the system. It seems reasonable to suggest that the system be first designed assuming causal connection, and then the final design be augmented with a further stage where the causal connection mechanism itself is designed. In this case, the infrastructure for causal connection could be tailored to the specific needs of the application at hand.

Note that the analysis documents are of course the same irrespective of whether the design is reflective and irrespective of the target language, so that they could even be reused for different implementations, some using reflection explicitly, and others using a mainstream (non reflective) language.

5   Related Work

Several authors within the Reflection field have considered the application of reflective techniques to address non-functional software requirements. Hürsch and Videira-Lopes [14] highlight the relevance of an approach that separates multiple concerns (including functionality as one specific concern, as opposed to other non-functional concerns) both at the conceptual and implementation level. They provide a tentative classification of the concerns that may be separated in general software systems, and encompass the major techniques that may be used to separate them, namely *meta-programming*, *pattern-oriented programming*, and *composition filters*. Their discussion is somewhat less specific than that provided by this paper, as their concept of separation of concerns is not necessarily achieved via the use of re ective techniques (i.e., meta-programming). Most of other related e2orts propose *design approaches* (rather than analysis approaches) for structuring a software system in such a way that non-functional requirements are addressed by a system s meta-level(s) and thus cleanly separated from functional (base level) code. As we basically aim at supporting a smooth transition from analysis to design via re ection, re ective design approaches to the enforcement of non-functional properties provide us with some hints as to what the *result* of this process (that is, the resulting design) should look like. Stroud and Wu [27] discuss a re ective approach to the dynamic adaptation of nonfunctional properties of software systems. In their approach, security, persistence and replication properties are transparently added to an existing system (even available in black-box form) and easily tailored to any speci2c environment onto which the system is downloaded. Their paper explicitly tackles the issue of separating functional and non-functional requirements and reusing meta-objects implementing non-functional properties. Several authors addressed the transparent addition of fault-tolerance features to a software system via re ection, e.g. [1] (that applies channel rei2cation to communication fault-tolerance) [10] (that employs re ective N-version programming and both active and passive replication mechanisms) [20] (that employs re ective server replication) and [15] (that employs re ective checkpointing in concurrent object-oriented systems). As mentioned above, other non-functional issues that were demonstrated to be e2ectively tackled via re ection include persistence [17], atomicity [26], and authentication [2,22,25].

Also related to the topic of this paper is our work on Architectural Re ection (AR) [4,5,6]. In AR, a re ective approach is adopted for reifying the *software architecture* of a software system. While the de2nition of the architecture of a system is usually regarded as belonging to (early) design, there are cases where *requirements* on the architecture of a system should be considered from the outset (i.e., the need for integration with legacy systems, the need to reuse COTS components, and so on). Architectural properties of both the whole system and of single objects may be addressed in a re ective approach like that suggested in this paper. Other authors have considered addressing architectural properties of objects using a meta-level; for example, [12] proposes a re ective object-oriented pattern for the separated de2nition of an object s behavior, and [18] proposes the R-Rio system for system s dynamic recon2guration through a re ective description of the system s software architecture. Also strictly related to our work is [28], that proposes to use a re ective approach in analysis (within the context of component-based software development), although it is clearly the intention of the authors that re ection be kept as a basic mechanism through design to implementation.

6   Conclusions and Future Work

This paper is intended to suggest how traditional OO analysis could be extended in order to cope with non-functional requirements in a cleaner way than supported by current methods. It suggests that a re ective approach could be taken, whereby a system s speci2cation is partitioned into levels (i.e., in way that is orthogonal to a *functional* partitioning), where the base level includes information on the domain, and the other levels include information on the system. This partitioning into levels could then be mapped easily onto a re ective architecture where requirements related to the system are re2ned into meta-objects that augment base-objects with non-functional properties. We propose the general lines of a modi2ed object-oriented analysis methodology (which can be applied in any context, e.g., using UML and a method such as Objectory[3]) where non-functional issues are dealt with in a re ective fashion.

While the approach can be used independent of the adoption of re ective principles in *design* (or implementation), we also believe that this paper also provides some useful suggestion for the design of re ective systems themselves. To the best of our knowledge, few e2orts have been made to propose extensions or adaptations of OO methods, methodologies, and processes to OO re ective systems. In our view, the best way to design a re ective system is that of considering it in a re ective perspective from the outset, i.e., from analysis. This means that the analysis phase should include a partitioning of the system s requirements into levels as that proposed here.

Of course, this is just a "vision" paper. We plan to continue this work by considering the issues raised in this paper in more detail. In particular, we would like to progress in at least two directions. First, we will study in greater detail how the ROOA may 2t with mainstream OO notations, meta-models, methods, and methodologies (starting from the UML meta-model and related processes and methods). As ROOA necessarily leads to a de2nition of the overall structure of the *system* from the 2rst stages of analysis, it would probably 2t best with methods that include an early de2nition of architecture, such as the already mentioned Rational process. We believe that a very interesting side e2ect of this study would be that of clarifying, in a sense, the essence of (OO) re ection. In other words, while traditional OO concepts have been deeply understood and clearly formalized in notations such as UML, OO re ective concepts, in our view, are usually perceived as belonging to a lower abstraction level than basic OO concepts such as inheritance, associations, and so on. We believe that re ective concepts will tend to become ever more ubiquitous in object-oriented development, and that a precise understanding of their meaning, at the highest abstraction level possible, is strongly needed.

As a second line of research, we would like to investigate how di2erent re ective models apply within ROOA. We plan to investigate how the di2erent models apply to the speci2cation of traditional non-functional requirements. We believe that this will hardly lead to identifying the *best* model. Rather, it is likely that non-functional issues can be classi2ed according to what re ective model is required to express them most clearly (i.e., no single model applies in all cases).

Acknowledgements. This work has been supported by DISCo (Department of Informatics, Systems and Communication), University of Milano Bicocca.

References

1. Massimo Ancona, Walter Cazzola, Gabriella Dodero, and Vittoria Gi-anuzzi. Channel Rei cation: a Reflective Approach to Fault-Tolerant Software Development. In *OOPSLA'95 (poster section)*, page 137, Austin, Texas, USA, on 15th-19th October 1995. ACM. Available at http://www.disi.unige.it/person/CazzolaW/references.html.

2. Massimo Ancona, Walter Cazzola, and Eduardo B. Fernandez. Reflective Authorization Systems: Possibilities, Bene ts and Drawbacks. In Jan Vitek and Christian Jensen, editors, *Secure Internet Programming: Security Issues for Mobile and Distributed Objects*, Lecture Notes in Computer Science 1603, pages 35 51. Springer-Verlag, July 1999.

3. Grady Booch, James Rumbaugh, and Ivar Jacobson. *The Uni ed Modeling Language User Guide*. Object Technology Series. Addison-Wesley, Reading, Massachussetts 01867, 3 edition, February 1999.

4. Walter Cazzola, Andrea Savigni, Andrea Sosio, and Francesco Tisato. Architectural Reflection: Bridging the Gap Between a Running System and its Architectural Speci cation. In *Proceedings of 6th Reengineering Forum (REF'98)*, pages 12 1 12 6, Firenze, Italia, on 8th-11th March 1998. IEEE.

5. Walter Cazzola, Andrea Savigni, Andrea Sosio, and Francesco Tisato. Architectural Reflection: Concepts, Design, and Evaluation. Technical Report RI-DSI 234-99, DSI, University degli Studi di Milano, May 1999. Available at http://www.disi.unige.it/person/CazzolaW/references.html.

6. Walter Cazzola, Andrea Savigni, Andrea Sosio, and Francesco Tisato. Rule-Based Strategic Reflection: Observing and Modifying Behaviour at the Architectural Level. In *Proceedings of 14th IEEE International Conference on Automated Software Engineering (ASE'99)*, pages 263 266, Cocoa Beach, Florida, USA, on 12th-15th October 1999.

7. Shigeru Chiba. A Meta-Object Protocol for C++. In *Proceedings of the 10th Annual Conference on Object-Oriented Programming Systems, Languages, and Applications (OOPSLA'95)*, volume 30 of *Sigplan Notices*, pages 285 299, Austin, Texas, USA, October 1995. ACM.

8. Scott Danforth and Ira R. Forman. Reflections on Metaclass Programming in SOM. In *Proceedings of the 9th Annual Conference on Object-Oriented Programming Systems, Languages, and Applications (OOPSLA'94)*, volume 29 of *Sigplan Notice*, pages 440 452, Portland, Oregon, USA, October 1994. ACM.

9. Francois-Nicola Demers and Jacques Malenfant. Reflection in Logic, Functional and Object-Oriented Programming: a Short Comparative Study. In *Proceedings of the IJCAI'95 Workshop on Reflection and Metalevel Architectures and their Applications in AI*, pages 29 38, Montreal, Canada, August 1995.

10. Jean-Charles Fabre, Vincent Nicomette, Tanguy Perennou, Robert J. Stroud, and Zhixue Wu. Implementing Fault Tolerant Applications Using Reflective Object-Oriented Programming. In *Proceedings of FTCS-25 Silver Jubilee*, Pasadena, CA USA, June 1995. IEEE.

11. Jacques Ferber. Computational Reflection in Class Based Object Oriented Languages. In *Proceedings of 4th Conference on Object-Oriented Programming Systems, Languages and Applications (OOPSLA'89)*, volume 24 of *Sigplan Notices*, pages 317 326. ACM, October 1989.

12. Luciane Lamour Ferreira and Cec lia M. F. Rubira. The Reflective State Pattern. In Steve Berczuk and Joe Yoder, editors, *Proceedings of the Pattern Languages of Program Design*, TR #WUCS-98-25, Monticello, Illinois - USA, August 1998.

13. Nicolas Graube. Metaclass Compatibility. In Norman K. Meyrowitz, editor, *Proceedings of the 4th Conference on Object-Oriented Programming: Systems, Languages, and Applications (OOPSLA'89)*, volume 24(10) of *Sigplan Notices*, pages 305 316, New Orleans, Louisiana, USA, October 1989. ACM.

14. Walter Hürsch and Cristina Videira Lopes. Separation of Concerns. Technical Report NU-CCS-95-03, Northeastern University, Boston, February 1995.

15. Mangesh Kasbekar, Chandramouli Narayanan, and Chita R. Das. Using Reflection for Checkpointing Concurrent Object Oriented Programs. In Shigeu Chiba and Jean-Charles Fabre, editors, *Proceedings of the OOPSLA Workshop on Reflection Programming in C++ and Java*, October 1998.

16. Gregor Kickzales, Jim des Rivieres, and Daniel G. Bobrow. *The Art of the Metaobject Protocol*. MIT Press, Cambridge, Massachusetts, 1991.

17. Arthur H. Lee and Joseph L. Zachary. Using Meta Programming to Add Persistence to CLOS. In *International Conference on Computer Languages*, Los Alamitos, California, 1994. IEEE.

18. Orlando Loques, Julius Leite, Marcelo Lobosco, and Alexandre Sztajnberg. Integrating Meta-Level Programming and Con guration Programming. In Walter Cazzola, Robert J. Stroud, and Francesco Tisato, editors, *Proceedings of the 1st Workshop on Object-Oriented Reflection and Software Engineering (OORaSE'99)*, pages 137 151. University of Milano Bicocca, November 1999.

19. Pattie Maes. Concepts and Experiments in Computational Reflection. In Norman K. Meyrowitz, editor, *Proceedings of the 2nd Conference on Object-Oriented Programming Systems, Languages, and Applications (OOPSLA'87)*, volume 22 of *Sigplan Notices*, pages 147 156, Orlando, Florida, USA, October 1987. ACM.

20. Juan-Carlos Ruiz-Garcia Marc-Olivier Killijian, Jean-Charles Fabre and Shigeru Chiba. A Metaobject Protocol for Fault-Tolerant CORBA Applications. In *Proceedings of the 17th Symposium on Reliable Distributed Systems (SRDS'98)*, pages 127 134, 1998.

21. Philippe Mulet, Jacques Malenfant, and Pierre Cointe. Towards a Methodology for Explicit Composition of MetaObjects. In *Proceedings of the 10th Annual Conference on Object-Oriented Programming Systems, Languages, and Applications (OOPSLA'95)*, volume 30 of *Sigplan Notice*, pages 316 330, Austin, Texas, USA, October 1995. ACM.

22. Thomas Riechmann and Jürgen Kleinöder. Meta-Objects for Access Control: Role-Based Principals. In Colin Boyd and Ed Dawson, editors, *Lecture Notes in Computer Science*, number 1438 in Proceedings of 3rd Australasian Conference on Information Security and Privacy (ACISP'98), pages 296 307, Brisbane, Australia, July 1998. Springer-Verlag.

23. James Rumbaugh, Michael Blaha, William Premerlani, Frederick Eddy, and William Lorensen. *Object-Oriented Modeling and Design*. Prentice-Hall, Englewood Cli s, NJ, 1991.

24. Robert J. Stroud. Transparency and Reflection in Distributed Systems. *ACM Operating System Review*, 22:99 103, April 1992.

25. Robert J. Stroud and Ian Welch. Dynamic Adaptation of the Security Properties of Application and Components. In *Proceedings of ECOOP Workshop on Distributed Object Security (EWDOS'98)*, in 12th European Conference on Object-Oriented Programming (ECOOP'98), pages 41 46, Brussels, Belgium, July 1998. Unite de Recherche INRIA Rhone-Alpes.

26. Robert J. Stroud and Zhixue Wu. Using Meta-Object Protocol to Implement Atomic Data Types. In Walter Oltho , editor, *Proceedings of the 9th Conference on Object-Oriented Programming (ECOOP'95)*, LNCS 952, pages 168 189, Aarhus, Denmark, August 1995. Springer-Verlag.

27. Robert J. Stroud and Zhixue Wu. Using Metaobject Protocols to Satisfy Non-Functional Requirements. In Chris Zimmerman, editor, *Advances in Object-Oriented Metalevel Architectures and Reflection*, chapter 3, pages 31 52. CRC Press, Inc., 2000 Corporate Blvd.,N.W., Boca Raton, Florida 33431, 1996.

28. Junichi Suzuki and Yoshikazu Yamamoto. Extending UML for Modeling Reflective Software Components. In Robert France and Bernhard Rumpe, editors, *Lecture Notes in Computer Science*, number 1723 in Proceedings of «UML»'99 - The Uni ed Modeling Language: Beyond the Standard, the Second International Conference, pages 220 235, Fort Collins, CO, USA, October 1999. Springer-Verlag.

29. Michiaki Tatsubori. An Extension Mechanism for the Java Language. Master of engineering dissertation, Graduate School of Engineering, University of Tsukuba, University of Tsukuba, Ibaraki, Japan, February 1999.

Towards a True Reflective Modeling Scheme

Jean Bézivin[1] and Richard Lemesle[1] [2]

[1] LRSG, University of Nantes,
2, rue de la Houssiniere, BP 92208
44322 Nantes cedex 3, France
jean.bezivin@sciences.univ-nantes.fr
[2] Societe Soft-Maint
4, rue du Chateau de l'Eraudiere, BP 588
44074 Nantes cedex 3, France
rlemesle@sodifrance.fr

Abstract Model engineering is taking a growing place in software development. To cope with the diversity of models, the OMG (Object Management Group) itself is now centering its activities on the emerging MOF (Meta-Object Facility) de ned for model interoperability. After discussing how the concept of a MOF has progressively emerged in the last ten years, we illustrate some advantages and limits of such a modeling language. We show that explicit de nitions of model and meta-model are lacking from the MOF speci cation and that a linking mechanism from a model to its meta-model is missing. We present the key role played by these concepts and their relations and we propose to de ne them explicitly within an improved meta-modeling framework. This proposition is based on a proprietary research platform which main contribution is to emphasize the central role played by the *meta* relation. Making this relation explicit in a true reflective modeling scheme allows us to present a much clearer structure of the overall modeling architecture.

Keywords: Models, Ontologies, Meta-modeling, Model engineering, Reflection, UML, MOF.

1 Introduction

Re ection is the name given to a design principle that allows a system to have a representation of itself in a manner that makes it easy to adapt the system to a changing environment. Quoting from the Re ection 96 workshop [6], re ective and meta-level techniques have now matured to the point where they are being used to address real-world problems in such areas as programming languages, operating systems, databases and distributed computing. It is the purpose of this paper to show that the same techniques are now entering the domain of modeling and that they are already playing there a central role.

The arrival of the Uni2ed Modeling Language UML [9,14] strengthens this feeling as well as the acceptance of the MOF in December 1997 [8] and of the

W. Cazzola et al. (Eds.): Reflection and Software Engineering, LNCS 1826, pp. 21 38, 2000.
© Springer-Verlag Berlin Heidelberg 2000

XMI (XML Metadata Interchange) in January 1999 [12] clearly opens the debate on the key contribution of modeling and knowledge representation techniques to object technology. This paper presents some of the practical problems resulting from the multiplicity of models and ontologies in the current forms of software systems development. More particularly it discusses the necessary re ective properties of a meta-model architecture.

1.1   Re ection: From a Programming to a Modeling Viewpoint

Fig. 1 shows a typical Smalltalk browser. In addition to the 2ve panes, the usual property of this browser is the class/instance switch at the bottom of the second upper pane. This radio button is used to switch between the level of objects and that of classes. In the 2rst case, the browser is displaying the instance methods of the selected class, while in the second case, it is displaying the class methods of the selected class.

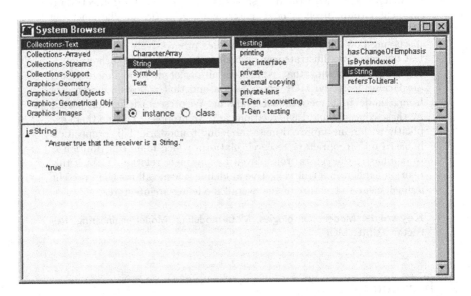

Fig. 1. A Smalltalk browser with its instance/class radio button to switch between the level of objects and that of classes.

It is ironic to observe that, on some recent CASE tools, a similar switch is appearing. It serves to indicate that the UML drawing corresponds either to a UML model or to a MOF model, i.e. that one is working respectively on level M^1 (the model level) or level M^2 (the meta-model level). These levels share many similarities and it is normal that similar tools and procedures may apply to them (Fig. 2). In the case we are discussing here, it would have been obviously a waste of energy to design a drawing tool specially for each level. The decision to use the standard UML notation was thus an obvious decision to take. Then, the switch could thus be useful to recall the current modeling level.

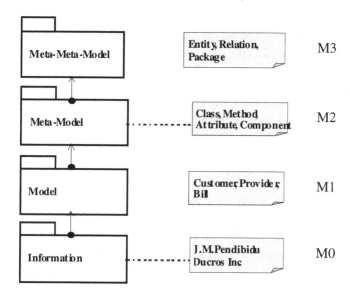

Fig. 2. The four level architecture framework as described in MOF,CDIF and UML documentation.

This paper 2rst introduces the MOF re ective scheme, which is gaining wide acceptance as an OMG standard recommendation. The following limitations of such a re ective core will be detailed:

the absence of a Meta-Model meta-entity,
the absence of a Model meta-entity,
thus, the absence of a "meta" relation between a model and its meta-model,
and the absence of a "meta" relation between an entity and its meta-entity.

Then our own re ective core, based on the sNets formalism [2] and 2lling these gaps, will be presented. To conclude, the paper shows how our re ective core can be mapped to the corresponding parts of the MOF, the CDIF meta-model [1] , and the sNets formalism.

2   Why the MOF Should be Reflective

After CORBA and UML, we may observe now a third wave of proposals at OMG with the MOF. One possible interpretation of this is that model engineering is progressively becoming a mainstream technology. Models and meta-models are presently being recognized as 2rst-class entities in the software development process. The MOF has emerged from the recognition that UML was one possible meta-model in the software development landscape, but that it was not alone. Facing the danger of having a variety of di2erent meta-models emerging and independently evolving (data warehouse, work ow, software process, etc.), there was an urgent need for an integration framework for all meta-models. Standardizing meta-models means providing facilities to exchange models based on such meta-models. The answer was thus to provide a language to de2ne meta-models, i.e. a meta-meta-model. This is the 2rst purpose of the MOF but some modeling tools also use it to be meta-model independent. This can be done by using some re ective facilities to discover the meta-model used during execution.

2.1   MOF = UML + CDIF

The MOF has borrowed much inspiration from CDIF. The CDIF community had been working since ten years on elaborating a similar framework based on a four-level architecture [1] (Fig. 2) which has been accepted as an organization framework for models, meta-models and meta-meta-models. The CDIF is an EIA (Electronic Industry Associates) standard structured around knowledge domains called "subject areas". The MOF may be seen as an integration of the main UML ideas within a CDIF-like framework.

Initially, UML was self-de2ned (Fig. 3.a). Progressively emphasis has shifted and the self-de2ned MOF has become the reference meta-meta-model at OMG (Fig. 3.b). Consequently other products are being de2ned in term of the MOF (Fig. 3.c). Not only UML, but also potential extensions of UML like a possible "UML for Business Objects". Among the di2erent e2orts for de2ning MOF-compliant meta-models, one may quote the Corba Model of Components, the Work ow initiative [10], the DataWarehouse initiative [13] or the Software Process Engineering work [11]. So, the MOF is becoming a widely adopted meta-modeling reference.

Let us take a closer look to the meaning of the relations described in Fig. 3. The relation between the ontological spaces *UML_FBO* and *UML* is de2nitively not the same than between *UML* and *MOF*. In the 2rst case, it is a relation meaning that *UML_FBO* is an extension (a superset) of *UML* while in the second case, it is a relation meaning that *UML* is de2ned using the *MOF* (the MOF is the meta-model of UML). Thereafter, we endeavor to explicitly de2ne all the relations we use. Then, the 2rst relation will be called *basedOn*, meaning that a model is based on a meta-model while the second relation will be called *extends*, meaning that a model is the extension of an other model. The example situation described in Fig. 3 shows the following relations:

basedOn (MOF, MOF);
basedOn(UML, MOF);
extends (UML_FBO, UML);

(a)   (b)   (c)

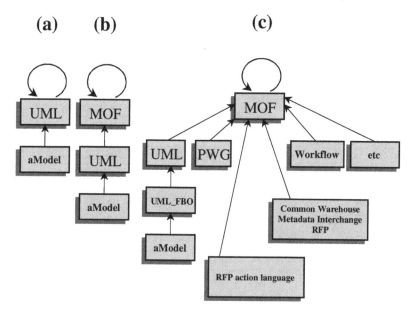

Fig. 3. From a self-de ned UML used for object modeling to a set of meta-models including UML and based on a self-de ned MOF.

As we see, it is essential to clearly de2ne the possible relationships between models, and meta-models as well as their semantics. The same thing have to be done for entities and meta-entities. Concerning the MOF context, the following questions remain unanswered:

What s a model?
What s a meta-model?
How can a model be related to its meta-model?
What s an entity?
How an entity is related to its meta-entity?

So, let us take a closer look to the MOF model.

2.2   A Closer Look to the MOF

The self-de2ned MOF contains basic mechanisms for de2ning meta-entities (called *Class* in MOF terms) and meta-relations (called *Association* in MOF terms) as illustrated by the simpli2ed scheme of Fig. 4. To cope with modularity, the MOF also de2nes a package meta-entity which acts as a container for meta-entities and meta-relations. A meta-model described using the MOF is generally composed of a root package containing all its de2nition. So, while there isn t any meta-model meta-entity in the MOF, a *Package* can be used to represent such a meta-model.

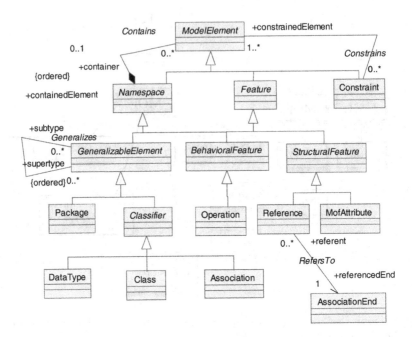

Fig. 4. A MOF 1.1 simpli ed model where the main meta-entities and their relations are presented.

With the MOF, the only relationship de2ned between packages (as previously stated, MOF meta-models can be represented by packages) is the *extends* relationship (a Package is a *GeneralizableElement* in the MOF and we can consider that our *extends* relationship can be mapped to the MOF generalization relationship). The *basedOn* relationship or its equivalent, which is a major relationship, is never explicitly de2ned, nor explicitly used.

To conclude on the MOF re ective scheme, we can see that two of the most signi2cant relationships are missing in its de2nition presented in Fig. 4. These two relationships are the *basedOn* relationship between a model and its meta-model (such a relationship is also called *instanceOf* but we don t want to use this term which may create confusion with our second relationship) and the *instanceOf* relationship between an entity and its meta-entity (representing its type). The 2rst relation means that every model must be de2ned using a meta-model while the second relation means that every entity has a type represented by a meta-entity. These two relations doesn t have the same meaning. For example, the sentence "the MOF is a self de2ned meta-model" indicates that we have the following two relations:

basedOn (MOF, MOF);
instanceOf(MOF, MetaModel);

while the sentence "UML is a meta-model de2ned using the MOF" means these
two other relations:

basedOn(UML, MOF);
instanceOf(UML, MetaModel);

It is essential to clearly de2ne the main meta-modeling meta-entities as well
as their relationships to avoid confusion about their meaning. This is the aim of
the following section.

3   A Reflective Modeling Core

This section presents a clearly de2ned re ective meta-model. This meta-model
will be compared thereafter to the MOF and other meta-modeling languages.
In our view on a re ective modeling core (presented on Fig. 5), the following
concepts and relations have to be de2ned:

an **Entity** concept,
a **Meta-Entity** concept,
an *instanceOf* relation de2ned between **Entity** and **Meta-Entity**,
a **Model** concept,
a **Meta-Model** concept,
a *basedOn* relation de2ned between **Model** and **Meta-Model**,
a *de nedIn* relation de2ned between **Entity** and **Model**,
and a *de nedIn* relation de2ned between **Meta-Entity** and **Meta-Model**.

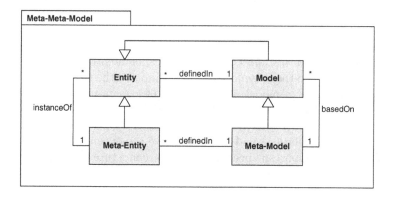

Fig. 5. A reflective core for meta-modeling.

In the Fig. 5, we have used the UML notation to represent our re ective core.
We consider that everything is an entity. A meta-model is a kind of (a subtype
of) model which is itself a kind of entity and a meta-entity is also a kind of
entity. This is de2ned by the inheritance relationships.

For more readability, the **Meta-Relationship** meta-entity has not been represented in Fig. 5. But in this 2gure, the rectangles are representing meta-entities while the relations between rectangles are representing meta-relations (Meta-relations have an *hasSource* link to their source type and a *hasDestination* link to their destination type).

In fact, such a core de2nes precisely the concepts of **Entity**, **Model**, **Meta-Entity**, **Meta-Model** and **Meta-Relationship**, as well as the main meta-relations between them such as the*instanceOf* relationship between an entity and its meta-entity, and the *basedOn* relationship between a model and its meta-model. The 2rst relation is re ectively used in the Fig. 5 to state that:

> *instanceOf(Entity, Meta-Entity);*
> *instanceOf(Meta-Entity, Meta-Entity);*
> *instanceOf(Model, Meta-Entity);*
> *instanceOf(Meta-Model, Meta-Entity);*
> *instanceOf(instanceOf, Meta-Relationship);*
> *instanceOf(basedOn, Meta-Relationship);*
> *instanceOf(Entity:de nedIn:Model, Meta-Relationship);*
> *instanceOf(Meta-Entity:de nedIn:Meta-Model, Meta-Relationship);*
> *instanceOf(Meta-Meta-Model, Meta-Model);*

The *basedOn* relation is also used there to state that our meta-meta-model is re ective:

> *basedOn(Meta-Meta-Model, Meta-Meta-Model);*

This relation links explicitly a model and its meta-model. It means that the model is expressed using the set of concepts and relationships de2ned in the meta-model. We can state that UML is de2ned with the MOF using this *basedOn* relation. But we can also state that a particular object model is de2ned with UML with the same relation.

Every entity has an *instanceOf* relation to its meta-entity. This clearly shows the di2erence between the *instanceOf* relationship and the *basedOn* relationship. So, when we say that a model is an instance of a meta-model, we are talking about our *basedOn* relationship, not our *instanceOf* relationship. A model have always an *instanceOf* relationship to the meta-entity **Model**: a model "is a" model (*instanceOf* relation) and a model "have a meta-model" (*basedOn* relation). This is very important because layered architecture of models and meta-models is based on such relations.

3.1   Meta-modeling: How Many Layers?

A classical problem is the number of layers used in meta-modeling. The root layer is always present and usually known as the meta-meta-model. This is the re ective root of this layered architecture. The next layer always represents meta-models. These meta-models are de2ned using the language de2ned in the meta-meta-model (the meta-meta-model is almost always unique). The next layer always represents models. Each model is de2ned using the language de2ned by one meta-model (its own meta-model). At this point, you can either consider the architecture is complete, or you can also add another layer to describe data. And some people may go further and use an unlimited number of layers to represent data. But we have to keep in mind that the number of layers depends on the instantiation relation used between entities from each of these levels (or layers). In order to explain how these di2erent layers are identi2ed, let s take the example of a common architecture using four layers.

Layer	Contents	Example
Meta-Meta-Model	Language to describe meta-models	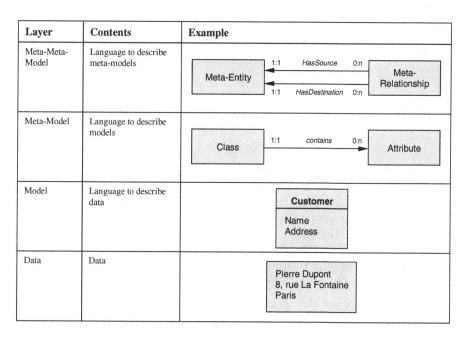
Meta-Model	Language to describe models	
Model	Language to describe data	
Data	Data	

Fig. 6. The four layer common architecture and its content explained.

A four-layer common architecture

This is the architecture used by CDIF and the MOF model. The four layers are presented in Fig. 6. Layered architecture is associated to a given instantiation relationship and there must be a precise de7nition of this *instanceOf* relationship to determine to which layer an entity belongs.

Given such a relation, we have the following axioms:

A layer contains entities.
Stating that an entity belongs to a layer means that this entity has an *instanceOf* relation to an entity from the previous layer (the previous layer of the 7rst layer is itself).

In the previous examples, there are several entities and each of them has an instantiation link. So, the Fig. 7 show the instantiation links de7ned for these entities. These links allow us to determine the layer containing entities.

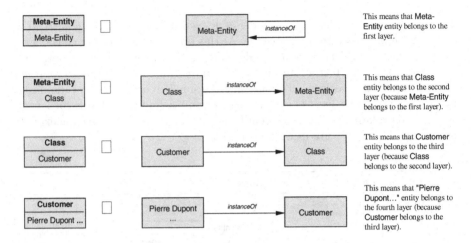

Fig. 7. Instantiation links making the separation between layers.

On the meaning of the instantiation links

The Fig. 7 seems to be consistent with the previous axioms. But lets take a closer look to the latest *instanceOf* relationship. We have previously stated that such a **global** relationship is de7ned between an entity and its meta-entity. The latest relationship is between a customer (**Pierre Dupont** is a **Customer**) and a class (**Customer** is a **Class**). Can we say that this latest relation is the same as our **global** *instanceOf* relationship since this one led to a class which de7nes a **local** type in an object modeling context only?

In this speci7c case, this relationship is an *instanceOf* relationship between an object and its class **in an object model**. Such a relationship exists **only** in such an object model. This relationship has the same name as our **global** modeling *instanceOf* relationship, but its meaning is di7erent. It is also de7ning a type, but not the same kind of type. In fact, in our global modeling context, the entity **Pierre Dupont** has an *instanceOf* link to the **Object** meta-entity de7ned in the object meta-model. Then, the relation between **Pierre Dupont** and its class **Customer** is renamed *instanceOf*$_{(2)}$. Such a relation is de7ned by a meta-relation between the **Object** meta-entity and the **Class** meta-entity in a meta-model representing the object paradigm as shown by Fig. 8.

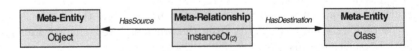

Fig. 8. *instanceOf*$_{(2)}$ meta-relationship de nition between **Object** meta-entity and **Class** meta-entity in an Object meta-model.

This relation is called *instanceOf*$_{(2)}$ to di7erentiate it from our *instanceOf* relationship de7ned in Fig. 5. And this previous relation will be called *instanceOf*$_{(1)}$ afterwards. Then, the fourth and last scheme represented in Fig. 7, will be replaced by that of the Fig. 9.

Fig. 9. *instanceOf*$_{(2)}$ relation used in the model layer.

Then, using a clearly de7ned instanceOf$_{(1)}$ relationship in order to separate layers, Fig. 6 leads to Fig. 10 in which these relations are shown. Using such a de7nition, we can only represent three modeling levels (the bold line in the Fig. 10 represents an inheritance relationship that is out of the scope of this paper).

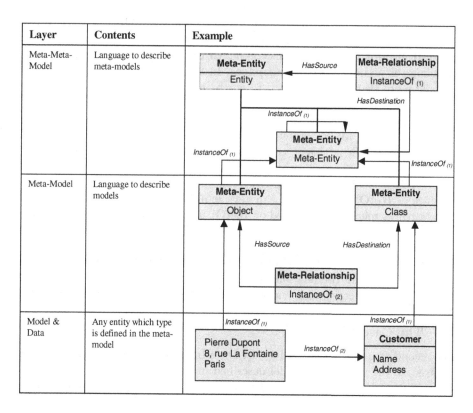

Fig. 10. A three layers architecture based on an explicit *instanceOf* relationship.

We want to point out that if we don t clearly de7ne such an *instanceOf* relationship, we can state anything. And it makes no sense to base so many things on so few foundations. The layer count in a layered modeling architecture is based on such a non-existent relationship. This may explain why some speak about 3 levels, others about 4 levels and others about *n* levels.

4   Reflective Core in Current Modeling Formalisms

In this section, we show how the entities of the proposed re ective core are de7ned in the current mainstream meta-meta-models. These meta-meta-models are the MOF, the CDIF meta-meta-model and our own formalism called sNets. First, we will take the example of the MOF [8].

4.1   The Case of the MOF

The MOF is a self-de7ned meta-meta-model and its core de7nition has already been described in Fig. 4.

In such a de7nition, a MOF meta-entity can be de7ned using a **Class**, a meta-model can be de7ned using a **Package** and the relationship between a **Class** and its **Package** (our *de nedIn* relationship between a **Meta-Entity** and its **Meta-Model**) can be de7ned using an association called *contains* between a **ModelElement** (**Class** is a subtype of **ModelElement**) and a **Namespace** (**Package** is a subtype of **Namespace**). In the MOF model package, there is nothing more that can be mapped to our re ective core scheme (Fig. 5).

The MOF also provides a re ective package. This package needs to be imported by all the MOF compliant meta-model. So, the MOF model package itself imports it. Then, this re ective package contains a class called **RefObject** which needs to be the root super type of all the MOF classes. This means that this **RefObject** can act as our **Entity** concept. Every MOF entity is at least an instance of **RefObject**, and we can get the meta-entity of such an entity using a *meta_object* relationship de7ned on **RefObject** (see Fig. 11). This means that the *meta_object* relation can act as our *instanceOf* relation.

However, even with this re ective package, the MOF does not provide a concept of **Model**, and the relationships related to this concept (*basedOn* between a model and its meta-model, and *de nedIn* between an entity and its model).

4.2   The Case of CDIF

The second example is the CDIF (Case Data Interchange Format) format, which is based on the meta-meta-model described in Fig. 12.

In such a de7nition, you can see that a CDIF meta-entity is de7ned using a MetaEntity, a meta-model is de7ned using a SubjectArea and the relationship between a meta-entity and its subject area (our *de nedIn* relationship between a meta-entity and its meta-model) is de7ned using an association called

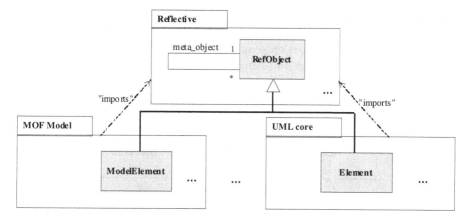

Fig. 11. The reflective package and the MOF.

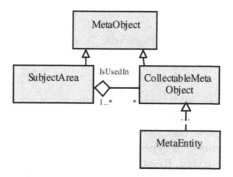

Fig. 12. The CDIF meta-meta-model.

"isUsedIn" between a collectible meta-object (MetaEntity is a subtype of Col-lectableMetaObject) and a subject area. So, in the CDIF meta-model, there is nothing more that can be mapped to our re ective core scheme (Fig. 5).

Now, if we take a look to the CDIF Integrated Meta-model, which is the set of all the subject areas de7ned using the CDIF meta-meta model, we can see that each of these subject areas must extend a Foundation Subject Area which de7nes RootObject meta-entity which acts as the root of all meta-entities [5]:

"The Foundation Subject Area provides the basic de nitions which under-pin the remainder of the CDIF Integrated Meta-model. It consists of an At-tributableMetaObject called RootObject, which is purely abstract, and acts as the root of the Attributable-MetaObject Hierarchy."

This means that this **RootObject** can act as our **Entity** concept. So, CDIF as well as the MOF, doesn t de7nes the concept of **Model**, and the relationships related to this concept (*basedOn* between a model and its meta-model, and *de nedIn* between an entity and its model).

4.3   The Case of sNets

The sNets formalism is based on semantic networks. A part of the sNets core de7nition is described in Fig. 13 (using the UML notation).

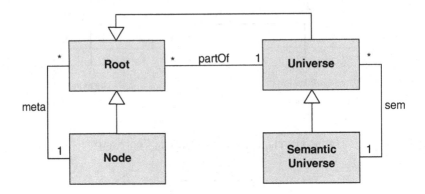

Fig. 13. A part of the sNets core de nition (UML notation).

In the sNets formalism, a node represents every entity. Every node has a type, which is also represented by a node (of type **Node**). And every node of type **Node** is a subtype of the node **Root** represented in Fig. 13. So every entity has a *meta* link to a node of type **Node** and a *partOf* link to a node of type **Universe**. This means that **Root** can be seen as our **Entity** concept, **Node** can be seen as our **Meta-Entity** concept, **Universe** can be seen as our **Model** concept, *meta* can be seen as our *instanceOf* relationship and *partOf* can be seen as our *de nedIn* relationship.

In sNets, there is also the concept of meta-model. A meta-model is represented by a node of type **SemanticUniverse**. It is a subtype of **Universe** (as Meta-Model is a subtype of Model in Fig. 5). And the relationship *basedOn* between a model and its meta-model is also de7ned by the *sem* link between a **Universe** and a **SemanticUniverse**.

In sNets, if a model is de7ned using a particular meta-model, the only entities it can contain will be those with meta-entities de7ned in the meta-model. In the same way, if a meta-model is de7ned with a particular meta-meta-model, the only meta-entities allowed would be those with meta-entities de7ned in the meta-meta-model. This means that a **SemanticUniverse** can only contains meta-entities with types de7ned in the meta-meta-model. So, the *partOf* relationship between an **Entity** and its **Model** can also be used between a **Meta-Entity** and its **Meta-Model**.

The sNets formalism is the only one, which support all the concepts and relationships represented in Fig. 5.

4.4   Core Concepts Compared

Figure 14 is a summary of the de7nition of the core concepts previously presented. The common concepts of these formalisms are only the Meta-Entity and the Meta-Model concepts. While the only relationship found in all these formalisms is the *de nedIn* relationship between meta-entities and meta-models. The *instanceOf* relationship, which is one of the most important relationship, only appears in the MOF (with its re ective package) and in sNets. Unfortunately such a relationship is not well documented in the MOF speci7cation document.

	MOF only	MOF & Reflective	CDIF	sNets
Meta-entities:				
Entity	N/A	Reflective::RefObject	MetaEntity "RootObject"	Node "Root"
Meta-Entity	Class "Class"	Class "Class"	MetaEntity "MetaEntity"	Node "Node"
Model	N/A	N/A	N/A	Node "Universe"
Meta-Model	Class "Package"	Class "Package"	MetaEntity "SubjectArea"	Node "SemanticUniverse"
Meta-relationships:				
instanceof	N/A	meta_object() defined in Reflective::RefBaseObject	N/A	Link "meta"
definedIn (between meta-entities & meta-models)	Association "contains"	Association "Contains"	MetaRelationship "IsUsedIn"	Link "partOf"
definedIn (between entities & models)	N/A	N/A	N/A	
basedOn	N/A	N/A	N/A	Link "sem"

Fig. 14. Summary table of core concepts de nitions.

5   Conclusion

Meta-level architectures are being put to work in the area of software modeling [3,12,7]. Following more than one decade of work on the subject, important communities are now starting to base their practical development on such frameworks. This is particularly the case of the OMG Meta Object Facility.

What we have suggested in this paper is that the common four layer meta-level modeling architecture, classically found in most proposal is probably not the best choice. We have argued that a common misunderstanding in this domain comes from the existence of multiple di7erent *instanceOf* relations and that the architectural choices are based on the supposed uniqueness of this relation. Nowadays, we may consider the MOF-based activity (de7nition of new meta-models) as de7ning the basis for a new technology, so we need its architecture to be consistent if we want a good meta-modeling framework.

By comparing three similar architectures (CDIF, a non-evolving standard; sNet a research prototype and MOF an industrial recommendation), we have been able to understand more precisely the impact of self-de7nition techniques in model engineering. We have tried to show that many options may still be subject to discussion.

We are now witnessing rapid changes in the domain of model engineering. Introduction of new technological possibilities may have consequences that are going beyond surface changes. One of these consequences is that re ectivity seems now to be at reach in the modeling area.

The arrival to maturity of precise and inter operable modeling (i.e. the situation where every model is based on an explicit meta-model and all meta-models are based on the same meta-meta-model) makes it possible to consider a regular framework of connected models. In this organization, the boundary between run-time and development-time characteristics is becoming very loose. More important, entities belonging to di7erent models may now communicate. This possibility comes out of the fact that the meta-meta-model de7nes standard interfaces to given middleware technology like CORBA. As a consequence, a run-time object may now interrogate a linked development-time object, in order for

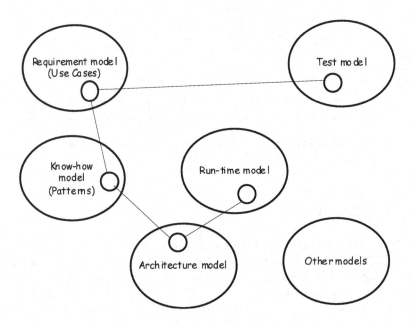

Fig. 15. Frameworks & models.

example to access certain QoS or certain deployment choices. This is why we may state that with MOF-like technology, model introspection is already today a practical possibility.

Beyond this, we may envision not only introspective but also fully re ective possibilities to become soon available. As a matter of fact, entities of the various models are precisely de7ned and traceability may be easily established between them. The models become much more than simply descriptive: they may also have reactive behavior. An execution object may interrogate a linked architectural item, triggering other requests to a pattern item, a use case item, a test item, and so on (Fig. 15).

The technical feasibility of such frameworks now seem established. How will this a7ect the way systems will be built in the next decade remains an open question.

Acknowledgements. We would like to thank particularly Stéphane Ducasse for all its suggestions, ideas and help in writing this paper.

References

1. Jean Bezivin, Johannes Ernst, and Woody Pidcock. Model Engineering with CDIF. In *post-proceedings, Summary of the workshop*, Vancouver, October 1998.
2. Jean Bezivin, Jerome Lanneluc, and Richard Lemesle. Representing Knowledge in the Object-Oriented Lifecycle. In *Proceedings of TOOLS PACIFIC'94*, pages 13 24, Melbourne, December 1994. Prentice Hall.
3. Stephen Crawley, Scott Davis, Jadwiga Indulska, Simon McBride, and Kerry Raymond. Meta Information Management. In *Proceedings of 2nd Formal Methods for Open Object-based Distributed Systems (FMOODS97) Conference*, pages 21 23, Canterbury, United Kingdom, July 1997.
4. Stephen Crawley, Scott Davis, Jadwiga Indulska, Simon McBride, and Kerry Raymond. Meta-Meta is Better-Better. In *Proceedings IFIP WG 6.1 International Working Conference on Distributed Applications and Interoperable Systems*, October 1997.
5. EIA. CDIF Framework for Modeling and Extensibility. Technical Report EIA/IS-107, EIA, January 1994.
6. Gregor Kiczales. *Proceedings of Reflection'96*. Springer Verlag, San Francisco, April 1996.
7. Microsoft. Microsoft Repository Product Information, Open Information Model Overview. Technical report, Microsoft, 1999.
8. Object Management Group. OMG/MOF Meta Object Facility (MOF) Speci ca-tion. OMG Document AD/97-08-14, OMG, Framingham, Mass., 1997.
9. Object Management Group. OMG/UML Uni ed Modeling Language UML Notation Guide. OMG Document AD/97-08-05, OMG, Framingham, Mass., November 1997.
10. Object Management Group. OMG/BOM Workflow Management Facility Speci - cation. OMG Document BOM/98-01-11, OMG, 1998.
11. Object Management Group. OMG/SPE Analysis and Design PTF, Software Process Engineering Request for Information, Version 1.0. OMG Document AD/98-10-08, OMG, November 1998.

12. Object Management Group. OMG/XMI XML MetaData Interchange (XMI) Proposal to the OMG OA&DTF RFP3 : Stream Based Model Interchange Format (SMIF). OMG Document AD/98-10-05, OMG, October 1998. Adopted at the Washington Meeting, (January 1999).
13. Object Management Group. OMG/CWMI Common Warehouse Metadata Interchange Request For Proposal. OMG Document AD/98-09-02, OMG, 1998 September.
14. Rational Software. UML Speci cation Version 1.3R9. Technical report, Rational Software, January 1999.
15. Clemens Szyperski. *Component Software: Beyond Object-Oriented Programming.* Addison Wesley and ACM Press, Readings, MA, USA, 1998.
16. Jos Warmer and Anneke Kleppe. *The Object Constraint Language Precise Modeling with UML.* Object Technology Series. Addison Wesley, Readings, MA, USA, 1999.

Declarable Modifiers:
A Proposal to Increase the Efficacy of Metaclasses

Ira R. Forman

IBM
Austin, TX
forman@acm.org

Abstract The amount of information available to metaprogrammer during intercession is limited. If a metaprogrammer has more information about the intentions of a programmer, the metaprogrammer can create more useful facilities. This paper proposes that object-oriented programming languages be designed so that metaprogrammers can declare new modifiers for methods and instance variables. Class programmers can use these modifiers to communicate intentions during intercession to the facilities created by metaprogrammers. This paper presents an extension to Java that has metaclasses. The intercessional features of the metaclasses are enhanced with the ability to declare both method and field modifiers. These modifiers are used by class programmers to communicate with a metaclass and control the effect of its intercession.

1 Introduction

Metaclasses can be used to implement many class transformations. However, the available information about a class limits the number of transformations that can be programmed with metaclasses. By increasing this information, the efficacy of metaclasses can be increased. This observation arose during several years of metaclass programming starting in 1992. This work reached the public with version 2.1 of the SOMobjects Toolkit [14], which was released by IBM in 1994. To increase the available information, this paper proposes that metaprogrammers (who write metaclasses) declare new modifiers that class programmers can apply to methods and instance variables. Subsequently, the metaclass checks for these modifiers when participating in the construction of the class (written by the programmer).

Our line of thinking was influenced by the trend in language design in which the number of modifiers has increased. Eiffel introduced a flexible indexing clause to provide information for tools that archive and retrieve classes. Despite this step forward, the indexing clause has no impact on the meaning of the program. Java introduces more modifiers than C++ for controlling the properties of classes, methods, and fields. One modifier use not allowed by Java is synchronized in front of class. An important observation is that this could have been achieved in SOM with a metaclass. One is led to the need for declarable modifiers by combining this observation, the trend of increasing modifiers in language design,

W. Cazzola et al. (Eds.): Reflection and Software Engineering, LNCS 1826, pp. 39–57, 2000.
© Springer-Verlag Berlin Heidelberg 2000

and the di7culties in programming certain kinds of class transformations in SOM.

The ideas presented in this paper have been tested in SIOP2, which simulates the successor to the metaobject protocol that was presented in [9]. Beyond the examples in [9], SIOP2 was used to implement a library of software patterns [10]. A copy of SIOP2 can be obtained by writing to the author at `forman@acm.org`.

This paper is organized as follows. Section 2 gives a description of JEM, a notation that extends Java with metaclasses, and additional background on programming metaclasses. Section 3 describes the kind of problem that a metaprogrammer faces when trying to write highly useful metaclasses. Section 4 presents the solution to our problem and an example of the solution. Section 5 discusses the issues concerning the use of multiple modi7ers (which implies the composition of metaclasses).

2   Background

To present the usefulness of declarable modi7ers, a notation is needed. This section presents JEM, Java extended with metaclasses. Currently, JEM has neither a formal semantic model nor a compiler. JEM is interesting in itself, but is not the point of this paper. The complete description of JEM is contained [8].

2.1   JEM is an Extension of Java

The core of the Java object model is embodied in the classes named Object and Class. Class is a subclass of Object. Object is an instance of Class and Class is an instance of itself. Object is the root of the inheritance hierarchy. This con7guration is depicted in Figure 1 along with a class object for Dog, a class that is declared as follows.

class Dog   ...

Although odd looking, the circularities in this diagram result from the evolution in the design of object-oriented programming systems that began with SmallTalk-80 [11]. There is a detailed explanation of why Figure 1 looks as it does in Chapter 2 of [9]. All classes are objects and a *metaclass* is a class whose instances are classes. In Java, Class is the only metaclass and all classes are instances of Class.

Throughout this paper, we use diagrams drawn with the conventions of Figure 1 to illustrate the meaning of JEM constructs. JEM is an extension of Java. That is, if one does not employ metaclasses, then one can understand a JEM program by using its Java meaning. This implies that all of the familiar concepts of Java hold for JEM. Figure 1 also depicts the basic con7guration for JEM. A class de7nes instance variables and methods. A method de7nition can be either an introduction or an override. The instance variables and method supported by a class are those that it either introduces or inherits.

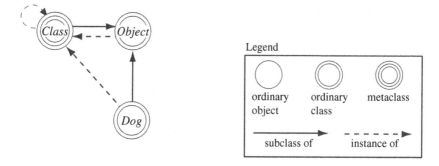

Fig. 1. The basic conguration of both a Java system and a JEM system.

JEM (like Java) is a class-based programming language, which means that an object responds to the methods that its class supports (introduces or inherits). In this respect, classes are like ordinary objects in that a class responds to the methods supported by its metaclass. Java classes respond to the methods supported by Class, which are the methods introduced by Class and the methods inherited from Object. The same is true for JEM with the extension that JEM facilitates the creation of metaclasses other than Class.

To properly explain JEM, we need to introduce a new concept into the vocabulary of object-oriented programming. We all know that a class supports a set of methods that may be invoked on its instances. The usual operational semantic model speci7es that to each class there is a method table that binds the method identi7er to a *code pointer*, which designates the control point to which control is passed when a method is invoked. This model is not su7cient to explain JEM.

For JEM, a *method table* binds a method identi7er to an *implementation chain*. An implementation chain is a list of code pointers. For a class una7ected by any metaclass, the implementation chain for each method contains the code pointers for each override and the base implementation (de7ned to be the code pointer associated with the method when it was introduced). Execution of a method begins with the 7rst code pointer in the implementation chain and an invocation of the **super** method executes the next code pointer in the implementation chain.

2.2   The Declaration of a Metaclass

Metaclasses are desirable because a new dimension in modularity (and thus, reuse) is attained. *Putting Metaclasses to Work* [9] shows how to think about a metaclass as a class transformation. This allows the factoring of a property of a class away from any classes that have that property. Some examples of properties that may be so factored are

Synchronized – wrap all method invocations in critical section
Traced   – output information about method calls and returns
Persistent   – ensure all changed objects are saved on permanent storage

Implementations of the 7rst two (and others) may be found in [9]; the third may be found in [19]. Factoring on the basis of class transformations is a useful programming technique that is defended in [7] and [9].

In Java, Class is 7nal and, thus, cannot be subclassed. JEM relaxes this constraint and allows the subclassing of Class. Any descendant of Class is a metaclass (as is Class, too), because the descendant inherits from Class the template for making a class (that is, all of the instance variables that constitute a class along with their initializations). Therefore, by subclassing Class, one can write a new metaclass that is highly reusable, because it can embody a class property independently of the classes that have the property.

Let us illustrate the above by writing in JEM part of the code for the metaclass Synchronized, which places all methods of a class within a critical section. Figure 2 shows the code on the left and the diagram of the class hierarchy on the right. Because a class is being declared, Synchronized appears as an instance of Class on the right. Because Class is being extended, Synchronized also appears as a subclass of Class.

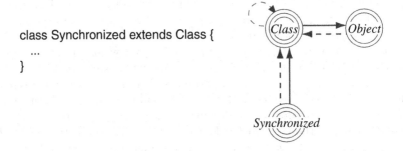

class Synchronized extends Class {

    ...

}

Fig. 2. Fragment of the Synchronized metaclass.

Below we do explain to how to program the Synchronized metaclass, but 7rst let us describe how metaclasses are used.

2.3   Using Metaclasses

In JEM, the metaclass for a class is declared by writing the metaclass name along with the other class modi7ers. For example, to declare a class named SynchronizedDog that is a subclass of Dog and an instance of the metaclass Synchronized, one would write:

Synchronized class SynchronizedDog extends Dog

Combining this statement with those that create Figure 1 and Figure 2 yields the structure depicted in Figure 3. The default metaclass in JEM is Class if no metaclass is mentioned in front of the key word class. Placing the metaclass

reference among class modi7ers is appropriate, because as a class transformation, the metaclass modi7es the class. This section presents the use of a single
metaclass among the modi7ers. The use of multiple metaclass names among the
modi7ers is possible and is discussed in Section 5.

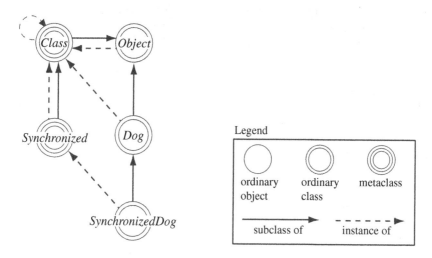

Fig. 3. The class objects upon which SynchronizedDog depends.

2.4   Intercession During Class Construction

Class must be extended with intercessional capability, which means that the
metalevel must be able to a7ect the execution of methods. A complete list of
the methods that give JEM intercessional capability is contained in [8]. The
writing of the Synchronized metaclass requires a few such methods. One method
is addMetaclassOverride, which is introduced by Class with the signature

    void addMetaclassOverride(Method m, Method r)

where m is a method supported by the target class and r is a re ective method.
addMetaclassOverride modi7es the method table so that r is invoked before the
currently existing chain of implementations for m. The method r must have the
same signature and return value as m except if r is declared re ective (see below).
    There are two more methods that must be added to Class. Following [9],
JEM allows intercession only during class construction, which means during the
time that the class object is loaded. JEM introduces two methods, initializeClass
and readyClass, in its Class that facilitate intercession. These two methods are
introduced with the following signatures.

    void initializeClass( )
    void readyClass( )

A metaclass can declare an override of either method. An override of initial-izeClass uses intercessional methods to modify the class object being constructed. An override of readyClass uses the introspective methods to ensure the transformation implemented by its declaring metaclass is compatible with those of other metaclasses. The class loader 7rst invokes initializeClass and then readyClass. After readyClass is executed on a class object, no further changes are allowed.

Let us illustrate the above by completing the metaclass Synchronized, which places all methods of a class within a critical section. In Figure 4, initializeClass (which is a method of Class) is called during the construction of an instance of Synchronized to achieve the desired transformation. In this case, for each method of the class being constructed, the method table entry is modi7ed (by addMetaclassOverride) so that the method acquireReleaseSemaphore acts as an override for each method of a class that is an instance of Synchronized. The following numbered points further explain the code in Figure 4 and correspond to the circled numbers in the 7gure.

1. The method getSupportedMethods is introduced by Class with the signature

   Method[] getSupportedMethods( )

   It returns an array of all methods introduced or inherited by the class on which it is invoked.

2. The expression acquireReleaseSemaphore.method evaluates to an object of class Method. This is like a Java expression of the form <classname>.class, which evaluates to the corresponding class object. Note that the .method expression can only be used within the scope of the method name.

3. The modi7er re ective indicates that the method invocation is to be re-ected, that is, treated as an object. Therefore, the parameters to a re ective method are
   - the target of the method call,
   - a Method object that represents the called method,
   - and an Object[] that contains the parameters to the called method.

   The use of an object array to re ect the parameters of a method call is consistent with Java in that the invoke method of class Method uses an object array for the parameter list. Primitive values are wrapped when the object array is created. The modi7er re ective may only be used inside of a metaclass. A re ective method must be declared private.

4. In the de7nition of acquireReleaseSemaphore, the expression super.m(pl) is evaluated dynamically. That is, super binds to the parent of the class that is the target of the call to addMetaclassOverride. A compiler can discern this case because the parameter m is Method valued, rather than being a literal method name. This super invocation in acquireReleaseSemaphore requires only one parameter of type Object[], because it is written in the context of a re ective method.

The above items imply a rather large and interesting set of additions to Java to make it convenient for re ective programming. Such additions are clearly useful because the capability in Figure 4 cannot be programmed within Java.

```
class Synchronized extends Class {

  void initializeClass() {                              ①
    super.initializeClass();
    Method[] methods = this.getSupportedMethods();                    ②
    for (int i = 0; i < methods.length; i++) {
      this.addMetaclassOverride( methods[i], acquireReleaseSemaphore.method );
    }
  }              ③

  reflective private
  Object acquireReleaseSemaphore( Object target, Method m, Object[] pl ) {
    synchronized( target ) {
      return super.m( pl );
    }
  }              ④
}
```

Fig. 4. Simple Synchronized metaclass.

2.5 Development Organizations

The software development for JEM envisions two roles being involved. One is the *metaprogrammer*, who writes the metaclass Synchronized. The second is the *programmer*, who writes the class SynchronizedDog.

JEM is a single inheritance language, which gives it an interesting property:

Each ancestor of a metaclass except for   (JEM Property 1)
Object is a metaclass.

Recall that all descendants of Class are metaclasses. JEM Property 1 holds because there is only one inheritance path from a metaclass and that path must lead back to Class. Object is the superclass of Class and creates the minor awkwardness in the statement. JEM Property 1 is not true for systems with multiple inheritance, where a metaclass must have one path that leads back to Class but can also have other paths on which there are ordinary classes.

The effect of this property is that the work of metaprogrammers is segregated from that of programmers with respect to the flow of definitions implied by inheritance. Programmers can use JEM just as they use Java. In addition, programmers have new power available through using metaclasses as class modifiers. If, to achieve this improvement, the programming model for metaprogrammers is a major extension Java, then so be it. There are no metaprogrammers today who will be upset by the JEM extension to Java.

3 The Problem

When a metaclass is used as a modi7er, it transforms the whole class. This leads to a problem: suppose the programmer of SynchronizedDog wishes to exempt some methods from being wrapped in the critical section. To handle this situation, the metaprogrammer must enable the metaclass so as to allow the programmer to express the intention that particular methods should not be placed inside of the critical region. Here the metaprogrammer is severely limited. One solution is to require the programmer to add (or override) a method to express these intentions.

Let us try to program this kind of solution. To express exemptions, the metaprogrammer requires that the programmer write a static method named isMethodSynchronizedExempt, which has signature

boolean isMethodSynchronizedExempt(String methodName, Class[] paramTypes)

that returns true if the method speci7ed by the parameters is de7ned for the class and should be exempt from synchronization by the Synchronized metaclass. isMethodSynchronizedExempt must be static because it must be called during class construction (and for the sake of this discussion we assume there is no problem in doing so). The metaprogrammer writes the Synchronized metaclass as shown in Figure 5. The standard getMethod of java.lang.Class is used to determine if the class (being constructed) responds to the static method isMethodSynchronizedExempt. If not, the NoSuchMethodException is raised and all methods are placed in the critical region (this is in the clause where NoSuchMethodException is caught). If no exception is raised, then the placing a method inside the critical region must be guarded by a call to isMethodSynchronizedExempt. The invocation of isMethodSynchronizedExempt is done with the invoke method of the class Method. This has to be done because the metaprogrammer does not have a static literal with which to write the call to this static method. The invocation is done with parameters that are retrieved from the Method object.

The metaclass in Figure 5 is not easy to write. In addition, this design hides several nasty problems that have been passed on to the programmer by the metaprogrammer.

- isMethodSynchronizedExempt is expected to be a static method that is written by the programmer. The metaprogrammer cannot declare the interface so that the compiler can check if the method is implemented properly.
- There are two formal parameters to isMethodSynchronizedExempt used to identify the method. These are awkward to use when the programmer writes isMethodSynchronizedExempt.
- When subclassing a Synchronized class, the programmer is left with the problem of how to aggregate the exemptions of ancestor classes. In Java, one cannot use super to invoke a static method and we do not wish to change Java for the programmer.

Another possible solution is to require the programmer to declare a static variable with a particular name if the method is to be exempt. For example, if

```
class Synchronized extends Class {

  void initializeClass() {
    super.initializeClass();
    Class[] paramTypes = new Class[1];
    paramTypes[0] = String.class;
    try {
      Method isMethodSynchronizedExempt
                  = this.getMethod( "isMethodSynchronizedExempt", paramTypes );
      Method[] methods = this.getSupportedMethods();
      Object[] actualParams = new Object[2];
      for (int i = 0; i < methods.length; i++) {
        actualParams[0] = method[i].getName();
        actualParams[1] = method[i].getParameterTypes();
        if ( ! isMethodSynchronizedExempt.invoke( null, actualParams ) ) {
          addMetaclassOverride( methods[i], acquireReleaseSemaphore.method );
        }
      }
    } catch ( NoSuchMethodException e ) {
      for (int i = 0; i < methods.length; i++) {
        addMetaclassOverride( methods[i], acquireReleaseSemaphore.method );
      }
    } catch ( SecurityException e ) {
      // This cannot happen because the metaclass has access to all methods.
    }
  }

  reflective private
  Object acquireReleaseSemaphore( Object target, Method m, Object[] pl ) {
    synchronized( target ) {
        return super.m();
    }
  }
}
```

Fig. 5. Synchronized metaclass that uses a method to specify exemptions.

the method bark is to be exempt, the programmer is required to declare a static boolean with the name barkIsSynchronizedExempt. This solution has similar problems to the 7rst. Neither of the above designs is a satisfactory solution to the problem of how the programmer should express intentions with respect to properties of individual methods. The fundamental issue is that using either methods or instance variables for this kind of communication is tedious to program and leads to complex code. The next section introduces a new approach.

4   A Proposed Solution

Let us revisit the source of power of object-oriented programming — the synergy of knowledge representation and programming. Consider the following linguistic interpretation of the evolution of computer programming. In the 1950s and 1960s, programming was about commanding the computer — verbs. In the 1970s, this approach proved deficient. A new paradigm arose in which the specification of abstract data types and then classes — nouns — became foremost for the programmer. This paradigm, object-oriented programming, has evolved throughout the 1980s and 1990s. Although powerful and useful, object-oriented programming has proved deficient in isolating properties of objects — adjectives — so that the code that implements a property can be reused. This linguistic interpretation is completed by noting that metaclasses correspond to adjectives, because a metaclass transforms a class, which is the analog of an adjective transforming a noun.

Now given the above view, our problem has a simple interpretation: a metaclass only provides a property to be associated with an entire class. But a solution to our problem requires a way to associate an arbitrary property with other parts of a program, in particular, methods and instance variables. By following the linguistic interpretation, a solution to our problem is achieved by allowing a metaprogrammer to declare modifiers[1] that can be associated with methods and instance variables.

The solution to our problem is for JEM to allow a metaprogrammer to declared modifiers for methods and instance variables. These modifiers can be used in the list of modifiers at the beginning of a declaration of a method or an instance variable. These modifiers obey the following rules.

- A modifier is declared with either of the following statements.

    field modifier <comma-separated-list-of-modifiers>
    method modifier <comma-separated-list-of-modifiers>

  where field, method, and modifier are keywords. Such declarations may only be written inside of a metaclass declaration. (Adding new keywords interferes the compatibility of existing Java programs with JEM, but we are not going to worry about that here.)
- A modifier must be declared before it can be used.
- A modifier declaration has as scope the metaclass in which it is declared, any subclass of that metaclass, and any class that uses that metaclass or any of its subclasses. However, the scope is limited by class access modifiers to the scope of the metaclass name. That is, if the metaclass as package visibility, then so do any modifiers declared in the metaclass.

---

[1] You may have noticed that this section started with our linguistic interpretation in which methods are thought of as verbs. In addition, methods are usually named with verb phrases. However, the modifiers that are typically associated with methods are not adverbs but adjectives, for example in Java, public, synchronized, abstract, and so on. This may seem inconsistent, but it is not, because in a reflective programming system, the methods are embodied as objects. That is, the adjectives are applied to the objects for example, instances of class Method. The designers of Java did well by using the term modifier, which is neutral with respect to adjectives and adverbs.

– If the use of a modi7er is ambiguous, an error is generated. This can happen because multiple metaclasses can participate in the construction of a class (see Section 5). Disambiguation can be achieved by using the declaring metaclass name as a quali7er.

4.1   Example of the Solution

With the addition of declarable modi7ers, the Synchronized metaclass is written as shown in Figure 6.

```
class Synchronized extends Class {

  method modifier Unsynchronized;

  void initializeClass() {
    super.initializeClass();
    Method[] methods = getSupportedMethods();
    for ( int i = 0; i < methods.length; i++ ) {
      if ( !methods[i].hasModifier( Unsynchronized ) ) {
        addMetaclassOverride( methods[i], acquireReleaseSemaphore.method );
      }
    }
  }

  reflective private
  Object acquireReleaseSemaphore( Object target, Method m, Object[] pl ) {
    synchronized( target ) {
      return super.m();
    }
  }
}
```

Fig. 6. Synchronized metaclass that implements the Unsynchronized modi er.

Little is changed from our 7rst solution in Figure 4 other then the following two items.

– The modi7er declaration binds the literal Unsynchronized to a unique object of class Modi er.
– The loop now has a test that checks if the method should be unsynchronized. The test uses the method hasModi er, which is added to the interface of class Method with signature
     boolean hasModi er(Modi er)
hasModi er returns the boolean true if the modi7er speci7ed in the parameter is associated with the method and false otherwise.

As an example of how the metaclass in Figure 6 is used, consider the Dog class, which is defined as follows.

```
class Dog extends Object {
    String name = "Fido";
    String getName() { return name; };
}
```

Below the SynchronizedDog class can be derived from the Dog class. If one wishes to exempt a method from the synchronization one just declares an override with no method body, which adds the modifier to the method.

```
Synchronized class SynchronizedDog extends Dog {
    Unsynchronized String getName();
}
```

The override of getName with no method body has the same meaning as writing the following.

```
Synchronized class SynchronizedDog extends Dog {
    Unsynchronized String getName() { super.getName(); }
}
```

We started with the idea that a metaclass is a transformation (modifier) for an entire class. This led to the problem that the metaprogrammer does not always have enough information about the intentions of the class programmer, which in turn led to the problem of increasing the communication between the two. Our solution enables the metaprogrammer to declare new modifiers that are used by the class programmer to declare intentions. This very general solution has aspects that require further comment.

4.2   Inheritance of Modifiers

We have extended the meaning of modifiers for three JEM entities: metaclass identifiers used as modifiers in class declarations and metaprogrammer-declared identifiers used as modifiers in method and instance variable declarations. Let us now examine the inheritance issues related to these modifiers.

For reasons explained in Chapter 3 of [9], the class hierarchy (which includes the metaclasses) must adhere to this invariant:

The metaclass for a class must be a descendant of or equal to the metaclasses for each of its parent classes.

Enforcing this invariant has the effect that a (metaclass) modifier is inherited. This effect is called *inheritance of metaclass constraints*, because when a metaclass is used as a modifier, that modifier is treated as a constraint on the actual metaclass for the class being constructed and the constraints are accumulated when deciding on the metaclass. As an example, consider

```
class Collie extends SynchronizedDog { ... }
```

In this case, the class Collie has the Synchronized property (as do all other descendants of SynchronizedDog).

When overriding a method, the modifiers of the overridden method are inherited by the overriding method. This decision is dictated by inheritance of metaclass constraints. If the metaclass modifier is inherited, the method modifiers must be inherited, too. Continuing the example, if Collie is derived from SynchronizedDog as follows

```
class Collie extends SynchronizedDog {
    final String getName();
}
```

then the getName method for Collie is Unsynchronized, because modifiers are inherited as well as implementation. This issue does not arise for instance variables (fields), because instance variables cannot be overridden. That is, a declaration of an instance variable with the same name as one in an ancestor class declares a new instance variable (and hides the ancestor's).

4.3   Declaring Multiple Modifiers

A metaclass may declare multiple modifiers, which may be applied to the same method or instance variable. The metaprogrammer is obligated to determine the meaning for such situations.

This is the same as the problem that the language designer must solve when defining modifiers for the language. The Java language designers specified interactions of the access modifiers in Section 8.4.3 of [12]. The metaprogrammer is in a real sense extending the programming language (as was observed in [16]). The metaprogrammer must carefully define and enforce the meaning in cases were multiple modifiers apply to an entity. The metaobject protocol must have appropriate facilitates to do so.

For example, the Synchronized metaclass might declare both Unsynchronized and Synchronized as modifiers. Note that the Synchronized modifier would have the same meaning as Java's synchronized modifier. In this case, metaprogrammer might change the loop in initializeClass to look as follows.

```
for ( int i = 0; i ¡ methods.length; i++ ) {
    if ( !methods[i].hasModifier( Unsynchronized )
       || methods[i].hasModifier( Synchronized ) ) {
         addMetaclassOverride( methods[i], acquireReleaseSemaphore.method );
    }
}
```

This means that if both modifiers are present the Synchronized modifier has precedence. This is only one of several possibilities; all of which must be studied by the metaprogrammer with the goal of making the metaclass as easy to use as possible.

5   Using Multiple Metaclass Modifiers in a Declaration

The use of multiple metaclass modifiers in a declaration brings us to the issue of how properties compose. JEM provides a framework in which metaprogrammers can write a metaclass that embodies a property that can be used and reused by programmers. As we see below, JEM also provides a framework that composes metaclasses when the class programmer asks for multiple properties to be endowed to a class. It is the obligation of the metaprogrammer to use the metaobject protocol to ensure that no other metaclass can interfere with the working of his metaclass.

5.1   Multiple Metaclass Modifiers in a Class Declaration

Multiple metaclasses can be used in the declaration of a class. The meaning of such constructions was studied in [9]. For example, consider the following JEM declarations.

```
class Dog { ... }
class Persistent extends Class { ... }
class Synchronized extends Class { ... }
Persistent Synchronized class PersistentSynchronizedDog extends Dog {}
```

The first line declares an ordinary class. The second and third line declare two metaclasses as we have already explained. For the purpose of this section, we care only about the relationships among these classes, not what they do (for a discussion of how to use a metaobject protocol to implement persistence, see [19]). The fourth line can be somewhat mysterious unless you have read [9]. The class PersistentSynchronizedDog must have a metaclass, but neither Persistent nor Synchronized is an adequate metaclass. The metaclass for PersistentSynchronizedDog must be the multiple inheritance join of Persistent and Synchronized as is depicted in Figure 7. This multiple inheritance join of the metaclasses — called a *derived metaclass* — is constructed by the programming system; it is a new metaclass constructed solely for the purpose of being the metaclass for PersistentSynchronizedDog and, thus, ensuring that PersistentSynchronizedDog is both persistent and synchronized.

In JEM, neither the programmer nor the metaprogrammer can write code that specifies that a class has multiple parents. Thus, syntactically, JEM is a single-inheritance language like Java. JEM is defined so that derived metaclasses are produced by the system as needed. Recall JEM Property 1: Each ancestor of a metaclass except for Object is a metaclass. This property implies that the JEM programming model for class programmers is the same as that of Java, because an ordinary class (written by a class programmer) can never be used a superclass for a metaclass. That is, the implications of derived metaclasses are never the concern of the class programmer.

JEM has a second property that is equally interesting:

A derived metaclass cannot be   (JEM Property 2)
the ancestor of a metaprogrammer-written metaclass.

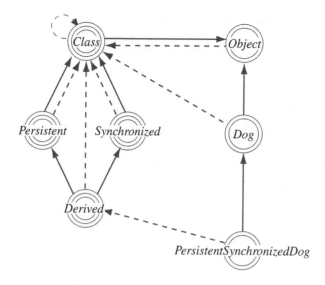

Fig. 7. The class objects upon which the PersistentSynchronizedDog depends.

This is because derived metaclasses are not statically declared and have no literal name that can be used to write a subclass. This implication of this property is that the derived metaclass are neatly segregated at the bottom of the inheritance hierarchy from the metaprogrammer-written metaclasses.

JEM Property 2 implies that the programming model for the metaprogrammer is almost a single inheritance model, too. It is a single inheritance model in the sense that when the metaprogrammer writes a metaclass, the meaning of that metaclass as a class transformation is determined by a single inheritance programming model. This facilitates the writing of stand-alone metaclasses in JEM. By "stand alone," we mean a metaclass that is not composed with other metaclasses. This leads to an important obligation of the metaprogrammer — the need to analyze the composability of a newly written metaclass with other metaclasses (which is done when a derived metaclass is created by the system). In this case, the metaprogrammer must understand multiple inheritance joins. Further, it is the obligation of the metaprogrammer to use the introspective part of the metaobject protocol to examine the class under construction to ensure that the requirements of his metaclass are satisfied by the derived metaclass (that is, no other metaclass has transformed the class in contradictory way). If this examination uncovers a problem, then an exception should be thrown during class construction. To facilitate this examination, the JEM metaobject protocol has the method named readyClass. It is called after initializeClass at a time in class construction when changes to the class are no longer allowed. The tests performed by readyClass is similar to design rule checking [4].

5.2   Redundant Metaclass Modifiers

The JEM syntax allows a metaclass to be used multiple times in the declarations of a class and its ancestors. For example,

```
Persistent class X { }
Persistent class Y extends X { }
```

where Persistent is a metaclass. Because of inheritance of metaclass constraints, reuse of a metaclass in a descendant of a class has no effect. It is best that an error be issued in such cases, because there may be intervening classes. Consider the following example.

```
Persistent class X { }
Synchronized class Y extends X { }
Persistent class Z extends Y { }
```

where Synchronized is also a metaclass. The class X has Persistent instances. Because Y extends X, the instances of Y are Synchronized Persistent, not the other way around. The order of application is important. That is, a Persistent Synchronized object is not necessarily the same as Synchronized Persistent object. In this case, the second use of Persistent must be ignored so that instances of Z are instances of Y. If this is not the case, Z would be constructed by applying the transformations implied by metaclasses in the reverse order of their application to Y. By ignoring the second use of Persistent rather than signaling an error, the programmer may be led to thinking that a Persistent Synchronized Z class is being created, while actually a Synchronized Persistent Z is being created.

This design decision (to exclude multiple metaclass usage in an inheritance) also obviates some nasty problems with the order disagreement among classes in the inheritance hierarchy. For example, consider the following three declarations.

```
Persistent class X { }
Synchronized class Y extends X { }
Persistent Synchronized class Z extends Y { }
```

Here the programmer of Z desires a Persistent Synchronized class, but this disagrees with its superclass. The declaration of Z must be an error, because the order of the metaclasses disagrees with the order in which the metaclasses are applied in the inheritance hierarchy.

6   Directions for Future Research

This paper contains part of a proposal that intended to increase the power of programming with metaclasses. Despite the attractiveness of the proposal, it is not perfect. Below are several points that require further study.

- First and foremost, JEM is a language proposal that has neither been implemented nor used. The proposal [8] is available from the author. The declarable modifier concept of this paper is independent of JEM. However, if further work reveals a problem with JEM, then the usefulness of declarable modifiers is diminished until a substitute for JEM can be created. Please, feel free to write me with any questions or comments about JEM.

- In theory, the obligation of the metaprogrammer to ensure that all metaclasses compose is an $\mathcal{O}(n^2)$ problem, because all pairs of metaclasses must be checked for composability. In practice, metaclasses rarely share resources, and those that they do share usually involve a position in the implementation chain for a method. Together [9] and [10] show that a closely coordinated group can produce a large set of mutually composable metaclasses. The next step is to produce a set of rules for producing a set of composable metaclasses when multiple metaprogrammers cannot communicate with each other (such as in producing a library of metaclasses).

- A metaclass cannot have an ordinary class as an ancestor. In theory, this limits reuse, because one cannot inherit functionality implemented by a class into a metaclasses. This is the downside of not having multiple inheritance. It seems to be a good tradeoff, but we will not know for sure until JEM has been implemented and used.

- The reflective modifier is a way of reflecting part of the call stack. SOM did this through its dispatch/redispatchStub facility (which was based on Smalltalk's dispatch method). The modifier only partially meets the goals of reflection because the metaprogrammer still cannot look at the entire call stack.

As for related research, depending how one looks there are either many or few precedents for this proposal for declarable modifiers. Don Batory used similar ideas in examples of the JTS program generator [3] and he suspects others in program generator research have done so. There are three precedents to note.

- A compile-time metaobject protocol is quite similar to a program generation system. OpenC++ [5] implements declarable keywords that can appear before the class keyword, a type name, or the new keyword. Despite this, there are major differences between OpenC++ and JEM that start with the JEM emphasis on the metaclass as the unit of modularity for metalevel activity. The OpenC++ "instantiates" statement is an imperative metaclass declaration. Our position is that a metaclass declaration must be treated as constraint (see Chapter 3 of [9]). This is more than a mere syntactic difference. In JEM, metaclasses are the interpreters of the declarable modifiers placed in front of a class. Another implication of this difference is the JEM view that modifiers should be inherited. In addition, declarable modifiers may not be put in front of an OpenC++ method declaration. OpenC++ has a successor OpenJava [6], which appears to apply the same compile-time techniques to preprocess Java.

- The adaptable method concept of Lead++ [2] allows the programmer to dynamically choose a method implementation based on a boolean-returning computation on a set of environmental objects. Although the Lead++ does achieve its adaptability goal, Lead++ does not satisfy our goal of facilitating a wide range of class transformations.

– The indexing clause of Eiffel [17] does allow a programmer to associate arbitrary attributes with a class, but these attributes can have no impact on the definition of the class.

Our research into metaclasses (as presented in [9]) is one way to factor class-based object-oriented programs to achieve greater reuse. There are several related efforts that define other factorings: mixins [7], composition filters [1], adjustments [18], aspects [16], and subjects [13]. None of these have proposed declarable modifiers.

7   Conclusion

Metaclasses are an effective means for programming class transformations. However, there are many transformations that require a granularity of information below that of the entire class. This paper explores how such information could be provided by extending an object-oriented programming language to allow new modifiers to be declared for use with methods and instance variables. These modifiers are declared by the metaprogrammer in a metaclass definition. They are used by the class programmer to control the class transformation implemented by the metaclass. Furthermore, the proposal recognizes that the metaprogrammer and the programmer are involved in a cooperative venture to create a beneficial software system.

Acknowledgements. Many thanks go to Don Batory, Walter Cazzola, Scott Danforth, Nate Forman, and Doug Lea for their thoughtful comments on this paper.

References

1. Mehmet Aksit, Lodewijk Bergmans, Jan Bosch, Ken Wakita, and Akinori Yonezawa. Abstracting Object Interactions Using Composition Filters. In *Proceedings of ECOOP'93, Workshop on Object-Based Distributed Programming*, LNCS 791, pages 152–184, Kaiserslautern, Germany, July 1993.
2. Noriki Amano and Takuo Watanabe. An Approach for Constructing Dynamically Adaptable Component-Based Software System Using LEAD++. In Walter Cazzola, Robert J. Stroud, and Francesco Tisato, editors, *Proceedings of the 1st OOPSLA Workshop on Object Oriented Reflection and Software Engineering (OORaSE'99), pages 1-16.* Denver, CO, November 1999.
3. Don Batory. private communication. (For information on JTS see http://www.cs.utexas.edu/users/schwartz), February 2000.
4. Don Batory and Bart J. Geraci. Composition Validation and Subjectivity in GenVoca Generators. *IEEE Transactions on Software Engineering (special issue on Software Reuse)*, pages 67–82, February 1997.

5. Shigeru Chiba. A Meta-Object Protocol for C++. In *Proceedings of the 10th Annual Conference on Object-Oriented Programming Systems, Languages, and Applications (OOPSLA'95)*, volume 30 of *Sigplan Notices*, pages 285–299, Austin, Texas, USA, October 1995. ACM.

6. Shigeru Chiba, Michiaki Tatsubori, Marc-Olivier Killijian and Kozo Itano. OpenJava: A Class-based Macro System for Java. In Walter Cazzola, Robert J. Stroud, and Francesco Tisato, editors, *Reflection and Software Engineering*, Lecture Notes in Computer Science 1826. Springer-Verlag, June 2000.

7. Matthias Felleisen, Matthew Flatt, and Shriram Krishnamurthi. Classes and Mixins. In *Proceedings of the 25th ACM SIGPLAN-SIGACT Symposium on Principles of Programming Languages*, pages 171–183, January 1998.

8. Ira R. Forman. JEM: A Proposal for Extending Java with Metaclasses. to be published.

9. Ira R. Forman and Scott H. Danforth. *Putting Metaclasses to Work*. Addison-Wesley, 1999.

10. Nate B. Forman. Metaclass-Based Implementation of Software Patterns. Masters report, University of Texas at Austin, December 1999.

11. Adele Goldberg and David Robson. *SmallTalk-80: The Language and Its Implementation*. Addison-Wesley, Reading, Massachussetts, 1983.

12. James Gosling, Bill Joy, and Guy Steele. *The Java Language Specification*. The Java Series ... from the Source. Addison-Wesley, Reading, Massachussetts, 1996.

13. William H. Harrison and Harold Ossher. Subject-Oriented Programming (A Critique of Pure Objects). In *Proceedings of OOPSLA'93*, pages 411–428, September 1993.

14. IBM. SOMobjects Developer Toolkit Reference Manual. Reference Manual Version 2.1, IBM, October 1994.

15. Gregor Kickzales, Jim des Rivières, and Daniel G. Bobrow. *The Art of the Metaobject Protocol*. MIT Press, Cambridge, Massachusetts, 1991.

16. Gregor Kiczales, John Lamping, Anurag Mendhekar, Chris Maeda, Cristina Videira Lopes, Jean-Marc Loingtier, and John Irwin. Aspect-Oriented Programming. In *11th European Conference on Object Oriented Programming (ECOOP'97)*, Lecture Notes in Computer Science 1241, pages 220–242, Finland, June 1997. Springer-Verlag.

17. Bertrand Meyer. *Eiffel: The Language*. Prentice-Hall, 1994.

18. Mira Mezini. *Variational Object-Oriented Programming Beyond Classes and Inheritance*. Kluwer Academic Publisher, 1998.

19. Andreas Pæpcke Eds. *Object-Oriented Programming: The CLOS Perspective*. MIT Press, 1993.

Managing Evolution Using Cooperative Designs and a Reflective Architecture

Emiliano Tramontana

Department of Computing Science,
University of Newcastle upon Tyne,
Newcastle upon Tyne, NE1 7RU, UK
Emiliano.Tramontana@newcastle.ac.uk

Abstract The separation of concerns is important to attain object oriented systems which can be easily evolved. This paper presents a reflective architecture which enforces the separation of concerns by allocating functional, interaction and synchronization code to different levels. A variant of collaborations (CO actions) is used to capture interactions between objects and avoids spreading the description of interactions among the participating objects. Functional and interaction code are also separated from synchronization code by means of metalevel components. Introducing changes into the reflective architecture to consider evolution needs is facilitated by the loose coupling of different concerns. Hence, changing a concern often consists of modifying only one component of the reflective architecture. The paper describes the reflective architecture in terms of a case study. The evolution of the reflective implementation of the case study is compared with the evolution of an alternative implementation and the benefits of the proposed architecture are shown by using an evolution metric.

1 Introduction

Object oriented systems consist of a collection of interacting objects. In such systems interactions are mixed with functional code and spread among several objects. Therefore, both objects and interactions are difficult to express and reuse. When those systems need to evolve, the code is difficult to understand, since it mixes functionalities of objects with their interactions, and difficult to modify, since a change in an object might cause all the interacting objects to change.

Several approaches, which can be grouped under the name of *collaborations* (or *contracts*), have been proposed to describe sets of interactions between objects, and to avoid interactions being scattered among objects [24,29]. However, most of these approaches do not enforce a clear separation between functional and interaction aspects, so changing one implies also changing the other [2,3,14]. Other approaches which achieve such a separation require extending the existing object oriented model, thus compromising the feasibility of implementations using standard object oriented languages [12,19].

W. Cazzola et al. (Eds.): Reflection and Software Engineering, LNCS 1826, pp. 59–78, 2000.

This paper uses *cooperations* to represent interactions between objects, and a reflective architecture for implementing software systems using objects and cooperations [8,9]. In a *cooperative object oriented* design relationships between objects are only captured by cooperations. A reflective implementation of a cooperative object oriented design allocates cooperations at the metalevel, thus enhancing the evolution of software systems, and providing a means of implementing the control of access to objects transparently from the objects [10,28]. The aim of the present paper is to show, using a case study, how the reflective architecture supports evolution. Some evolution scenarios are analysed for the case study and an evolution metric is presented to quantify the effort to change the reflective system. The evolution scenarios are compared with the equivalent evolution of an alternative implementation of the case study.

This paper is an extended version of [28] which presents the detail of a reflective architecture implementing a cooperative object oriented design, and where the enhancement provided by the reflective implementation is quantified by an evolution metric. A different version of the case study was previously presented in which evolution was discussed in the context of a cooperative object oriented design [27].

The paper is structured as follows. Section 2 describes the cooperative object oriented design and how it enhances evolution. Section 3 introduces the relevant background concerning reflection and the motivation for using reflection in our approach. Section 4 shows the cooperative object oriented design of a case study and its reflective implementation. Section 5 analyses evolution scenarios for the case study and compares the reflective implementation with an alternative one. The related work is presented in section 6 and eventually conclusions are presented in section 7.

2   Cooperative Object Oriented Design and Evolution

Object oriented systems consist of a collection of interacting objects. Interactions are usually described within objects, thus a complex set of interactions is difficult to express since it is scattered among objects. In a *cooperative object oriented (COO)* design, the object oriented model is extended by explicitly representing collaborative activities between objects which are expressed in terms of *cooperative actions (CO Actions)* [8,9]. Instances of CO actions are called *cooperations*. Using the COO design, objects are employed to model components' behaviour, and cooperations are used to model interactions between objects. A CO action specifies the collaborative activity of its participating objects and the pre-conditions, invariants and post-conditions associated with a collaborative activity. These express the respective conditions for a group of objects to start, hold and finish a cooperation.

Classes of a COO design are not aware of each other. The behaviour of a class is described only in terms of its own methods. This yields the construction of classes which are easy to understand and modify, since they do not mix functional and interaction code. Classes are also likely to be reused, because they are not specialised with interaction code. Similarly, since interactions between classes are described as CO actions and clearly separated from classes, they are easy to express and likely to be reused.

Changes that reflect evolving needs of a system can be incorporated only in the definition of new interactions among the existing components of the system. Hence, a COO design can evolve by changing only its CO actions, while classes remain unchanged. The diagram in figure 1 represents a COO design. Boxes illustrate classes, rounded boxes illustrate CO actions and lines connect a CO action with its participating classes. The three classes of the diagram participate to CO action COActionA, and its evolution attained by defining CO action COActionB. Consider a system which handles data for flight reservations. The classes of figure 1 then represent flights, customers, and tickets. CO action COActionA is responsible for booking tickets and thus describes interaction between those classes. Evolution of the system may necessitate changing the rules for booking a ticket, for example allowing a flight to be held for a while without being paid. That evolution scenario is incorporated into a new CO action (COActionB) describing a new set of interactions between the classes. Those classes remain unchanged when defining the new CO action.

A COO design can also evolve by changing classes. The CO actions where the changed classes participate can still be used as long as the methods used and the roles the classes play remain unchanged.

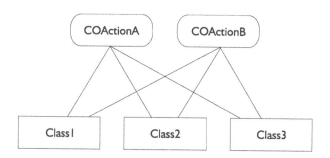

Fig. 1. Evolution of a COO design.

3   Reflective Architecture for Supporting Evolution

A reflective software system is a software system which contains structures representing aspects of itself that enable the system to support actions on itself [23]. A reflective architecture consists of a baselevel and a metalevel, where objects and metaobjects are respectively implemented. Two major reflective approaches have been identified [5,13]: communication reification and metaobject model. In the former approach the metalevel represents and operates on messages between objects, whereas in the latter the metalevel represents and operates on objects.

In the metaobject model, metaobjects are instances of a class able to intercept messages sent to their associated objects. The interception of messages allows metaobjects to perform some computation on the messages before delivering them to the objects, therefore making it possible to intertwine different concerns. The execution of an object's method can be suspended to verify constraints, to achieve synchronization, etc. [1,17].

A key concept in reflection is that of transparency: in a reflective system baselevel objects are not aware of the presence of metalevels above them. Thus, the development of objects is independent of that of metaobjects, and the connection of metaobjects to objects is performed without changing any of them.

In a COO design, objects and cooperations are easier to evolve and more likely to be reused because they only describe functional and interaction code, respectively. Evolution of COO systems can be attained by assuming that objects remain unchanged while cooperations can be modified or replaced. In the reflective implementation of a COO design, objects and cooperations are located respectively at the baselevel and metalevel. Different levels of a reflective architecture can be used to implement different parts of the same application, as in the Operating Systems Apertos [21] and Mach [25]. The metalevel adds functionalities to the baselevel, since the behaviour of the latter is altered by metalevel computation.

Reflection enhances evolution by allowing aspects of objects to be customised at the metalevel [18], and by encapsulating into the metalevel the part of an application more likely to change when new requirements are taken into account [4]. Since cooperations are located at the metalevel, this encapsulates the part of a COO system which is more likely to change when such a system evolves. Replacing cooperations is facilitated because of the clear division between baselevel and metalevel.

The evolution of COO systems is also enhanced by separating the application software from the control of the access to objects by several cooperations. The concurrency control is implemented by managers associated with objects and cooperations, which are located at the metalevel.

The reflective architecture supports evolution since it provides the separation of functional and interaction aspects, the hiding of the complexity of a changeable application, and the separation between concurrency control and application, which makes it possible to change both application and concurrency control independently.

4   COO Design and Reflective Architecture of a Case Study

To describe the reflective implementation of a COO design we use the electronic height control system (EHCS), which aims to increase the driving comfort by adjusting the chassis level to different road conditions [26]. It controls the height of a vehicle by regulating the individual height of the wheels through pneumatic suspensions. Figure 2 illustrates the physical system which is composed of four wheels, each of which has a valve and a height sensor, connected to a compressor and an escape valve. For each wheel of the vehicle, the height of the suspension is increased by opening the wheel valve, closing the escape valve and pumping in the air, and decreased by opening the escape and wheel valves, and blowing off the air.

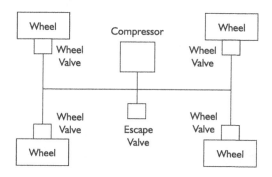

Fig. 2. Electronic height control system.

4.1   COO Design of the EHCS

The COO design of the EHCS is achieved by mapping each physical component into a class and describing interactions between such classes using CO actions. As figure 3 illustrates, the COO design of the EHCS is composed of classes: Compressor, EscapeValve, Wheel, WValve and HeightSensor; and CO actions: DecreaseSP, IncreaseSP, and ReadSP. In the diagram, CO actions list the participants of their collaborative activity.

Classes. Class Compressor provides a method which starts and stops the compressor pumping air and a variable which holds the state of the compressor. Class EscapeValve provides methods for opening and closing the escape valve, and a variable holding the state of the valve. Class Wheel provides methods for increasing and decreasing the set point of the height of the wheel, and a variable which holds the height of a wheel. Class Wheel is composed of two other classes: class HeightSensor which can read the height of a wheel; and class WValve which provides methods to open and close the valve of the wheel, and a variable holding the state of the valve.

Since in a COO design a class does not incorporate interactions, it can only be described in terms of its own methods. In the COO design of the EHCS class Compressor is not aware of the other classes such as, for example, EscapeValve and Wheel. However, class Wheel is aware of classes HeightSensor and WValve since it is composed of those two classes. Nevertheless, the interactions between such classes are also described by means of CO actions.

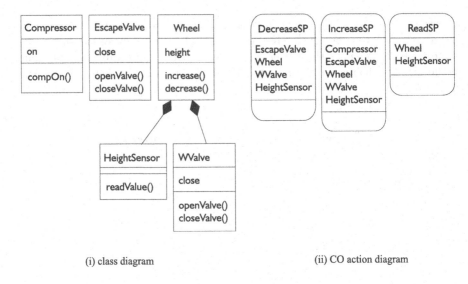

(i) class diagram   (ii) CO action diagram

Fig. 3. COO design of the EHCS.

CO Actions. CO actions are defined by their four methods: `pre()`, `inv()` and `post()` to check pre-conditions, invariants and post-conditions, respectively, and `coll()` to execute the collaborative activity involving a set of objects. Each CO action is implemented into a metaobject to keep it clearly separated from application objects and other CO actions.

CO actions `IncreaseSP` and `DecreaseSP` respectively describe how to attain an increase and a decrease in the height of a suspension. The former CO action activates methods of objects `:Compressor` and `:WValve`; and checks conditions on other objects to start, hold, and properly end the collaborative activity. CO action `ReadSP` describes how to read the height of a suspension. The value of the height is provided by method `readValue()` of class `HeightSensor` and it is stored in variable `height` of class `Wheel`. The activation of cooperation `:ReadSP` is carried out by cooperation `:IncreaseSP`, thus `:ReadSP` is a nested cooperation. To keep this description simple detail about nested cooperations will be given in the following sub-section.

When describing a CO action a new class is created. Such a class inherits from the abstract class `Cooperation` a method (`collab()`) which is responsible for activating the methods which check preconditions, execute collaborative activity, and check postconditions. Method `collab()` is also responsible for starting a new thread which checks the invariants while the collaborative activity is executed. Moreover, class `Cooperation` provides the primitives which allow the introspection of baselevel objects.

In the following we show an example of CO actions, which is the Java code of CO action `IncreaseSP`.

```
class IncreaseSP extends Cooperation {
```

```
protected int SetPoint = 100;
protected Object compressor, escapevalve, wheel, wvalve,
    heightsensor;

// initialization code

public boolean pre() {
    if (introspect(escapevalve,"close") &&
        introspect(wheel,"height") < SetPoint) return true;
    return false;
}

public boolean inv() {
    if (introspect(escapevalve,"close") &&
        ! introspect(wvalve,"close") &&
        introspect(compressor,"on")) return true;
    return false;
}

public boolean post() {
    if (introspect(escapevalve,"close") &&
        introspect(wheel,"height") > SetPoint) return true;
    return false;
}

public void coll() {
    returnRef1 = invokeMethod(wvalve, "openValve", null);
    returnRef2 = invokeMethod(compressor, "compOn", null);
    returnRef3 = invokeMethod(wvalve, "closeValve, null);
    isOK = readSP.collab(wheel, heightsensor);
}
}
```

The code has been developed using Dalang, a reflective version of Java [30]. Dalang implements metaobjects as wrappers for objects to allow interception of method calls of the object. Metaobjects exist during run-time, so they can be dynamically created, destroyed, and associated to objects. A meta configuration file is used to determine the association of metaobjects with objects. A run time adaptive version of the EHCS case study was previously presented [11].

The reflective implementation of a COO design does not depend on a particular reflective language. Thus, the code could be produced using other reflective languages that allow interception of method calls and introspection of objects, such as: OpenC++ [6], OpenJava [7], metaXa [15].

4.2   Reflective Architecture of the EHCS

To produce a reflective implementation of a COO design, each object is associated with an *object manager* and each cooperation with a *cooperation manager* [10,28]. However, as explained in the following, nested objects and nested cooperations can generate a different reflective architecture. Object and cooperation managers are used to provide support to the application and their responsibilities include control of access to objects in a concurrent environment.

When some objects in the COO design are parts of an enclosing object, the reflective architecture can be changed in order to optimise the implementation. In this case the manager of the enclosing object can provide its services for the inner objects, and those objects do not need their own managers. It is essential, nevertheless, to assure that the inner objects are relevant to the other objects of the system if only related with its enclosing object.

Figure 4 shows the reflective architecture of the COO design of the EHCS. To simplify the reflective architecture, not every object has been associated with an object manager. Objects `:WValve` and `:HeightSensor` can be considered inner objects of `:Wheel` and so the services provided by object manager `:WManager` for `:Wheel` are also used by those two inner objects.

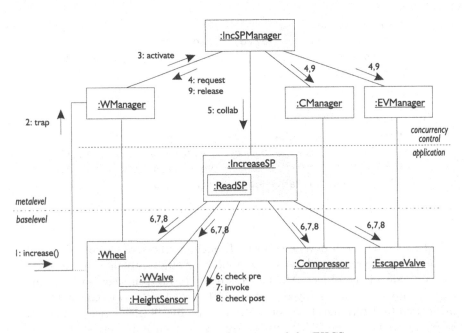

Fig. 4. Reflective architecture of the EHCS.

Object Managers. The role of an object manager is to control the access to its associated object, and to establish the rules for cooperations to invoke the services of that object. Another service that can be provided by an object manager is the invocation of a cooperation manager when control is trapped at the metalevel.

Concurrency control can be achieved by evaluating the state of the object, thus the object manger handles the rules which check the object state and determines whether to grant access to the object. Another way to achieve concurrency control is by enforcing mutual exclusion. To allow synchronization between threads two methods are provided to request an object for 'read' accesses and 'write' accesses, respectively, readRequest() and writeRequest(). The object manager allows multiple 'read' accesses while denying all 'write' accesses, or allows only one 'write' access while denying all the others. Two other methods are provided to release the object (readRelease() and writeRelease()).

The result of a request depends on the state of the object associated with the object manager. The object manager will return a failure indication if the associated object cannot be used. Hence an object manager implements a *balking* policy; however, other policies such as *guarded suspension, rollback/recovery*, etc. can be also implemented [20].

In the EHCS concurrency control has to be enforced since more than one :Wheel could ask to use the compressor at the same time. To implement the concurrency control object manager :CManager is able to inspect :Compressor to check whether the state of object :Compressor allows its use. Concurrency control can be enforced also by mutual exclusion, so :CManager will grant access only if the object :Compressor is not being used.

An object manager is described as a class which implements the interface defined by the generic ObjectManager, which consists of methods readRequest(), writeRequest(), readRelease(), writeRelease() and invokeMethod(). The implementation of object manager CManager when concurrency control is enforced by mutual exclusion is shown in the following. The synchronized keyword of Java is used to ensure that only one thread executes inside object :CManager at a given time. The methods of CManager update two variables according to the number of 'read' and 'write' accesses, and determine the availability of object :Compressor. When access is granted the reference to object :Compressor (i.e. target_obj) is passed to the requesting cooperation manager.

```
class CManager implements ObjectManager {

    protected Object target_obj = null;
    protected boolean intialization = true;

    protected int readers = 0;
    protected int writers = 0;

    public synchronized Object readRequest() {
        if (writers == 0) {
            readers++;
```

```
        return target_obj;
    }
    return null;
}


public synchronized Object writeRequest() {
    if (readers == 0 && writers == 0) {
        writers++;
        return target_obj;
    }
    return null;
}


public synchronized void readRelease() {
    if (readers > 0) readers--;
}


public synchronized void writeRelease() {
    if (writers > 0) writers--;
}


public void invokeMethod(Object target,
    String methodname, Object arg[], String metaParam) {
    if (intialization) init_reference(target);
}
}
```

Cooperation Managers. The services provided by a cooperation manager are the coordination of the requests for accessing a group of objects participating in a cooperation and the activation of the associated cooperation. A cooperation manager is also responsible for selecting alternative cooperations in case of failure when requesting objects, and for starting recovery actions if the executed cooperation cannot meet the post-conditions. Cooperation managers hold references to the object managers of the objects involved in a cooperation.

A cooperation manager acquires the rights to access objects participating in a cooperation by asking the respective object managers, then it gives the control to one of the associated cooperations. While enforcing control of access to objects, deadlock must be prevented or avoided, thus a cooperation manager implements a prevention or avoidance strategy.

In the EHCS cooperation manager IncSPManager is responsible for asking object managers to access objects :Compressor, :EscapeValve and :Wheel. When the access is granted by the object managers, IncSPManager will give control to cooperation :IncreaseSP. The following shows the Java code of IncSPManager. The interface of a cooperation manager, consisting of methods init() and activate(), is defined by the generic CooperationManager.

```
class IncSPManager implements CooperationManager {

    protected static CManager cmanager;
    protected static EVManager evmanager;

    // initialization code

    public void activate() {
        Object target0, target1, target2;
        target0 = wmanager.writeRequest();
        target1 = cmanager.writeRequest();
        target2 = evmanager.readRequest();
        if (target0 != null && target1 != null && target2 != null) {
            boolean isOK=increaseSP.collab(target0,target1,target2);
        }
        wmanager.writeRelease();
        cmanager.writeRelease();
        evmanager.readRelease();
    }
}
```

Nested Cooperations. Cooperations can be organised in a hierarchy, hence there is a top level cooperation which controls cooperations nested within it. Nested cooperations are lower level cooperations. Similarly to Moss's model of nested transaction, a nested cooperation is a tree of cooperations where the subtrees are either nested or flat cooperations [16]. Top level cooperations are able to organise the flow of control, determine when to invoke which cooperation, as well as carry out actual work, whereas leaf level cooperations only perform actual work. With respect to the concurrency control, all the objects held by a parent cooperation can be made accessible to its sub-cooperations.

In the proposed reflective architecture cooperation managers are associated only with top level cooperations. A cooperation manager is responsible for acquiring all the objects used by a cooperation tree. The accessing rights to the objects are then passed from the cooperation manager to the top level cooperation and from the latter to lower level cooperations.

In the COO design of the EHCS cooperation :ReadSP, which describes how to read the height of a suspension, is a nested cooperation of :IncreaseSP. In the reflective architecture cooperation manager IncSPManager is associated with cooperation :IncreaseSP, whereas no cooperation manager is associated with cooperation :ReadSP.

The collaborative activity of cooperation :IncreaseSP describes, among other things, the invocation of nested cooperation :ReadSP. The latter cooperation defines the interactions between objects :Wheel and :HeightSensor. The accessing rights to such objects are passed from :IncreaseSP to :ReadSP.

Flow of Invocations. The following describes the sequence of invocations for activating :IncreaseSP in the reflective architecture illustrated in figure 4. When increase() of :Wheel is invoked (1), the call is intercepted (2) by object manager :WManager which activates cooperation manager :IncSPManager (3). The latter requests access to the objects involved in the cooperation (4). When access has been granted by all the object managers, control is given to cooperation :IncreaseSP (5). At the application level, cooperation :IncreaseSP checks whether the pre-conditions are satisfied (6). Once the check returns true, the collaborative activity starts (7), and the invariants are checked. As part of the collaborative activity of cooperation :IncreaseSP, cooperation :ReadSP is activated to update the value of variable height of Wheel. When cooperation :ReadSP finishes the control goes back to cooperation :IncreaseSP where the post-conditions are checked (8). Finally, the control goes back to the cooperation manager which can release the objects (9).

5   Evolution of the EHCS

A COO system evolves by evolving its classes, CO actions, control to access objects, or adding some classes. The proposed reflective architecture facilitates evolution by providing separation between objects, cooperations and control of access to objects. Each element of the architecture can be easily changed, with little impact on the other elements. Although the proposed reflective architecture better supports evolution of COO systems when only changing their CO actions, it also supports changes of classes and managers. In this section we propose some evolution scenarios that might affect the EHCS and discuss the effectiveness of the proposed reflective architecture in dealing with changes.

The evolution of the reflective implementation of the EHCS will be compared with that of an alternative implementation which makes no use of CO actions nor reflection. A metric is used to measure the evolution effort for each implementation and to evaluate the effectiveness of the proposed reflective implementation.

The *alternative implementation* uses only the class diagram shown in figure 3 (i). However, classes Compressor, EscapeValve and Wheel provide methods that allow their acquisition and releasing (i.e. readRequest(), writeRequest(), readRelease() and writeRelease()). Method increase() of class Wheel describes the interactions between objects and consists of the calls to synchronize threads, the checking of preconditions, the execution of collaborative activity, etc. That is, it describes all the functionalities of IncSPManager, IncreaseSP and ReadSP of the reflective implementation. Analogously, method decrease() of class Wheel describes the functionalities of DecSPManager, DecreaseSP and ReadSP.

5.1   Evolution of Interactions

Suppose that the EHCS has to evolve by implementing a specialised control algorithm which is able to accommodate gravel as a new type of road. The new control algorithm describes a set of interactions between the existing classes to regulate the height of the suspension (for example, defining a new set point). The change in the reflective implementation for expressing the new requirement is restricted to the definition of a new CO action, `IncreaseSPGravel`. Cooperation manager `IncSPManager` will be changed to select one of two cooperations: `:IncreaseSP` or `:IncreaseSPGravel`, while classes and all the other CO actions and managers remain unchanged. In general changes in CO actions do not involve any changes in the related classes, since the reflective architecture makes classes not aware of the CO actions in which they participate.

Suppose now that the new control algorithm, which regulates the height of the suspension when the road is gravel, has to be introduced into the alternative implementation of the EHCS. The new control algorithm will be defined as a new method of class `Wheel` (i.e. `increaseGravel()`), which implements synchronization and interaction code (similarly to method `increase()`). Modifying class `Wheel` is difficult since it describes several concerns. Moreover, although only the interaction code is new, calls for synchronization and starting of threads have to be rewritten. As a result the code implementing `increaseGravel()` will be much longer than the code for `IncreaseSPGravel` of the reflective implementation and more difficult to write.

5.2   Evolution of Concurrency Control

Suppose that the physical system changes by introducing a new type of compressor which permits air to be pumped to more than one wheel at the same time. A different policy is then adopted to handle the use of the compressor so that more than one access is allowed for object `:Compressor` at the same time. The change in the reflective implementation consists of the definition of a new object manager for object `:Compressor` that will replace the old one. All the classes, CO actions and managers remain unchanged. In general changes in object managers have no impact on the other elements of a COO system. In fact, object managers interact only with cooperation managers and objects. Since cooperation managers are not involved with the rules of accessing objects, and objects are not aware of object managers changing object managers do not impact other elements.

When the new synchronization code is introduced in the alternative implementation of the EHCS, class `Compressor` needs to be updated by changing the methods which allow synchronization. Evolving the alternative implementation requires more effort than evolving the reflective one, since the rules for accessing the objects are not clearly separated from other functionalities of class `Compressor`.

5.3   Evolution of Classes

The EHCS can evolve by changing its classes to reflect changes in the physical elements where they are mapped. For example, class `Compressor`, which initially provides one method both to start and stop the compressor, could be changed to implement two methods, instead of one, one for each activity. Thus, method CompOn() has to be changed and method CompOff() is added. In the reflective implementation the only element, other than Compressor, which needs to be updated is CO action IncreaseSP.

Another example is when the physical system changes to accommodate an escape valve for each wheel, and the software needs to be restructured. In this scenario class EscapeValve can be considered an inner class of Wheel (the same as class WValve), so object manager EVManager is not necessary anymore, instead WManager will be used. Cooperation manager IncSPManager is changed to refer to object manager WManager, class Wheel needs to be changed to incorporate EscapeValve, and CO action IncreaseSP is changed to refer to the new inner object of Wheel. The other classes and their respective object managers remain unchanged.

Modifying classes is the sort of evolution scenario that can start substantial changes in systems based on the COO design. However, from the first example we can observe that when a class changes its interface only the CO actions which use that class have to be modified, whereas object and cooperation managers remain the same. From the second example, we can see that changing the structure of the classes implies changes in the CO actions and their respective cooperation managers, but not in all the classes and their respective object managers.

When method compOff() is added to the alternative implementation of the EHCS class Compressor is updated. Also method increase() of class Wheel is updated. Since method increase() intertwines fragments of code describing synchronization and interactions, evolving the alternative implementation is much more difficult than evolving the reflective implementation.

When class EscapeValve becomes an inner object of class Wheel in the alternative implementation, class Wheel will be changed accordingly and its method increase() will be updated to refer to it. Again method increase() has to be modified. Class EscapeValve does not need methods for synchronization anymore, so it needs to be modified as well.

5.4   Evolution Metric

An evolution metric is a number that represents the effort necessary to evolve a fragment of code. It quantifies the effort to understand the code, to modify it and to write a new fragment of code. The effort to understand and modify a code is related to the tangling between different concerns of the code, since tangled code is difficult to understand and to modify. When modifying a tangled code it is necessary to mentally untangle it, therefore the more tangled the code the more difficult it is to evolve.

According to [22] the tangling ratio of a code is calculated by means of the following:

$$Tangling = \frac{\text{\# of transition points between different concerns of the code}}{LOC} \quad (1)$$

The transition points are the points in the source code where there is a transition between fragments of code dealing with different concerns. The concerns considered in this paper are the implementation of the functionality, the synchronization of threads and the interactions between objects. For example, referring to cooperation manager `IncSPManager` synchronization code is represented as non-underlined code, whereas the interaction code which consists of activating a cooperation is underlined. Then, a transition point occurs between the non-underlined code and the underlined one and another transition point occurs between the underlined code and the non-underlined one.

The evolution metric cannot be equal to the tangling ratio since a code implementing only one concern has a tangling ratio equal to zero. Instead the effort to evolve such a code is greater than zero. The *evolution ratio*, calculated according to the following, considers the effort to understand and modify a code.

$$Evolution = \frac{\text{\# of transition points between different concerns of the code} + 1}{LOC} \quad (2)$$

Table 1 summarises the measurements of transitions and lines of code (LOC) and the evolution ratio of each object of the reflective and alternative implementation of the EHCS.

Table 2 summarises the average evolution ratio for the scenarios of evolution described above for the two implementations of the EHCS.

The evolution ratio of a group of classes is the average evolution ratios of such classes. For example, the third row of table 2 refers to the introduction of method `compOff()`, which in the reflective implementation consists of modifying cooperation `IncreaseSP` and class `Compressor`, and in the alternative implementation consists of modifying class `Wheel` and class `Compressor`. Thus, the figures of the third row of table 2 are the average evolution ratios of the classes involved.

The figures of table 2 suggest that evolving the reflective implementation requires less effort than evolving the alternative one, for all the scenarios that have been considered. However, the evolution metric reflects only partially the effort to evolve a code, since, while it measures the effort to understand and modify a code, it does not quantify the effort to write a new fragment of code. We expected that the figures of the first row were not so close to each other, while the figures of the second row were more close to each other. For example, a change

Table 1. Evolution ratios.

	Reflective EHCS			Alternative EHCS		
	transitions	LOC	evolution	transitions	LOC	evolution
Wheel	0	15	7 %	27	94	30 %
Compressor	0	6	17 %	7	28	29 %
EscapeValve	0	13	8 %	9	35	29 %
HeightSensor	0	5	20 %	0	5	20 %
WValve	0	13	8 %	0	13	8 %
WManager	0	48	2 %			
CManager	0	36	3 %			
EVManager	0	36	3 %			
ReadSP	0	24	4 %			
IncreaseSP	0	29	3 %			
IncSPManager	4	21	24 %			
DecreaseSP	0	27	3 %			
DecSPManager	4	19	26 %			

Table 2. Comparison of evolution ratios.

	Reflective EHCS	Alternative EHCS
Evolution of interactions	24 %	30 %
Evolution of concurrency control	3 %	29 %
Evolution of classes (i)	10 %	29.5%
Evolution of classes (ii)	11 %	29.5%

into the alternative implementation could necessitate writing a fragment of code specifying several concerns, and the same change into the reflective implementation could require the adding of code specifying only one concern (or vice versa), thus the effort just to write new code would have a different impact for the two implementations. We argue that the disagreement in our expectations is due to the lack of the evolution metric to quantify the effort to write a new fragment of code.

6   Related Work

Other approaches have been developed to separate functional and interaction code. The Composition Filters approach extends the conventional object oriented model with message filters [2]. Incoming messages pass through the input filters and outgoing messages pass through the output filters. Filters are used to pass messages to other objects (internal or external) and to translate messages. The Composition Filter model can be used to define Abstract Communication Types which are objects describing interactions among objects. When a message received by an object is accepted by a particular filter, named Meta filter, this is passed to an Abstract Communication Type object to handle it.

The Mediator design pattern is an object that encapsulates how a set of objects interact [14]. Mediator promotes loose coupling by keeping objects from referring to each other explicitly. It is responsible for controlling and coordinating the interactions of a group of objects. Each participant of a collaborative activity knows its mediator object and communicates with the mediator whenever it would have otherwise communicated with other colleagues.

Ducasse et al. propose to extend the object oriented model by using connectors [12]. Connectors specify dependencies between objects, and maintain and enforce all the activities between objects. A connector is a special object describing all the information relating to the interactions of objects, including data conversion, interface adaptation, synchronization and coordination.

Kristensen et al. define the concept of activity to describe collaborations between objects [19]. An activity is a modelling and language mechanism that may be used to capture the interplay between groups of objects throughout at different points in time. When the activity abstraction mechanism is objectified, it depicts the relationships that link interacting objects. To support the mapping from design with activities onto implementation entities, some language constructs have been proposed to be added to the existing object oriented languages. An activity is described by a relation-class, an extension of a standard class able to relate the participants of an activity.

In the Layered Object Model layers encapsulate objects and messages sent to or from an object are intercepted by the layers [3]. When a message is intercepted, the layer evaluates the contents and determines the appropriate action. The layered object model extends the object model providing some layer types (adapter, observer, etc.), and it can be also extended with new layer types.

All the above approaches have similarities with our work: they all provide means of explicitly describing interactions between objects into an explicit entity, however some of them lack a clear separation between objects and their interactions, thus changing one of them impacts the other [2,3,14]. Other approaches extend the object oriented model and so they do not allow implementation using standard object oriented languages [12,19].

7   Conclusions

Building a software system that can evolve to incorporate any requirements is impossible. Often systems can be evolved only to incorporate changes that are predictable during their development. However, it is possible to characterize general principles which result in easily evolvable systems. We argue that those principles include the separation between different concerns and the provision of the appropriate architectural support. The support for evolution is provided by considering objects independent of each other and allocating components which coordinate the interaction between objects. The increased number of components for representing a system in terms of the reflective architecture is effective in separating different concerns and reduces complexity since the various components can be understood and altered independently.

When systems implemented using the reflective architecture are evolved objects do not necessarily need to change, instead cooperations are able to capture new object configurations. Reflection has been used to separate different parts of a system, to provide means to intertwine synchronization, interaction and functional code, and to place at the metalevel the part of the system more likely to change.

A case study has been used to show the reflective architecture and some of its evolution scenarios have been described and compared with an alternative architecture. An evolution metric has also been presented to quantify the effort of evolving a system and to characterize the enhancement of evolution due to the reflective architecture.

Ongoing research concerns the expansion of the services provided by object and cooperation managers in order to allow the handling of role-based cooperative designs and of cooperations in a distributed environment. The consistency and effectiveness of the evolution metric is being tested for other evolution scenarios. Moreover, we foresee the inclusion into the evolution metric of means of measuring the effort to write a new fragment of code.

References

1. Mehmet Aksit. Composition and Separation of Concerns in the Object-Oriented Model. *ACM Computing Surveys*, 28A(4), December 1996.

2. Mehmet Aksit, Ken Wakita, Jan Bosch, Lodewijk Bergmans, and Akinori Yonezawa. Abstracting Object-Interactions Using Composition-Filters. In Rachid Guerraoui, Oscar Nierstrasz, and Michel Riveil, editors, *Proceedings of the Workshop on Object-Based Distributed Programming at the European Conference on Object-Oriented Programming (ECOOP'93)*, volume 791 of *Lecture Notes in Computer Science*, pages 152–184, Berlin, Germany, 1993. Springer-Verlag.

3. Jan Bosch. Superimposition: A Component Adaptation Technique. *Information and Software Technology*, 1999.

4. Frank Buschmann, Regine Meunier, Hans Rohnert, Peter Sommerlad, and Michael Stal. *Pattern Oriented Software Architecture: A System of Patterns*. John Wiley & Sons, 1996.

5. Walter Cazzola. Evaluation of Object-Oriented Reflective Models. In *Proceedings of the ECOOP'98 Workshop on Reflective Object-Oriented Programming and Systems*, Brussels, Belgium, July 1998. Extended Abstract also published on ECOOP'98 Workshop Readers, S. Demeyer and J. Bosch editors, LNCS 1543, ISBN 3-540-65460-7 pages 386-387.

6. Shigeru Chiba. A Metaobject Protocol for C++. In *Proceedings of the 10th Annual Conference on Object-Oriented Programming Systems, Languages, and Applications (OOPSLA'95)*, volume 30 of *Sigplan Notices*, pages 285–299, Austin, Texas, USA, October 1995. ACM.

7. Shigeru Chiba and Michiaki Tatsubori. Yet Another java.lang.Class. In *Proceedings of the ECOOP'98 Workshop on Reflective Object-Oriented Programming and Systems*, Brussels, Belgium, 1998.

8. Rogerio de Lemos and Alexander Romanovsky. Coordinated Atomic Actions in Modelling Object Cooperation. In *Proceedings of the 1st International Symposium on Object-Oriented Real-Time Distributed Computing (ISORC'98)*, pages 152–161, Kyoto, Japan, 1998.

9. Rogerio de Lemos and Alexander Romanovsky. Exception Handling in a Cooperative Object-Oriented Approach. In *Proceedings of the 2nd IEEE International Symposium on Object-Oriented Real-Time Distributed Computing*, pages 1–8, Saint Malo, France, 1999.

10. Rogerio de Lemos and Emiliano Tramontana. A Reflective Architecture for Supporting Evolvable Software. In *Proceedings of the Workshop on Software and Organisation Co-Evolution (SOCE'99)*, Oxford, UK, August 1999.

11. Rogerio de Lemos and Emiliano Tramontana. A Reflective Implementation of Software Architectures for Adaptive Systems. In *Proceedings of the Second Nordic Workshop on Software Architectures (NOSA'99)*, Ronneby, Sweden, 1999.

12. Stéphane Ducasse, Mireille Blay-Fornarino, and Anne-Marie Pinna-Dery. A Reflective Model for First Class Dependencies. In *Proceedings of the Conference on Object-Oriented Programming Systems, Languages and Applications (OOPSLA'95)*, pages 265–280, Austin, Texas, October 1995.

13. Jacques Ferber. Computational Reflection in Class Based Object Oriented Languages. In *Proceedings of the ACM Conference on Object-Oriented Programming Systems, Languages and Applications (OOPSLA'89)*, volume 24 of *Sigplan Notices*, pages 317–326, New York, NY, 1989.

14. Eric Gamma, Richard Helm, Ralph Johnson, and Richard Vlissides. *Design Patterns: Elements of Reusable Object-Oriented Software*. Addison-Wesley. Reading, MA, 1994.

15. Michael Gölm and Jürgen Kleinöder. Implementing Real-Time Actors with Meta-Java. In *Proceedings of the ECOOP'97 Workshop on Reflective Real-time Object-Oriented Programming and Systems*, volume 1357 of *Lecture Notes in Computer Science*, Berlin, Germany, 1997. Springer-Verlag.

16. Jim Gray and Andreas Reuter. *Transaction Processing: Concepts and Techniques*. Morgan Kaufmann Publishers, San Mateo, California, 1993.

17. Walter L. Hürsh and Cristina V. Lopes. Separation of Concerns. Technical Report NU-CCS-95-03, Northeastern University, 1995.

18. Gregor Kiczales. Towards a New Model of Abstraction in Software Engineering. In Akinori Yonezawa and Brian C. Smith, editors, *Proceedings of the International Workshop on New Models for Software Architecture'92*, pages 1–11, Tokyo, Japan, 1992.

19. Bent B. Kristensen and Daniel C. M. May. Activities: Abstractions for Collective Behaviour. In Pierre Cointe, editor, *Proceedings of the 10th European Conference on Object-Oriented Programming (ECOOP'96)*, volume 1098 of *Lecture Notes in Computer Science*, pages 472–501, Berlin, Germany, 1996. Springer-Verlag.

20. Doug Lea. *Concurrent Programming in Java: Design Principles and Patterns*. Addison Wesley, Reading, MA, 1997.

21. Rodger Lea, Yasuhiko Yokote, and Jun-Ichiro Itoh. Adaptive Operating System Design Using Reflection. In *Proceedings of the 5th Workshop on Hot Topics on Operating Systems*, 1995.

22. Christina Videira Lopes. *D: A Language Framework for Distributed Programming*. PhD thesis, Northeastern University, 1997.

23. Patty Maes. Concepts and Experiments in Computational Reflection. In *Proceedings of the Conference on Object-Oriented Programming Systems, Languages and Applications (OOPSLA'87)*, volume 22 (12) of *Sigplan Notices*, pages 147–155, Orlando, FA, 1987.
24. Bertrand Meyer. *Object-Oriented Software Construction*. Prentice-Hall International Ltd, 1988.
25. Richard Rashid. Threads of a New System. *Unix Review*, 4(8):37–49, 1986.
26. Thomas Stauner, Olaf Müller, and Max Fuchs. Using HYTECH to Verify an Automative Control System. In O. Maler, editor, *Hybrid and Real-Time Systems*, volume 1201 of *Lecture Notes in Computer Science*, pages 139–153. Springer-Verlag, Berlin, Germany, 1997.
27. Emiliano Tramontana and Rogerio de Lemos. Design and Implementation of Evolvable Software Using Reflection. In *Proceedings of the Workshop on Software Change and Evolution (SCE'99)*, Los Angeles, CA, May 1999.
28. Emiliano Tramontana and Rogerio de Lemos. Reflective Architecture Supporting Evolution: a Case Study. In Walter Cazzola, Robert J. Stroud, and Francesco Tisato, editors, *Proceedings of the OOPSLA Workshop on Object Oriented Reflection and Software Engineering (OORaSE'99)*, pages 33–42, Denver, CO, November 1999.
29. Mike VanHilst and David Notkin. Using Role Components to Implement Collaboration-Based Designs. In *Proceedings of the 11th Annual ACM Conference on Object-Oriented, Programming Systems, Languages and Applications (OOPSLA'96)*, pages 359–369, San Jose, CA, October 1996.
30. Ian Welch and Robert Stroud. Dalang - A Reflective Java Extension. In *Proceedings of the OOPSLA'98 Workshop on Reflective Programming in C++ and Java*, Vancouver, Canada, 1998.

The Role of Reflective Middleware in Supporting the Engineering of Dynamic Applications

Fábio M. Costa, Hector A. Duran, Nikos Parlavantzas, Katia B. Saikoski,
Gordon Blair, and Geoff Coulson

Distributed Multimedia Research Group,
Department of Computing, Lancaster University,
Lancaster, LA1 4YR, U.K.
{fmc, duranlim, parlavan, saikoski, gordon, geoff}@comp.lancs.ac.uk
http://www.comp.lancs.ac.uk

Abstract The increasing complexity of building distributed applications has positioned middleware as a critical part of complex systems. However, current middleware standards do not address properly the highly dynamic and diverse set of requirements posed by important classes of applications, such as those involving multimedia and mobility. It is clear that middleware platforms need to be more flexible and adaptable and we believe that an open engineering approach is an essential requirement. More specifically, we propose the use of object oriented reflection based on a multi-model reflection framework as a principled way to achieve such openness. This leads to middleware that is flexible, adaptable and extensible, and, in consequence, capable of supporting applications with dynamic requirements.

1 Introduction

Engineering distributed applications is inherently more complex than non-distributed ones due to problems of heterogeneity and distribution. Middleware platforms aim to isolate developers from this extra complexity and have recently emerged as a critical part of distributed software systems. CORBA, DCOM and Enterprise Java Beans represent a few of the many competing technologies. The basic role of middleware is to present a unified programming model to developers that masks out distribution concerns and allows them to concentrate mainly on the application semantics.

The rapidly expanding visibility and role of middleware in recent years has emphasised the following problem. Traditional middleware is monolithic and inflexible and, thus, it cannot cope with the wide range of requirements imposed by applications and underlying environments. This is especially evident in the case of new application areas, such as multimedia, real-time, CSCW (Computer Supported Cooperative Work) and mobile applications, which have specialised and dynamically changing requirements. The problem has already been recognized and all current middleware architectures offer some form of configurability. However, this is typically piecemeal, ad-hoc and only involves selection between

W. Cazzola et al. (Eds.): Reflection and Software Engineering, LNCS 1826, pp. 79–98, 2000.

a fixed number of options. Clearly, a more systematic and principled solution to the problem is needed.

We believe that an open implementation approach is essential for developing flexible and adaptable middleware platforms. More specifically, the solution we propose adopts object-oriented reflection as a principled way to inspect and adapt the underlying open implementation. While reflection has principally been applied to languages and operating systems, we are convinced that middleware is the most natural level for reflective facilities. Our object-oriented meta-level architecture is based on the idea of structuring the meta-space in terms of orthogonal meta-models. Each of these meta-models provides dynamic adaptability of an independent set of middleware implementation aspects. In addition, reflective computation is performed under strictly controlled scope, since each meta-level entity acts upon a limited set of base-level entities.

This paper is structured as follows. Section 2 explores current distributed object platforms. Section 3 presents our arguments towards the need for the open engineering of middleware. Section 4 briefly describes computational reflection, which is the basis for our proposal. In section 5 we explain our approach to providing a reflective architecture for middleware, while in section 6 we present some early implementation results, notably a prototype meta-object protocol. In section 7 we present some examples of how reconfiguration takes place in our approach. Finally, section 8 discusses related work, and section 9 presents some concluding remarks.

2   Distributed Object Technologies

Object oriented technology has been combined with distributed computing to create a new generation of client/server technology: *distributed object computing*. The central idea of distributed objects is to have servers that expose objects, and clients that invoke methods on these objects locally or *remotely*. Such an environment is normally realised by providing an infrastructure that allows objects to interact transparently, independent of being in the same or in different address spaces.

Three main technologies are widely used as distributed object infrastructures: CORBA[9], Java RMI[20] and DCOM[4]. CORBA (Common Object Request Broker Architecture) is the distributed object platform proposed by the OMG (Object Management Group) which contains an open bus – the ORB (Object Request Broker) – on which objects can interoperate. Sun Microsystems developed its own Java ORB, called Java RMI (Remote Method Invocation). RMI provides a way for clients and servers running the Java Virtual Machine to interoperate. Microsoft also proposed its own solution for distributed object computing: DCOM (Distributed Component Object Model). DCOM architecture is an extension to Microsoft's component model (COM). While COM defines components and the way they are handled, DCOM extends this technology to support components distributed across many computers.

EJB (Enterprise Java Beans)[19], COM+[5] and CORBA Components[11] represent the latest trend in middleware platforms, which simplify even more the development of distributed component-based applications. The significance of these architectures lies in that they achieve a separation of concerns between the functional aspects of the application and the non-functional aspects such as distribution, resource management, concurrency and transactions. The latter aspects are managed by a container and the developers are freed from writing system code that deals with them.

As regards to flexibility and adaptability, we can see a clear trend towards opening up the implementation of middleware. For example, the CORBA specification defines interceptors as a way to open up internal aspects of the invocation path, allowing the injection of additional behaviour. Similarly, DCOM offers custom marshalling, which enables developers to bypass the standard remoting architecture to create customised connections. Moreover, EJB, COM+ and CORBA Components support declarative configurability of non-functional system aspects (e.g. transaction policies) using attributes. In all these cases, we can observe that the configurability is piecemeal and done using ad hoc and static (compile or deployment time) mechanisms. The implementation of the platform is mostly hidden and out of the control of the application developer.

3   The Case for Open Engineering of Middleware

While some business applications are based on the interaction of objects to exchange text (database query/update, etc.), others have more general requirements such as the exchange of multimedia data or need for run-time adaptation. For example, a company may be selling video on-demand services to clients whose connections to the network may vary significantly. Some clients may have high speed network connection, while others have more limited ones. Moreover, during the provision of services, some clients may face network congestion problems that may lead to the need for some kind of adaptation. This means that, in this example, the network conditions play important role in the provision of the service. The price a client pays for the service and the service itself are different for different clients.

These kind of applications require some flexibility from the underlying system. This is not provided by current middleware platforms in a principled way. This happens because the approach taken emphasises *transparency*, meaning that application developers do not need to know *any* details about the object from which the service is being required. But it also means that the developers do not get to know the details about the platform that supports the interaction as well. Therefore, it is not possible to provide the flexibility required.

This *black-box* approach is not suitable for developing flexible applications. Thus, it is necessary to design a distributed object platform that exposes its internal details and allows modifications to the way the infrastructure handles the interactions, for example, the way middleware deals with resource reservation.

Based on these observations we claim that middleware should provide several extra features in terms of adaptability, that is, *configuration* as a means of selecting specific operation at initialization time and *reconfiguration* as a means of changing the behaviour at run time. This can be done by inspecting the internal details of a system and changing them. Another important feature is *extension*. This allows new components to be introduced in the middleware in order to handle situations not already encountered.

For example, consider the transmission of audio over a channel whose through-put may change over time. Firstly, a *configuration* can be applied to establish the communication according to the channel (quality of audio is proportional to the throughput). Secondly, once the transmission is already running, *reconfiguration* will allow a filter to be introduced in order to reduce the audio quality due to a network congestion. Reconfiguration can happen again in case the network recovers its normal operation.

One can claim that adaptation could be performed at the operating system or application levels. However, adaptation at the operating system level is platform-dependent and requires a deep knowledge of the internals of the operating system. In addition, unwanted changes at this level could be catastrophic as every single application running in a node could be affected. Furthermore, some research in operating systems [7] and networking [8] has advocated leaving as much flexibility and functionality to applications as possible in order to satisfy the large variety of application requirements. On the other side, adaptation at the application level imposes an extra-burden to the application developer. Besides, the adaptation mechanisms developed at this level cannot be reused since they are application specific.

This leads us to emphasise that adaptations should be handled at the middleware level which ensures at the same time platform independence and isolation from the implementation details.

Based on these issues, we can say that traditional middleware platforms such as presented in section 2 are not suitable for flexible applications. An *open engineering* of middleware platforms would be a proper way to overcome this problem. In the next section we briefly review the concept of computational reflection, which is the basis for our approach.

4   Computational Reflection

A reflective system, as defined by Maes [17], is one that is capable of reasoning about itself (besides reasoning about the application domain). This definition implies that the system has some representation of itself in terms of programming structures available at run time. The process of creating this self-representation is known as reification. In addition, this self-representation needs to be causally connected with the aspects of the system it represents, in such a way that, if the self-representation changes, the system changes accordingly, and vice-versa.

In a reflective system, we call the base-level the part of the system that performs processing about the application domain as in conventional systems, whereas the meta-level is the term used to refer to the part of the system whose subject of computation is the system's self-representation. In an object-oriented environment the entities that populate the meta-level are called meta-objects, which are the units for encapsulation of the self-representation and the associated reflective computations. Thus the process of reification of some aspect of the system normally results in a meta-object being created. A further consequence of object-orientation is that reification can be applied recursively, such that meta-objects, as normal objects, can have associated meta-meta-objects and so on, opening the possibility for a tower of meta-objects, where each meta-object allows reflection on the meta-object below it. In practice, however, only a few levels are necessary and the topmost level can be hard-coded in the execution environment.

5 Our Approach

5.1 Applying Reflection to Middleware

As middleware platforms are just another kind of software platforms (such as programming languages and operating systems), applying reflection to them may follow the same principles. One has to identify the concepts and structures that compose the base-level, as well as the way they are going to be represented at the meta-level.

The base-level of a middleware platform can be considered as the services it provides, either implicitly or explicitly through its interfaces. Examples of such services are the communication of interactions among objects (with all the implicit activities it involves, such as marshalling, dispatching and resource management), the supporting services (e.g. name resolution and location, management of interface references, distributed object life cycle, relocation, migration, etc.), and other common services (e.g. security, transactions, fault tolerance and trading). Such services are usually modelled and implemented as cooperating objects, and the platform takes the form of a configuration of objects (although such a configuration is not normally visible at the base-level).

The meta-level consists of programming structures that reify such configurations of services and allow reflective computation to take place. It must cover the different aspects that are involved in middleware, such as the topology of configurations, the interfaces of the objects providing services, and the behaviour of such objects. The meta-level makes it possible to inspect the internals of the middleware and to alter its implementation, by means of well known meta-interfaces. For example, a new service can be added to the platform or an existing one can be reconfigured by appropriately using operations available at the meta-interfaces. The sources or invokers of such reflective computations may be the application which is running on top of the platform, or the platform itself, which may have mechanisms for quality of service monitoring that can trigger control actions involving reflection.

5.2 The Underlying Object Model

Both base- and meta-level of our reflective architecture for middleware are modelled and programmed according to a uniform object model. In what follows, we present the main concepts of this object model.

The basic constructs of the model are objects, which are also the units of distribution. Objects may have one or more interfaces, through which they interact with other objects, and each individual interface is identified by a unique interface reference, which contains enough information to allow the location of the implementation object and to get a description of the services it provides through the interface.

The programming model supports three kinds of interfaces in order to model the different styles of interactions an object may provide:

- *Operational interfaces* are meant to enable client-server style interactions, based on method invocation semantics. They consist of the signatures of the methods provided by the interface and (optionally) the methods required from other bound interfaces.
- *Stream interfaces* allow interactions by means of continuous flows of data, usually with temporal properties. Such a style of interactions is usually found in multimedia applications that involve the communication of audio and video data.
- *Signal interfaces* are meant to support one-way interactions that may have temporal (i.e. real-time) properties. The signal interaction style is more primitive than the other two, and may be used to model or implement them.

Objects may only interact through their interfaces, and such communication is achieved, primarily, by means of *explicit bindings*, which are first class objects in the model and encapsulate the services related to communications. Explicit bindings may be local (between objects in the same address space) or distributed (spanning different address spaces or machines) and their establishment may be requested either by a third party or by one of the objects to be bound.

The use of explicit binding objects is essential in order to provide a level of control over continuous media communications. This is due to the fact that a binding object is normally identified with an established connection among two or more parties. Explicit bindings allow, therefore, the exposure and manipulation of the mechanisms and properties involved in multimedia interactions, setting the context for their monitoring and adaptation.

However, for interactions with a transient nature, where the overheads or the programming effort involved in explicit binding establishment are often inconvenient, the model also supports *implicit bindings*. At the level of the programming model, an implicit binding is transparently created when an object gets an active interface reference of another object and uses it as a pointer to access its functionality (similarly to the way CORBA objects interact). As a consequence, implicit bindings provide no control over their internal implementation and are therefore unsuitable for applications requiring guaranteed levels of service [2].

Finally, quality of service (QoS) properties can be associated with the interactions among objects. This is supported by QoS annotations on the interacting interfaces and by the negotiation of contracts as part of the establishment of bindings. A complementary QoS management mechanism may then be used to carry out monitoring and control tasks based on such contracts.

5.3   Structure of the Meta-level

Basic Principles. As a consequence of the programming model introduced above, the basic constructs for reflective computation are *meta-objects*. The collection of the interfaces provided by the meta-objects are then referred to as the *meta-object protocol*, or simply MOP. In addition, as meta-objects themselves are objects, they can be reified as well (in terms of meta-meta-objects).

Procedural reflection is used, meaning that the reified aspects of the platform are actually implemented by the meta-objects. This is a somewhat primitive but powerful approach since it allows the introduction of completely new behaviour or functionality to the platform. Additionally, more elaborate declarative meta-interfaces can be built on top of the procedural meta-interfaces.

Another principle of our approach is the association of meta-objects with individual base-level objects (or set of objects) of the platform, with the purpose of limiting the scope of reflective computation. In this way, the effects of reflective computation are restricted to the reified objects, avoiding side-effects on other parts of the platform. Access to the meta-objects is dynamically obtained using a basic part of the meta-object protocol provided by the infrastructure, and making reference to the interface of the object being reified. If a requested meta-object does not exist yet, it is instantly created, which means that meta-objects are created on demand. Therefore, not necessarily all base-level objects have to have the overheads associated with reflection.

Finally, a crucial design principle is the adoption of a *multi-model reflection framework*, by applying separation of concerns to the meta-level itself. Several orthogonal aspects of the meta-level are identified and modelled by means of distinct meta-objects. This was motivated by the great complexity involved in a meta-level for middleware. By modelling (and implementing) each aspect as an independent meta-model, both the meta-level design and the use of reflective computation are made simpler. The concept of multi-model reflection was first introduced in AL-1/D [21], which defines a set of meta-models to deal with the different aspects normally found in distributed systems. AL-1/D, however, does not stress the importance of orthogonality between the meta-models, a feature which greatly improves their manageability. Currently, in our architecture, we have defined four meta-models, which are the subject of the next section: encapsulation, compositional, environment, and resource management. However, the framework is open, in the sense that other meta-models can be defined in order to model other aspects of middleware that may be identified in the future.

Meta-models. As discussed above, the meta-level is divided into independent and orthogonal meta-models, each one representing a different aspect of the platform. We categorise these meta-models according to the two well-know forms of reflection: structural and behavioural (also know as computational) [24]. In our architecture, structural reflection deals with the configuration of the platform, in terms of which service components it has (compositional meta-model), as well as the interfaces through which the services are provided (encapsulation meta-model). Behavioural reflection, on the other hand, deals with how services are provided, in terms of the implicit mechanisms that are used to execute invocations (environment meta-model) and the association of resources with the different parts of the platform (resources meta-model). The structure of the meta-space is illustrated by figure 1. In what follows, we analyse each of the meta-models in detail.

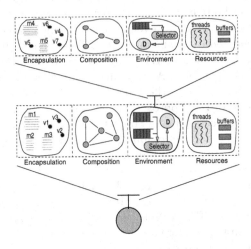

Fig. 1. Overall structure of meta-space.

Encapsulation. The *encapsulation meta-model* provides access to the representation of a particular interface in terms of its set of methods, flows or signals, as well as the interface attributes. It also represents key properties of the interface including its inheritance structure.

The level of access provided by a particular implementation of the encapsulation meta-model is dependent on the dynamic facilities that are present in the programming environment. For example, with compiled languages such as C access may be limited to inspection of the associated IDL interface. With more open languages, such as Java or Python, more complete access is possible, such as being able to add or delete elements (methods, flows, signals, and attributes) to or from an interface. This level of heterogeneity is supported by having a type hierarchy of meta-interfaces ranging from minimal access to full reflective access to interfaces. Note, however, that it is important that this type hierarchy is open and extensible to accommodate unanticipated levels of access.

Compositional. The *compositional meta-model* provides access to a compound object in terms of its configuration of components. The composition of an object is represented as an *object graph* [14], in which the constituent objects are connected together by edges representing local bindings. Importantly, some objects in this graph can be (distributed) binding objects, allowing distributed configurations to be created.

The compositional meta-model provides facilities for inspecting and manipulating the structure of the object graph, allowing access to individual components, as well as to insert or remove components. This meta-model is of crucial importance since it allows one to reify the configuration of the middleware platform and adapt it dynamically (such as to add new services). In particular, it allows one to reify the configuration of distributed binding objects, making it possible to inspect and change the internal binding components that implement the interaction mechanisms.

Environment. The *environment meta-model* represents the execution environment for the interfaces of objects in the platform. In such a distributed environment, this corresponds to functions such as message arrival, message queueing, selection, dispatching, and priority mechanisms (plus the equivalent on the sending side). In a similar design, the ABCL/R reflective language [24], collectively refers to these functions as the computational aspect of the base-level object.

Different levels of access are supported by environment meta-objects, depending on the dynamic capabilities of the execution environment. For example, a simple meta-model would only deal with the configuration of parameters of the existing mechanisms in the environment, such as the sizes and priority levels of the queues of arriving messages. More complex meta-models, however, would allow the insertion of additional levels of transparency or control over the actual implementation of such mechanisms. As with the encapsulation meta-model, this level of heterogeneity is accommodated within an open and extensible type hierarchy.

A further and crucial characteristic of the environment meta-model is that it is represented as a composite object. Hence, the environment aspect of the meta-space may be inspected and adapted at the meta-meta-level using the compositional meta-model. An example of such kind of adaptation would be to insert a QoS monitor at the required point in the corresponding object graph.

Resource Management. Finally, the *resource meta-model* is concerned with both the resource awareness and resource management of objects in the platform. Resources provide an operating system independent view of threads, buffers, etc. Resources are managed by resource managers, which map higher level abstractions of resources onto lower level ones.

Crucially, we introduce *tasks* as a logical activity that a system performs, e.g. transmitting audio over the network or compressing a video image. Importantly, tasks can span both object and address space boundaries. Each task in the system has a representation in the resource meta-space in terms of a *virtual task machine* (VTM). There is a one-to-one mapping between tasks and VTMs. Thus, a VTM represents all the abstract resources that a task uses for execution, such as threads and memory buffers. In addition, VTMs represent a unit of resource management, and may be seen as virtual machines in charge of executing their associated tasks.

The resources meta-space can therefore be viewed as three complementary hierarchies representing respectively resources, resource factories and resource managers at different levels of abstraction. The first one is the abstract resource hierarchy. VTMs are at the top of this hierarchy with raw resources at the bottom. Resource factories provide a second type of hierarchy. VTM factories are represented at the top of the hierarchy, whereas factories for lower level abstract resources lie at the levels below. Thirdly, we have a manager hierarchy. Managers defined at the top of the hierarchy are in charge of managing higher-level resources, e.g. VTMs, whereas managers next to the bottom manage lower-level resources, e.g. processors.

As an example, consider a particular instantiation of the resource framework shown in figure 2 below.

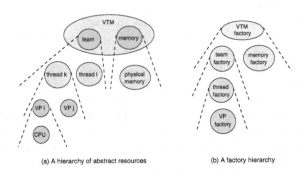

(a) A hierarchy of abstract resources   (b) A factory hierarchy

Fig. 2. Structure of the resources meta-space.

Firstly, the VTM has a hierarchy of processing resources, as shown in figure 2(a), where *user-level threads* run on top of *virtual processors* (kernel-level threads). At a higher level, a *team* abstraction represents two or more user-level threads within the VTM. Finally, at the bottom of this hierarchy we have a representation of a physical processor. Secondly, the VTM also has an abstract resource representing a memory buffer pool (*mem*), which in turn is a higher abstraction of physical memory. In a similar way, there is a hierarchy of abstract resource factories, as shown in figure 2(b). The VTM factory is composed by both the team factory and the memory factory. The team factory uses a thread factory, which in turn is supported by a virtual processor factory.

A complete description of the resource management entities that populate this meta-model can be found in [1] and [6].

6   Prototype Meta-object Protocol

We have implemented a significant subset of the architecture in order to allow the use and demonstration of its reflective features. The prototype consists of a base platform, which offers services for creating distributed bindings objects in order to support the communication between user entities. In addition, it provides meta-objects that implement each of the four meta-models described above, allowing dynamic adaptation of the platform. The implementation environment was based on Python, an interpreted object-oriented language that offers a powerful and flexible programming model which facilitates the implementation of the reflective features.

The prototype implements a simple meta-object protocol with enough expressiveness to illustrate the use of the meta-objects in meaningful scenarios. The prototype MOP consists of a basic part, which provides access to the meta-objects, and four other parts, which are specific to each of the meta-models respectively. We see this as an initial MOP, from which more elaborated ones can be devised following the idea of the hierarchy of meta-object protocols mentioned above. In what follows we present each of these parts of the MOP.[1]

Basic MOP. The basic part of the meta-object protocol, presented in table 1, consists of methods which are directly provided by the infrastructure.

Table 1. Meta-object protocol – basic part.

Method	Description
`encapsulation(interface)`	return a reference to the encapsulation meta-object that reifies the given interface
`composition(interface)`	return a reference to the compositional meta-object that reifies the given interface
`environment(interface)`	return a reference to the environment meta-object that reifies the given interface
`resources()`	provide access to the resource meta-space corresponding to the current address space; the operation returns a reference to the top-level abstract resource factory, i.e. the VTM factory.

As the table shows, the basic MOP has one method for each of the four meta-models, which returns an interface reference to the appropriate meta-object corresponding to a specific base-level entity. Note that in the case of the first three meta-models, the base-level entity corresponds to an interface, whereas for the resource meta-model, an address space is the base-level concept that is reified. Also note that if the meta-object does not exist, it is created.

Encapsulation MOP. The encapsulation part of the meta-object protocol (described in table 2) consists of methods to access and manipulate the reified features of an interface's encapsulation. These methods are all provided at the interface of the encapsulation meta-object.

Composition MOP. The compositional meta-object offers a meta-object protocol composed by the methods described in table 3. These methods are used for

---
[1] Note that all excerpts of code that appear hereafter, including the method signatures in the MOPs, are presented in Python syntax.

Table 2. Meta-object protocol - encapsulation part.

Method	Description
`inspect()`	return a description of the methods and attributes of the base interface
`addAttribute(attr_name, type, mode)`	add a new attribute to the base interface, with type and mode as given
`delAttribute(attr_name)`	remove the attribute from the base interface
`getAttribute(attr_name)`	return the value of an attribute
`setAttribute(attr_name, value)`	set the value of an attribute
`addProvMethod(method_sig, function)`	add a new method (of signature method_sig) to the row of methods provided by the interface
`delProvMethod(method_name)`	remove a provided method from the interface
`addReqMethod(method_sig)`	add a new method to the list of methods required (i.e. imported) by the interface
`delReqMethod(method_name)`	remove a required method from the interface
`addPreMethod(method_name, function)`	register the function as a pre-method for the named method
`delPreMethod(method_name)`	remove the pre-method of the named method
`addPostMethod(method_name, function)`	register the function as a post-method for the named method
`delPostMethod(method_name)`	remove the post-method of the named method

inspecting and manipulating the object graphs that represent the configuration of base-level compound objects.

Environment MOP. The meta-object protocol provided by the environment meta-object is as described in table 4. This is a fairly primitive MOP, in the sense that it does not offer a high level of structuring of the reified mechanisms in an interface's environment. Further extensions will, for example, allow the reification of particular mechanisms of the environment, such as queues of messages and dispatching mechanisms.

The current environment MOP is based on the concept of *before* and *after* computations, which consist of arbitrary processing that wraps the execution of every message received by a given interface. (Note that this is different from pre- and post-methods, which are assigned to particular methods, not to the whole interface.) The before computation can apply any sort of treatment to the message prior to delivering it to the interface's implementation object. Such treatment could be, for example, the delay of the message for a certain amount of time in order to smooth delay variations. Similar considerations apply to after computations. In addition, there can be a chain of before and after computations, where each individual one is identified by its own name. This functionality is similar to the idea of interceptors in CORBA.

Table 3. Meta-object protocol – compositional part.

Method	Description
`getComponents()`	return a list with the description of the components in the object graph; this description contains the component name, its type, and its kind (stub, filter, binding, etc.)
`getComponentsByKind(kind)`	return the components that conform to the given kind
`getBoundInterface(interface)`	return the interface that is locally bound to the given interface, if any.
`getLocalBind(obj1, obj2)`	return the names of the interfaces by which the two objects are locally bound (if there is a local binding between them)
`addComponent(comp_descr, position)`	add a new component to the object graph; the description of the new component consists of its name, type, kind, and any initialisation arguments; the position for its insertion is given by the names of the two adjacent interfaces between which the component is to be inserted (note that a new component can only be inserted between two existing interfaces; if there are any other interfaces to which it needs to be bound, the current MOP requires the corresponding local bindings to be explicitly established afterwards)
`delComponent(comp_name)`	remove the named component from the configuration (note that any broken local bindings need to be subsequently repaired)
`replaceComponent(comp_name, comp_descr)`	replace the named component with a new one (described in comp_descr as above); this equals to deleting the old component, adding the new one, as well handling any extra local bindings
`localBind(interf1, interf2)`	establish a local binding between the two named interfaces, if they are compatible (this is simply another way of accessing the local binding service provided by the infrastructure)

Table 4. Meta-object protocol – environment part.

Method	Description
`addBefore(name,function)`	add the function as a *before* computation in the environment of the base interface
`delBefore(name)`	remove the named *before* computation
`addAfter(name, function)`	add the function as an *after* computation in the environment of the base interface
`delAfter(name)`	remove the named *after* computation

Resource Management MOP. The meta-object protocol for the resources meta-model is described in table 5.

Table 5. Meta-object protocol – resources part.

Meta-object	Method	Description

Factory	`newResource(size,`
	`            mgntPolicy,`
	`            schedParam)`
		create an abstract resource of a given size and associate a management policy with it; scheduling parameters are passed in case of the creation of processing resources

Scheduler	`suspend(abstResource_id)` `resume(abstResource_id)`	suspend an abstr. processing resource resume an abstr. processing resource

Abstract resource	`getLLRs() /setLLRs(llrs)`
	`getHLR() / setHLR(hlr)`
	`getManager() /`
	`setManager(newMgr,param)`
	`getFactory() /`
	`setFactory(f)`
		get/set lower level resources
		get/set the higher level resource
		get/set the manager of this resource
		
		get/set the factory of this resource

As the table shows, the resources meta-space is composed by three kinds of meta-objects, according to the three complementary hierarchies of resource management discussed in section 5.3. Together, the meta-interfaces of these three kinds of meta-objects constitute the resources part of the MOP.

At each level of the resource management hierarchy, meta-objects implement these MOP meta-interfaces in a different way, depending on the abstraction level and on the type of the resources being managed. For instance, a team factory provides a different implementation for the operation `newResource()` than that provided by a thread factory or by a memory buffer factory. However, the overall meaning of this operation is consistent in all three cases.

7   Examples

In this section some example scenarios are presented to illustrate the use of the different meta-models to dynamically adapt the services provided by the platform.

Compositional Meta-model. Figure 3 shows a two-level binding object which provides the simple service of connecting the interfaces of two application objects. The purpose of such a binding may be, for example, to transfer a continuous stream of media from one object to the other. At run-time, some external monitoring mechanism notices a drop in the network throughput, demanding a reconfiguration of the binding object in order to support the negotiated quality of service. This reconfiguration may be in terms of inserting compression and decompression filters at both sides of the binding, hence reducing the actual amount of data to be transfered.

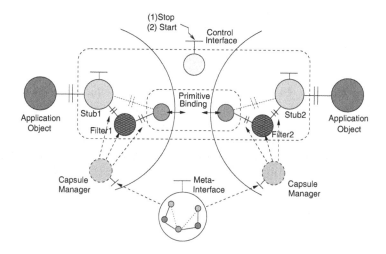

Fig. 3. Adaptation using the compositional meta-model.

As the picture shows, the compositional meta-object (`meta_obj`) maintains a representation of the binding configuration (the object graph). The compositional MOP provides operations to manipulate this representation, and any results are reflected in the actual configuration of components in the binding object. In this particular case, the following two calls are made to the meta-object:

```
meta_obj.addComponent(filter1, (stub1.interf2, prim_binding.interf1))
meta_obj.addComponent(filter2, (stub2.interf2, prim_binding.interf2))
```

By having a QoS control mechanism to call the above methods, the following effect is produced (for each call):

1. the previously existing local bindings between the stub and the primitive binding is broken;
2. the new filter object is created;
3. new local bindings are established to connect the interfaces of the filter to the interfaces of the stub and the primitive binding.

Note that the meta-object does the remote operations by calling special supporting services on the interface of the capsule manager at each side of the binding (i.e. operations `create_component` and `local_bind`).

Environment Meta-model. As another example of adaptation, consider a binding object used for the transfer of audio between two stream interfaces. In order to provide a better control of the jitter in the flow of audio data, the interface of the binding connected to the sink object can be reified according to the environment meta-model. The environment meta-object can then be used to introduce a *before* computation that implements a queue and a dispatching mechanism in order to buffer audio frames and deliver them at the appropriate time, respecting the jitter requirement.

Resources Meta-model. As a further example, we show how resource management adaptations can be achieved in our architecture by using the resources MOP (with the assistance of the encapsulation MOP). For this example, consider an application that transmits audio over the network, from an audio source to an audio sink object. For this purpose, we set up a stream binding as depicted in figure 4. Task 1 regards the activity of transmitting audio over the network. This (distributed) task is subdivided into two lower level tasks, task 2 and task3, for sending and receiving audio respectively.

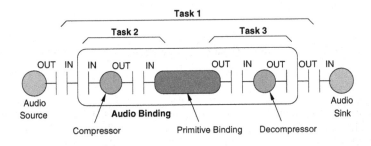

Fig. 4. A stream binding and its associated tasks.

As an example of fine-grained resource reconfiguration consider that the audio binding is initially using a rate monotonic scheduling strategy. However, over time some changes are introduced to the system, e.g. another similar audio binding is introduced. In this case, there might be a need to change the scheduling policy for a dynamic scheduling policy such as EDF. Consider that the new binding has been established from another site than the initial local site. As soon as the QoS mechanism detects a lack of processing resources in the remote site, the QoS manager performs the following operations, considering that the task dictionary vtmDict was obtained from the meta-space:

```
VTM3 = vtmDict.getVtm('receive')
team = VTM3.getLLRs()['TEAM']
thread = team.getLLRs()['THREADS'][0]
thread.setManager(EDFscheduler, schedParam)
```

The first line reifies the encapsulation meta-object concerning the interface OUT of the audioBinding object and then a VTM (Virtual Task Machine) dictionary of such interface is obtained. This dictionary maps the interface methods onto VTMs. The VTM that supports the execution of the operation *receive* is then retrieved. The lower-level resources of the VTM are then inspected through the getLLRs() operation of the resources MOP (this is an example of navigating the resource management hierarchy using the *get* operations described in table 5). As a result, the team of threads supporting the receive operation is obtained. Similarly, the team resource object is inspected and a particular thread is obtained. Finally, the scheduling policy of this processing resource is changed to an EDF policy by calling the setManager() operation of the resources MOP. Note that this is equivalent to expelling the thread from the current scheduler and subsequently admitting it to the EDFscheduler.

As an example of coarse-grained adaptation consider the same audio application. In case of a drastic shortage of resources due to dynamic changes to the environment of the application, one of the existing stream bindings may be suspended on behalf of the other. The binding associated with the VTM with lowest priority would be suspended. The QoS control mechanism would proceed as follows, after finding out which is the lowest priority distributed VTM, which happens to be VTM_x:

```
vtmSched = VTM_x.getManager()
vtmSched.suspend(VTM_x)
```

As a result, the VTM scheduler will suspend the corresponding VTM. The operation of suspending this VTM encompasses the suspension of the local and remote VTMs concerning the transmission and reception of audio streams respectively. This in turn involves the suspension of their corresponding underlying processing resources, e.g. threads.

8   Related Work

There has been a growing interest in using reflection to achieve adaptation at the middleware level. A pioneering piece of work in this area was the CodA meta-level architecture[18]. CodA decomposes the meta-level in to a set of fine-grained components that reify aspects such as message sending, acceptance and execution. However, it is difficult to support unanticipated changes in the meta-level due to the tight coupling of components.

In the FlexiNet [13] project, researchers at APM have experimented with a reflective middleware architecture that provides a means to dynamically modify the underlying protocol stack of the communication system. However, their solution is language specific as applications must be written in Java.

Researchers at Illinois [23] have developed a reflective ORB that provides facilities to dynamically modify the invocation, marshalling and dispatching of the ORB. However, the level of reflection is coarse-grained since only these elements of the ORB are reified. Further research at this institution has lead to the development of dynamicTAO [22], which is a CORBA-compliant reflective ORB supporting run-time distributed reconfiguration. One difference from our work is that this system do not make use of explicit meta-objects for reifying the

ORB. Instead they use a collection of entities known as component configurators. These components are in charge of both maintaining dependencies among system components and providing hooks for specific strategy implementations of the ORB (e.g. marshalling, scheduling, concurrency, etc). However, the focus is still very much on large-grained platform-wide configuration.

The work done in OpenCorba [15] follows a meta-class approach. In this system meta-classes allow reflective computation in order to control the behaviour and structure of all instances of a base-level class. In contrast, our work follows a meta-object principle, which allows a finer-grained (per-object) means to achieve adaptation. That is, changes to a meta-object are only spread to its corresponding base-level object.

Finally, note that OMG has standardised MOF (Meta Object Facility)[12] as a way of representing and managing meta information and XMI (XML Metadata Interchange) [10] as way for interchanging it. This effort is essentially different from our approach in the sense that it involves managing static meta-level descriptions of type systems rather than dynamic adaptation. However, the MOF can be used to represent the types of the meta-information that is used by meta-objects to perform reflection and dynamic adaptation. We are currently investigating this use of the MOF by implementing a second version of the reflective platform, which integrates the MOF concepts into our multi-model reflection framework.

9   Final Considerations

In this paper we have presented an approach for the open engineering of middleware. This leads to middleware that is flexible, adaptable and extensible and, in consequence, suitable to support applications with dynamic requirements.

Our approach applies reflection as a principled way of opening up the middleware implementation. The main points of our approach are: (1) *multiple meta-models*, which give us a means to separate different aspects of middleware implementation; (2) the use of *object graphs* as a uniform way to reify the platform configuration; and, (3) the use of *independent meta-spaces* for individual components of the platform which limits the scope of adaptation and provides a means for fine grained adaptation.

We have implemented a prototype in Python to demonstrate the main ideas. Notably, this implementation provides an initial meta-object protocol, which illustrates how reflective computation can be performed using the four meta-models. Although the prototype itself was limited to a single language environment, it has shown the feasibility of the general approach. Ongoing work is looking at lightweight component architectures as an efficient and language independent way to structure the implementation.

Our experience so far has shown that the approach is generic and powerful enough to cover a wide range of aspects of middleware. Moreover, the use of a uniform interface for adaptation contributes to reducing the complexity of developing dynamic and complex applications. On the other hand, the intrinsic openness of the approach might compromise the integrity of the platform (by unexpected or undesired adaptations). This was expected since we focused on the provision of flexibility. Further work will look at ways of alleviating this problem. For instance, we can benefit from experiences such as those presented in [3] and [16], which use software architecture principles to represent the static and dynamic properties of configurations. This would allow us to extend our compositional meta-model in order to use the rules of the architectural style for constraining and managing configuration adaptations.

Finally, several case studies are under development in order to evaluate the architecture in more realistic application scenarios.

Acknowledgments. Fábio Costa would like to thank his sponsors CNPq, the Brazilian National Council for Scientific and Technological Development and the Federal University of Goiás (UFG), Brazil. Katia Barbosa Saikoski would like to thank her sponsors, Federal Agency for Post-Graduate Education (CAPES), Brazil and Pontifical Catholic University of Rio Grande do Sul (PUCRS), Brazil. Hector A. Duran would like to thank his sponsor, the Autonomous National University of Mexico (UNAM).

References

1. Gordon Blair, Fábio Costa, Geoff Coulson, Fabien Delpiano, Hector Duran, Bruno Dumant, François Horn, Nikos Parlavantzas, and Jean-Bernard Stefani. The Design of a Resource-Aware Reflective Middleware Architecture. In *Second International Conference on Reflection and Meta-level architectures (Reflection'99)*, pages 115–134, St. Malo, France, July 1999.

2. Gordon Blair and Jean-Bernard Stefani. *Open Distributed Processing and Multimedia.* Addison-Wesley, 1997.

3. Gordon S. Blair, Lynne Blair, Valérie Issarny, and Apostolos Zarras Petr Tuma. The Role of Software Architecture in Constraining Adaptation in Component-based Middleware Platforms. In *IFIP/ACM International Conference on Distributed Systems Platforms and Open Distributed Processing (Middleware2000)*, IBM Palisades Executive Conference Center, Hudson River Valley, New York, USA, April 2000.

4. Microsoft Corporation. Microsoft COM Technologies - DCOM. Internet Publication - http://www.microsoft.com/com/tech/dcom.asp, March 1998.

5. Microsoft Corporation. Microsoft COM Technologies - COM+. Internet Publication - http://www.microsoft.com/com/tech/complus.asp, May 1999.

6. Hector Duran and Gordon Blair. A Resource Management Framework for Adaptive Middleware. In *3th IEEE International Symposium on Object-oriented Real-time Distributed Computing (ISORC'2K)*, Newport Beach, California, USA, March 2000.

7. Dawson Engler, M. Frans Kaashoek, and James W. O'Toole. Exokernel: An Operating System Architecture for Application-Level Resource Management. In *15th ACM Symposium on Operating System Principles*, pages 251–266, December 1995.

8. Sally Floyd, Van Jacobson, Ching-Gung Liu, Steven McCanne, and Lixia Zhang. A Reliable Multicast Framework for Light-weight Session and Application Level Framing. *IEEE/ACM Transactions on Networking*, pages 342–356, December 1995.

9. Object Management Group. CORBA Object Request Broker Architecture and Specification - Revision 2.2, February 1998.
10. Object Management Group. XML Metadata Information (XMI), October 1998.
11. Object Management Group. CORBA Components Final Submission. OMG Document orbos/99-02-05, February 1999.
12. Object Management Group. Meta Object Facility (MOF) Specification, Version 1.3 RTF, September 1999.
13. Richard Hayton. FlexiNet Open ORB Framework. Technical Report 2047.01.00, APM Ltd., Poseidon House, Castle Park, Cambridge, CB3 ORD, UK, October 1997.
14. Akihiro Hokimoto, K. Kurihara, and Tatsuo Nakajima. An Approach for Constructing Mobile Applications Using Service Proxies. In *ICDCS'96; Proceedings of the 16th International Conference on Distributed Computing Systems; May 27-30, 1996, Hong Kong*, pages 726–733, Washington - Brussels - Tokyo, May 1996. IEEE.
15. Thomas Ledoux. OpenCorba: A Reflective Open Broker. In Pierre Cointe, editor, *Proceedings of the 2nd International Conference on Reflection'99*, LNCS 1616, pages 197–214, Saint-Malo, France, July 1999. Springer-Verlag.
16. Orlando Loques, Alexandre Sztajnberg, Julius Leite, and Marcelo Lobosco. On the Integration of Configuration and Meta-Level Programming Approaches. In Walter Cazzola, Robert J. Stroud, and Francesco Tisato, editors, *Reflection and Software Engineering*, Lecture Notes in Computer Science 1826. Springer-Verlag, June 2000.
17. Pattie Maes. Concepts and Experiments in Computational Reflection. In Norman K. Meyrowitz, editor, *Proceedings of the 2nd Conference on Object-Oriented Programming Systems, Languages, and Applications (OOPSLA'87)*, volume 22 of *Sigplan Notices*, pages 147–156, Orlando, Florida, USA, October 1987. ACM.
18. Jeff McAffer. Meta-Level Programming with CodA. In Walter Olthoff, editor, *Proceedings of the 9th European Conference on Object-Oriented Programming (ECOOP'95)*, LNCS 952, pages 190–214. Springer-Verlag, 1995.
19. Sun Microsystems. Enterprise JavaBeans Specification Version 1.1. Internet Publication - http://java.sun.com/products/ejb/index.html.
20. SUN Microsystems. Java Remote Method Invocation - Distributed Computing for Java. Internet Publication - http://www.sun.com, 1998. White Paper.
21. Hideaki Okamura, Yutaka Ishikawa, and Mario Tokoro. AL-1/D: A Distributed Programming System with Multi-Model Reflection Framework. In *Proceedings of International Workshop on New Models for Software Architecture (IMSA'92)*, Tokyo, Japan, November 1992.
22. Manuel Román, Fabio Kon, and Roy Campbell. Design and Implementation of Runtime Reflection in Communication Middleware: the dynamicTAO Case. In *ICDCS'99 Workshop on Middleware*, Austin, Texas, June 1999.
23. Ashish Singhai, Aamod Sane, and Roy Campbell. Reflective ORBs: Supporting Robust, Time-critical Distribution. In *Proceedings of ECOOP'97 - Workshop on reflective Real-Time Object-Oriented Programming and System*, Finland, June 1997.
24. Takuo Watanabe and Akinori Yonezawa. Reflection in an Object-Oriented Concurrent Language. In Norman K. Meyrowitz, editor, *Proceedings of the 3rd Conference on Object Oriented Programming Systems, Languages and Applications (OOPSLA'88)*, volume 23(11) of *Sigplan Notices*, pages 306–315, San Diego, California, USA, September 1988. ACM.

Active Network Service Management Based on Meta-level Architectures

Alex Villazón and Jarle Hulaas

Centre Universitaire d'Informatique
University of Geneva
Rue Général Dufour 24
1211 Genève 4, Switzerland
{villazon, hulaas}@cui.unige.ch

Abstract The goal of this paper is to show the benefits of using reflective techniques and meta-programming in the context of active networks, i.e. networks where packets may contain code which programs the network's behavior. By having separate base-levels and meta-levels it is possible to increase the manageability of systems constructed with mobile code, since we may intercept and influence from the meta-level the activity taking place in the base-level. We focus here on resource management of services deployed over an active network and propose to this end an architecture as well as two alternative prototype implementations.

1 Introduction

Code mobility is becoming a key concept for modern distributed computing. It enables the dynamic deployment of distributed applications over the network, so that designers may better exploit available computational resources and optimize application distribution. As a particular paradigm of code mobility, the *mobile agent* paradigm enhances those features by incorporating the notion of autonomy, i.e. the possibility to decide where and when to migrate. Mobile agents are widely accepted as a promising enabling technology for the implementation of distributed systems because under certain conditions they are more interesting than classical approaches from the point of view of performance and flexibility [2].

In Active Networking, network packets are active entities (called *active packets*) that contain both data and code [33]. They can be seen as a very simple kind of mobile agents (they are notably autonomous). Thus, the moving code can be executed in the nodes that the packets cross, making possible the customization of the processing performed on packet fields. They can even modify and replace a given node's packet processing functions, thus enabling computations on user data inside the network and the tailoring of those functions according to application-specific requirements. A crucial concern with distributed applications is indeed their adaptability to particular requirements. Reflection and meta architectures are one means to achieve adaptability. In addition, mobile code technology gives extreme flexibility regarding distribution.

W. Cazzola et al. (Eds.): Reflection and Software Engineering, LNCS 1826, pp. 99–116, 2000.

Meta-programming permits the separation of functional from non-functional code. Functional code is concerned with computations about the application domain (base level), while non-functional code resides at some meta-level, supervising the execution of the functional code. This so-called *separation of concerns* is of great interest to software engineers since it makes design and maintenance of complex software much easier - and applications built with mobile code technology truly are complex pieces of software. We claim that the combination of mobility and meta-level manipulations gives a higher level of control and opens up interesting new possibilities.

A system supporting a meta-level will allow the incorporation of *meta objects* that may obtain information about any base-level object and/or control its execution. The system enables the redefinition of interactions between base-level entities (e.g. method calls, instantiations) through their management at the meta-level. Thus, when a client object sends messages to a service object at the base-level, a meta object may handle this call and execute additional computations and eventually invoke the method on the base-level service object. The set of rules governing the communications between base-level and meta-level entities is called a *meta-object protocol* (MOP).

In this paper we propose an active node architecture supporting a meta-level, the goal of which is to give the developer better control over active network services. For our purpose, which is to incorporate a management activity into an already deployed service, we describe alternative approaches making such manipulations possible by resorting to meta-programming techniques and meta-level manipulations. We investigate ways to control the execution of mobile entities by adding a meta-level that supervises services executing in the base-level environment. We consider management of active network service as a non-functional aspect. Thus, the supervision is performed by entities we call *meta-managers*, that interact with the base-level services through the MOP management interface. One of the major advantages of using meta-managers is that the information obtained from the execution of a service can be gathered and combined with similar information handed over by other meta-managers in order to enhance the overall service management. This leads to the possibility of modifying the behavior of the distributed service as a whole.

Several papers refer to "migration" as a non-functional aspect [6]. This is probably true for classical distributed systems. However, we claim that in the context of systems built around mobile code technology (e.g. active networks, mobile agents), mobility must not be considered as an orthogonal aspect, since those kinds of systems do not try to hide the notions of location and migration. In other words, the separation of functional and non-functional aspects must be enforced according to the specificities of the system, application and/or paradigm that is considered.

The rest of the paper is structured as follows: Section 2 gives an overview of what are active network services and how management at the meta-level can be performed. It also exposes the notion of meta manager. It discusses ways to make our managers mobile and emphasizes the strong relation between mobility, reflection and meta-level manipulations. An active network node architecture is presented, which makes meta-level management possible. Section 3 describes a complete example of an active network service and how to meta managers can be used. Section 4 describes two different prototype implementations that enable management tasks at the meta-level. The first one focus on meta-manager mobility and the second one on resource management handled at meta-level. Section 5 discusses related work. Finally, Section 6 concludes the paper.

2   Service Management

2.1   Active Network services

Active packets are very lightweight mobile entities that roam the network, performing simple actions with restricted scope (e.g. to transport data and apply simple filters [4]). An active network service is a set of several complex entities, also called *active extensions*, that are distributed and installed in different active network nodes. For the sake of simplicity, we will call each of those extensions a service (locally). Services are devoted to a particular role, allowing to modify and customize the packet processing function according to application-specific requirements. Services are not autonomous entities since their installation is triggered on demand of active packets. Several services can be installed in the same active node. Once installed, the services are accessible to every active packet that crosses a platform. It is also possible to install services that are restricted to a given application, i.e. we may limit access to the service. An (active) application is then composed by one or several specialized services installed in the active nodes and a flow of active packets that use those services. We may thus have several different concurrent active applications using the same infrastructure.

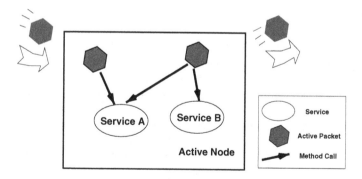

Fig. 1. Active packets and services in an active network node.

In a first, very simple model, active packets can be used to exchange management, control and service/application information between active nodes. This means that both application and management tasks are located at the same level. However, the addition of new functionalities to an active network service (e.g. in order to enable resource management) will cross-cut the structure of the whole service if such a unique level of execution prevails. For this reason we claim that a separation of base-level services from orthogonal functionalities must be enforced by introducing a meta-level into the active node. Such a separation allows a better structuring of services since their management can be handled *intrinsically*, i.e. from the inside of the system. We note that *self management* of active network systems is recognized as a crucial challenge [11]. We consider that enabling management at the meta-level is a step towards self-manageable active network systems.

2.2   Meta-management

Managing components "from the inside", is a notion that can be found in the context of classical distributed systems, e.g. in distributed network management [29], distributed fault management [1], and telecommunication services management [32]. The principle is to enforce the introduction of a management interface already during the design phase of the software engineering process, rather than adding interfaces a posteriori. This should also naturally enable more powerful management tasks. However, establishing a management interface in advance limits the possibility of extending and specializing management functionalities. The idea exposed in this article is to treat application management as an orthogonal aspect and to allow management modules to be incorporated afterwards. This means that the management activity takes place at the meta-level. In other words, we define the MOP as a management interface to avoid the definitive settlement of service management interfaces. It is thus possible to deploy new management functionalities a posteriori since management tasks are performed through the meta-level.

Active node architecture We propose an active network node architecture suitable for the requirements described above; it is composed of three different levels (see Fig. 2): the *active packet* level, the *base service* level and the *meta service* level. When compared to the basic architecture of Fig 1, we can see that such a separation corresponds to a generalization, where active packets and services are now clearly distributed in their respective areas, and with an additional meta-level needed to handle service management.

In our approach we integrate three different models of mobility [14] in the active network node. Thus, low-level mobile code is used at the active packet level; base services comply with remote evaluation and/or code-on-demand models (push/pull); finally meta-level entities are closer to the mobile agent model and need support as found at the service level for meta-level manipulations. This classification will be justified below.

In this architecture, meta-managers are software agents that manage active network services and run in their own meta-level environment. This execution

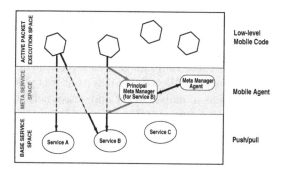

Fig. 2. An active network node supporting different levels.

environment must provide the necessary mechanisms for them to perform their management tasks, i.e. it must allow them to be bound to the underlying base-level services and to capture their activity. Two kinds of entities are defined at the meta-level: the *principal meta-managers*, which are associated to base-level services and intercept their activities, and the *meta-managers*, which perform the actual management tasks.

The combination with a principal meta-manager can be carried out when a service is installed in its execution environment. The composition of a base-level service with its principal meta-manager leads to an association that may be seen as a "unique" entity which provides the necessary support for the future insertion of meta-managers.

Principal meta-managers controls the execution of services and the inter-actions between active packets and base services. Each service has one or more meta-managers associated with it. Activities that must be captured and analyzed by meta-managers depend on the service functionality. Neither active packets nor base services are aware of the associated meta services, i.e. meta-managers work transparently. To this purpose, a behavioral reflective approach (also called computational reflection[21]) is probably the most appropriate for meta-manager integration since it allows to capture the activity in a well-structured and fine-grained manner.

Meta-managers are thus able to migrate under specific conditions and to collaborate with other similar managers in other nodes. Principal meta-managers handle migration and interactions between the associated meta-manager agents. This is an interesting issue, since they can be inserted independently of the service that they manage, and they can be coordinated in order to implement new sets of activities, for example, by exchanging information about the service under their supervision. The goal here is to exploit mobility as a feature rather than considering it as a disadvantage, because it is more difficult to manage a mobile service than a stationary one. For this reason, it is necessary to study the tradeoff between allowing meta-managers to migrate and how they handle base-level services under their supervision.

Finally, since meta-managers can directly intercept and modify the service behavior, security requirements at the meta-level are higher than those for simple active packets. This aspect cannot be neglected, because meta-services are injected at run-time and because they can gain access to the node's management and configuration infrastructure. We assume here that it is possible to apply the same security mechanisms as in mobile agent and active network systems, based on encryption, authentication, etc. [17,37]. However, in our current work, we focus on the structuring of services and meta-services; security issues will therefore be studied in future work.

3   An Active Network Service Example

In order to illustrate the usage of meta-managers, let us consider an active network application where active packets are used to transport multimedia data streams over an active network. Using active packets allows us to optimize bandwidth consumption for example. This is possible because active packets will avoid sending a high amount of data over links that have low bandwidth capacity. This is achieved through connectivity verifications on the active nodes that are crossed or through some filtering on packets [4,3].

The service is deployed in two phases. Active packets will first dynamically construct paths in the active network between the source and their multiple clients thanks to the capability of active packets to execute pieces of code while traveling. Path construction (the multicast distribution tree) can be performed in several ways. One possibility is to deploy *subscriber* active packets, sent by the clients, that implement forwarding pointers in the traversed nodes. A subscription "cache" code can be installed in intermediate nodes to avoid the subscribe implosion problem on the server [4,40]; it is thus not necessary that all subscription requests reach the server.

Once the paths are created, another kind of active packets is sent to transport the multimedia streams. They will perform several actions each time they arrive at a new active node: checking the number of clients subscribed to the current stream session and testing the bandwidth capacity of the links that connect to those clients. Then, some kind of filtering can be applied to the transported multimedia data (e.g. simply dropping secondary video packets for low bandwidth clients or performing somewhat more complex compressions) before finally redistributing the results to all links connected to clients (i.e. following the forwarding pointers). Installing executable code in intermediate nodes also avoids the $NACK$ implosion problem when an error occurs in the multicast distribution tree, since it becomes possible to generate a local retransmission rather than requesting the source to redistribute the stream [20].

Multiple similar competing services (see distribution paths associated to sources A and B in Fig. 3) can be deployed over the active network and share intermediate nodes. In this example, the original distribution service does not implement any resource consumption verification. Thus, the shared nodes will become overloaded if the distribution of active packets exceeds the node's capac-

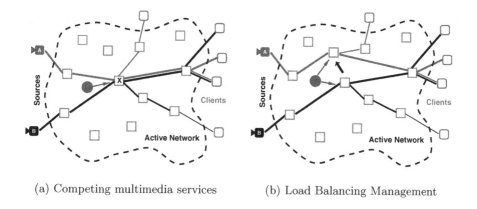

(a) Competing multimedia services   (b) Load Balancing Management

Fig. 3. Meta-management of load balancing in multimedia services over active networks.

ity to process the requested services. Each installed service potentially consumes
local resources on the node (CPU, memory and bandwidth). Active packets also
need resources to run the code that they transport. This implies that the Quality
of Service (QoS) will be degraded for customers if no resource management is
performed (see active node X on Fig. 3(a)).

By adding a meta-level we are able to add resource consumption verifications
and to adapt the (re)distribution of the service. Otherwise it would be necessary
to redesign the complete multimedia distribution active application in order to
integrate this orthogonal aspect. Meta-level manipulations allows a fine-grained
control of resource consumption by enabling verifications on the activity generated by services and active packets. A simple policy could be to disallow more
than n simultaneous instantiations of a given filtering service, each time the
queue length of unprocessed incoming active packets reaches a given threshold.

Since the management policy is integrated with the meta-level, and depends
on the type of reaction that is expected, we can exploit meta-managers as a
kind of collaborative software agents that use routing information to modify
and optimize the multicast distribution tree (this approach borrows its behavior
from biological systems, such as "ants-based" or "social insect" paradigm[5,13,
28]). Discovery meta-managers are initially sent to a downstream node (the next
node) to find a (reverse) backup route to the upstream node (the node before).
Once a route is found, the discovery meta-manager returns to the original node
and stores the backup routes. Only when needed, this information is used to
actually migrate the service code to another node. Finally, managers are sent to
update the distribution paths, which is simply done by replacing the forwarding
pointers previously installed by subscriber active packets with the already calculated backup route. This scenario describes a form of service load-balancing (see
Fig. 3(b)). Code mobility in active networks provides thus a very powerful technology for the implementation of such optimizations, as compared to the much

more static infrastructure offered by classical networks. The adoption of reflective architectures leads to a further level of flexibility, by helping to structure the code adequately.

4   Simulation and Prototype Implementation

We demonstrate two different simulations of the active node architecture described in Sec. 2.2, both combining an existing active network node (with limited support for meta manipulations) with external Java service applications. The reason for such a separation is that there exists no implementation of an active network node fully supporting computational reflection. It would be possible to implement a Java-based active node by resorting for example to a modified Java Virtual Machine (JVM) such as MetaXa [16]. MetaXa provides computational reflection through run-time insertion of meta-objects. However, the reliance on a modified JVM induces problems of portability and maintenance (i.e. every new release of the JVM must also be modified) and is in general not well suited because of trust and security concerns in the case of active network and mobile agent systems [37].

The active network system that we used is called MØ [36]. In this system, each active packet (called *a messenger*) is able to carry code that can be applied to its own data field. Moreover, some messengers may install procedures (services) that can later be used by other messengers which carry only a minimal code to load and apply the procedures to their own data field. The MØ programming language is similar to Postscript and has additional primitives for synchronization of threads, access to shared memory, accounting, secured installation and publication of services and creation of new messengers on the same platform (i.e. the messenger execution environment) and over the network. The messenger paradigm allows meta-level manipulations as will be described later.

The messenger platform provides a support for resource accounting and management that is based on a *market mechanism* [34,35]. Each platform sells its resources (memory, network bandwidth and CPU time) to messengers at prices that reflect the current availability and demand. Whenever a memory item has no *sponsor* left, the platform removes it from its memory. Note that this accounting is not only a way to perform distributed garbage collection but is also an important *resource control* mechanism that prevents forms of abuse like "denial of service" attacks and ensures that all incoming messengers will have equal chances to execute.

Unless the MØ active node is explicitly launched to run without support for resource accounting and sponsoring (by giving an infinite credit to all incoming messengers), MØ applications that where designed without specific code for resource management will not work as expected. Thus, programs must be redesigned and rewritten to handle it. For example, it is necessary to explicitly add some code that "feeds" all useful data and threads located on remote platforms. This is clearly an orthogonal aspect that can be handled at the meta-level.

In the following, we show why mobility is interesting at the meta-level, how the meta-level can be used for resource management and how to write base-level service code separately from resource management code. We also give some details of the implementation.

4.1   Meta-level with M∅

In a first prototype (see Fig. 4) we simulate the active network architecture described in Sec. 2.2, by separating the active packet level and the service level into different execution environments. The active packet level is implemented using M∅ messengers running on an M∅ active node. The service level is implemented using an external services application running on a Java Virtual Machine (JVM), on the same host or even on a remote one.

In this prototype, the meta-level has been simulated at the messenger level since the M∅ programming language provides a certain level of meta-programming and support for reflection. Messengers are able to manipulate and modify their own code and data, and to create a modified copy of themselves, e.g. to dynamically incorporate some extended functionalities. This kind of manipulation allows us for example to modify the way messengers access services. This can be performed using some kind of messenger code modifier (or compiler) that is itself written in M∅ and manipulates the messenger code while it is loaded and executed on the platform [19]. This approach is similar the Java bytecode rewriting technique in use in the JOIE toolkit [9], which permits the modification of any Java class bytecode in order to insert new methods, remove them or change attributes.

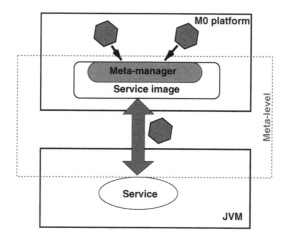

Fig. 4. Simulation of meta-management at M∅ active packet level.

The Java application can create messengers that are sent to a MØ platform where messengers are executed. However, the Java application cannot execute incoming MØ code (no Java-based MØ interpreter is currently available). Rather than executing the code, we have defined a very simple protocol to install, load and use services. When a messenger is received, the payload is extracted (as a string) and it is bound to a predefined request. The data transported by the messenger is used as argument to call a predefined method. Thus, all communications between the external Java services and MØ active packets take place by means of messengers: messengers are used to transport requests to the Java application and also to return answers to the messenger platform (see Fig. 4).

Messengers can trigger service installation by Java applications by supplying the URL of the service byte-code. An ad-hoc class loader is used in the Java application to retrieve the service code and store it in a local repository. Each Java service class has a *service image* i.e. a service proxy written in MØ allowing messengers to access the service. After instantiating a Java service, the application will retrieve the associated MØ service image code and create a messenger that will install the service image on the requesting MØ platform [27]. This is similar to the JINI framework [30], where services exploit mobile code to indicate how remote clients shall interact with them.

Each service provides the customized MØ code that is necessary for other messengers to access the service. The service image is represented as a set of callable procedures or methods (MØ code) that are securely installed in a local service repository and are accessible only to authorized messengers. Calling this code will result in the creation of an emissary messenger that migrates to the Java application in order to trigger the real service method call.

A meta-level service is here simulated by modifying the way method calls are performed, before sending the "real" invocation to the service object in the external Java application. MØ service images can be modified dynamically, because authorized messengers are allowed to modify and extend with meta-level code the implementations of method invocations.

In the present example, we inserted some code to perform statistics on service usage (simply by incrementing a meta-level counter each time an active packet calls the service). When a given threshold is reached, the creation of an "alarm" messenger is triggered. This messenger simply migrates to the monitoring application running elsewhere to notify about this event. Finally, the monitoring application can send a management messenger to the meta-level, telling not to forward the method call to the base-level service, e.g. because the external service is overloaded.

This simple example shows that even if the usage of low-level manipulations initially allows a limited set of management activities, the integration of mobility at the meta-level will however give extreme flexibility to this approach. Notice that in this first simulation, we did not enable the resource accounting mechanism on the MØ platform. In this simpler setting, service images residing on MØ platforms do not have to be "fed" with virtual money by the corresponding

Java-based remote services. This issue will be used in the following simulation to illustrate a more concrete example of resource management at the meta-level.

4.2   Meta-level with Java

In this second prototype, the meta-level was simulated by using a wrapper for the Java service object (see Fig.5). The mechanism for method call binding between the active packets and the Java service object is the same as described above. This time, however, it was not possible to perform similar code manipulations on the Java-based service since it is not allowed to modify the code of an already installed Java service.

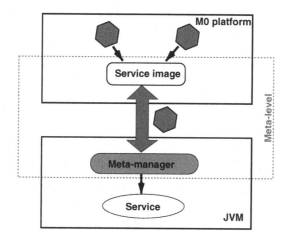

Fig. 5. Simulation of meta-management at external Java application.

Different approaches can be followed to add more sophisticated meta-level manipulations in Java. Five possibilities can be considered:

- (a) integration of meta-level code during the compilation. This approach is called *compile-time MOP* resolution [31];
- (b) using a customized (modified) JVM that supports a meta-level [16,12, 26];
- (c) customizing a Java Just-in-Time compiler to enable reflection as it converts the bytecode into native machine code [22];
- (d) dynamic generation of wrapper classes that allow interception of method invocation [38,7];
- (e) generating a modified class, while loading the original class bytecode and before it is instantiated inside the JVM [39,9,8];

Even if solutions (b) and (c) are powerful, they have not been considered because they are not portable.

A first implementation was based on approach (a) with compile-time reflection to integrate meta-services in a well-defined and structured way. We used the OpenJava framework [31] in order to automate the creation of service wrappers. Here each meta-service is created by processing of base-level source code. Even if this solution allows a clean separation of both base and meta-services, it is not possible to easily insert a meta-service afterwards. Moreover, the service source code must be available. Also, the base-level service is somehow aware of the meta-service, even if they are separate entities.

Our second implementation is a *Reflective Active Node* based on the Javassist framework [8], where both compile-time and load-time techniques are exploited. Javassist does not require any modification of JVM and enables load-time structural reflection for Java applications. Javassist is actually based on approaches (d) and (e). It is a very powerful framework that hides low-level bytecode modifications giving the programmer the possibility to concentrate on application design. The Java bytecode is modified at load-time and metaobjects are dynamically attached. The "assisted" bytecode modifications allows to tune the method call mechanism, the access to class attributes, to add/remove methods, to create a new class from scratch and even to change the instantiation mechanism. Javassist compiles the modified classes at run-time without resorting to any external compiler and produces immediately loadable bytecode.

Our Reflective Active Node allows active packets to install, load and use services that are transparently managed through the meta-level integrated through Javassist. Fig. 6 shows some relevant components of the Reflective Active Node. For example, the ServiceMediator is the bridge between active packets and services. It contains the predefined protocol allowing to install, load and use services. The ServiceInterface contains the minimal set of method definitions that allows active packets to use a given service. Every service must implement this interface and adequately customize its own methods. Two different classloaders are used: the JVM system classloader, and the `javassist.Loader`. The latter gives support for specialized user-defined loaders, such as the ReflectiveLoader, which itself performs bytecode modifications to insert metaobjects when loading new services on the node.

In Fig. 6 we can see, for example, that the RoutingService has been loaded and modified. The ReflectiveLoader has attached the corresponding Principal-MetaManager and MetaManager metaobjects. Neither a service's concrete implementations nor its metamanagers are considered known at compile-time, and can therefore be implemented separately. Notice that the resulting RoutingService class implements a new interface (called Metalevel) allowing to obtain the associated metaobject. Of course the ServiceInterface interface is conserved so that clients can use the service normally and methods calls are transparently redirected to metamanagers.

Resource management at the meta-level In order to demonstrate how meta-managers can implement resource management modules, we used the Re-

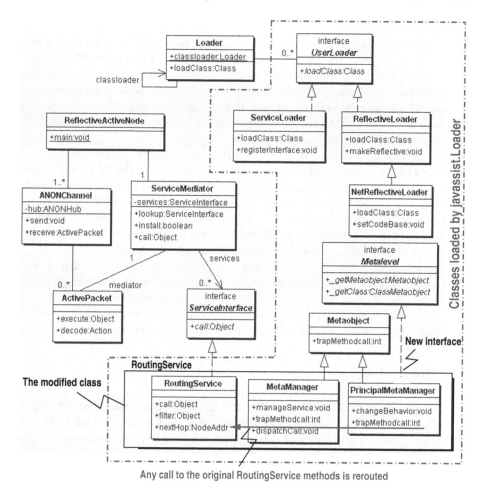

Fig. 6. UML class diagram of the reflective active node.

flective Active Node with an MØ platform; this time however, the resource accounting and sponsoring mechanism of the MØ platform is enabled.

Recall that every time a service is loaded on the node, an MØ service image (i.e. a proxy) must be installed on the client platform. Furthermore, every change in the Java service must also be reflected on its MØ image. If no meta-level is defined, the service programmer must integrate tricky MØ code in the Java service implementation to cope with this new requirement: special code must e.g. be added to each messenger before it is sent to the MØ platform in order to take into account resource consumption.

Each time a new service image is pushed, messengers must be sent periodically to feed the needed data structures. Otherwise, the platform will discard them. Other systems based on mobile code, like Jini [30] use a similar mechanism called *leasing*: objects are destroyed if their lease is not refreshed within a predefined interval. Meta-managers are delegated to send sponsoring messengers to keep alive all the data structures installed by the service on the MØ platform. The MOP provides information about the MØ objects that must be sponsored, the frequency, and the encrypted keys giving access to shared sponsoring accounts. The base-level service developer does not write any MØ code related to resource management. Moreover, the service implementation is independent of any particular sponsoring mechanisms.

In the example described here, resource management is performed at the meta-level for one side of the service: the image stored on the MØ platform. We do not discuss resource management or accounting for the Java service itself. The current implementation of the JVM does not provide such mechanisms. However, we can cite JRes [10], which provides a resource accounting interface for Java programs. Interestingly, JRes follows and approach similar to Javassist, since it is also based on load-time bytecode rewriting techniques.

Our experience described in [27], where a similar combination of MØ and Java was used, has shown that programming services becomes very complex and error-prone without a clean structural separation between resource management code and base-level code. By handling the sponsoring mechanism at the meta-level, we have a better control on the future development of services.

5   Related Work

To our knowledge, the literature related to mobility in meta-level architectures is rather scarce. In the context of distributed objects, we can cite CodA/Tj [23], which provides a computational model supporting migration, remote references and replication using a collection of distributed objects. Their object model separates the state and the execution of an object into different meta-components. This means that an object can store its state in one space but execute in another. Thus, the object's state and execution can migrate independently. Even if CodA/Tj does not follow the mobile agent paradigm (e.g. since messages between different spaces are handled using a remote method call mechanism), it is interesting to see that mobility at the meta-level is a research topic that has been explored in other contexts.

Resource management is very desirable in the domain of active networks. Resource Controlled Framework for Active Network Services (RCANE) [24] provides robust control and accounting of system resources. It is implemented over the Nemesis Operating System and allows execution and resource accounting of untrusted code written in a safe language. Services are loaded on the active node and associated to a *session* that allows resource accounting. Sessions can be seen as static resource managers for services. The service loader does not allow to associate customized managers as described in this paper.

Maude [25] is a high-performance reflective language and system supporting both equational and rewriting logic specification and programming for a wide range of applications. Reflection is used to support analysis of formal specifications. Maude is used to develop new security models and proof techniques that will be needed for secure active networks. The goal is to provide the active network architecture with a formal language technology that will allow formal transformation of specifications into mobile code and to support verification of security properties.

In the context of mobile agents, there is no work directly related to meta-level manipulations and structuring. However, slightly similar work - the addition of extra code to a mobile agent system - has been reported. It is based on source code modification to e.g. enable transparent migration of Java-based mobile agents [15], where the automatically inserted code takes care of saving the agent's state before migration and of reconstructing it on arrival at the destination host. Another example of agent source code modification can be found in [18] where additional, non-structured code is incorporated in order to ease the debugging of mobile agents. This is achieved through explicit calls to a debugger process between every instruction code of the debugged agent. Thus, even if those approaches are not directly related to meta-programming, since the resulting agent exhibits no separation between functional and non-functional aspects, it shows that new ways of combining different aspects inside mobile agents is a strongly desired feature.

6   Conclusion

This paper describes the need for flexible structuring mechanisms in the world of active networks. Meta-level manipulations is a promising way to achieve this, especially because of the resulting openness, which enables the programmer to customize the structure of the system. In particular, we wanted to show: (1) that it is necessary to be able to add non-functional aspects to already deployed active network services, and (2) that a solution, with a clean layering of orthogonal responsibilities, is made possible by meta-level architectures. We also argue that mobility must not be considered as a non-functional aspect in systems built around mobile code.

An active network node architecture with support for a meta-level is illustrated. We describe how we implement such an architecture, in the context of active networks service management, by combining an existing active network node with an external application. We introduce the notion of meta-managers that supervise the execution of services in the active node. Two different prototype implementations are described. In the first one, we show the advantage of having support for mobility at the meta-level. The second one shows an example of resource management performed through meta-managers. In both prototypes, we consider the interception of interactions between base-level services and active packets as a basis for service management. In our current approach we focus on a somewhat restricted MOP, the goal being to incrementally explore extensions which generalize the realm of possible management activities. Introspection of base-level activities could then for instance be exploited to allow for even more interesting management scenarios.

Acknowledgements. This work was funded by the Swiss National Science Foundation grant 20-54014.98.

References

1. Vito Baggiolini and Jürgen Harms. Towards Automatic, Run-time Fault Management for Component-Based Applications. In J. Bosh and S. Michell, editors, *ECOOP'97*, volume 1357 of *LNCS*, 1998.
2. Mario Baldi and Gian Pietro Picco. Evaluating the Tradeoffs of Mobile Code Design Paradigms in Network Management Applications. In R. Kemmerer and K. Futatsugi, editors, *Proceedings of the 20th International Conference on Software Engineering (ICSE'97), Kyoto (Japan)*, April 1998.
3. Mario Baldi, Gian Pietro Picco, and Fulvio Risso. Designing a Videoconference System for Active Networks. In K. Rothermel and F. Hohl, editors, *Mobile Agents. Second International Workshop, MA'98*, volume 1477 of *LNCS*, Stuttgart, Germany, September 1998.
4. Albert Banchs, Wolfgang Effelsberg, Christian Tschudin, and Volker Turau. Multicasting Multimedia Streams with Active Networks. In *IEEE Local Computer Network Conference LCN'98*, pages 150–159, Boston, MA, October 1998.
5. Eric Bonabeau, Florian Henaux, Sylvain Guérin, Dominique Snyers, Pascale Kuntz, and Guy Theraulaz. Routing in Telecommunications Networks with "Smart" Ant-Like Agents. In *Intelligent Agents for Telecommunications Applications '98*, 1998.
6. Walter Cazzola, Robert Stroud, and Francesco Tisato. OORASE'99. In *OOPSLA'99 Workshop on Reflection and Software Engineering*, November 1999.
7. Shigeru Chiba. Javassist — A Reflection-based Programming Wizard for Java. In *Reflective Programming in C++ and Java, OOPSLA'98*, Vancouver, Canada, 1998.
8. Shigeru Chiba. Load-Time Structural Reflection in Java. In *ECOOP 2000*, Sophia Antipolis and Cannes, France, 2000.
9. Geoff Cohen and Jeffery Chase. Automatic Program Transformation with JOIE. In *USENIX Annual Technical Symposium*, 1998.
10. Grzegorz Czajkowski and Thorsten von Eicken. JRes: A Resource Accounting Interface for Java. In *Proceedings of OOPSLA '98*, Vancouver, Canada, October 1998.
11. Information Technology Office DARPA. *Active Networks online information.* http://www.darpa.mil/ito/research/anets/challenges.html.
12. José de Oliveira. Reflection for statically typed languages. In *European Conference on Object Oriented Programming ECOOP*, 1998.
13. Gianni Di Caro and Marco Dorigo. Mobile Agents for Adaptive Routing. In *Proceedings of the 31st Hawaii International Conference on Systems*, January 1998.
14. Alfonso Fuggetta, Gian Pietro Picco, and Giovanni Vigna. Understanding Code Mobility. *IEEE Transactions on Software Engineering*, 24(5), May 1998.
15. Stefan Fünfrocken. Transparent Migration of Java-Based Mobile Agents: Capturing and Reestablishing the State of Java Programs. In K. Rothermel and Hohl Fritz, editors, *Mobile Agents. Second Internation Workshop, MA'98*, volume 1477 of *LNCS*, Stuttgart, Germany, September 1998.
16. Michael Gölm. Design and Implementation of a Meta Architecture for Java. Master's thesis, University of Erlangen-Nurnberg, Germany, January 1997.

17. Michael S. Greenberg, Jennifer C. Byington, and David G. Harper. Mobile Agents and Security. *IEEE Communications Magazine*, pages 76–85, July 1998.
18. Melissa Hirschl and David Kotz. AGDB: A Debugger for Agent Tcl. Technical Report PCS-TR97-306, Dartmouth College, Hanover, NH, USA, February 1997.
19. Jarle Hulaas, Alex Villazón, and Jürgen Harms. Using Interfaces to Specify Access Rights. In Jan Vitek and Christian D. Jensen, editors, *Secure Internet Programming*, volume 1603 of *LNCS*, pages 453–468. Springer Verlag, 1999.
20. Li-wei H. Lehman, Stephen J. Garland, and David L. Tennenhouse. Active Reliable Multicast. In *IEEE INFOCOM'98*, San Francisco, USA, March 1998.
21. Pattie Maes. Computational Reflection. Technical Report 97-2, Artificial Intelligence Laboratory, Vrieje Universiteit Brussel, 1987.
22. Satoshi Matsuoka, Hirotaka Ogawa, Kouya Shimura, Yasunori Kimura, Koichiro Hotta, and Hiromitsu Takagi. OpenJIT A Reflective Java JIT Compiler. In *Proceedings of OOPSLA '98 Workshop on Reflective Programming in C++ and Java*, November 1998.
23. Jeff McAffer. Meta-Level Architecture Support for Distributed Objects. In *International Workshop on Object-Orientation in Operating Systems IWOOS'95*, 1995.
24. Paul Menage. RCane: A Resource Controlled Framework for Active Network Services. In Stefan Covaci, editor, *Active Networks, Proceedings of the First International Working Conference, IWAN'99, Berlin*, volume 1653 of *LNCS*, June 1999.
25. Josè Meseguer and Carolyn Talcott. *MAUDE: A Wide-Spectrum Fprmal Language for Secure Active Networks*. http://www-formal.stanford.edu/clt/ArpaActive/.
26. Alexandre Olivia, Luis Eduardo Buzato, and Calciolari Islene. The reflective architecture of guaraná. http://www.dcc.unicamp.br/ oliva.
27. Pierre-Antoine Queloz and Alex Villazón. Composition of Services with Mobile Code. In *First International Symposium on Agent Systems and Applications (ASA'99) and Third International Symposium on Mobile Agents (MA'99) ASA/MA'99*, Palm Springs, California, USA, October 1999.
28. Ruud Schoonderwoerd, Owen E. Holland, and Janet L. Bruten. Ant-like Agents for Load Balancing in Telecommunications Networks. In *The First International Conference on Autonomous Agents*, ACM Press, 1997.
29. Morris Sloman. Management Issues for Distributed Services. In *IEEE Second International Workshop on Services in Distributed and Networked Environments (SDNE 95)*, Whistler, British Columbia, Canada, June 1995.
30. Sun Microsystems Inc. *Jini Connection Technology*. Sun Microsystems Inc., http://www.sun.com/jini, 1999.
31. Michiaki Tatsubori. An Extension Mechanism for the Java Language. Master's thesis, Graduate School of Engineering, University of Tsukuba, Ibaraki, Japan, February 1999.
32. Telecommunication Information Networking Architecture Consortium TINA-C. *Service Architecture Version 5.0*, June 1997.
33. David L. Tennenhouse, Jonathan M. Smith, W. David Sincoskie, David J. Wetherall, and Gary J. Minden. A Survey of Active Network Research. *IEEE Communications Magazine*, pages 80–86, January 1997.
34. Christian Frederic Tschudin. Funny Money Arbitrage for Mobile Code. In *Proceedings of the Second Dartmouth Workshop on Transportable Agents*, September 1997.
35. Christian Frederic Tschudin. Open Resource Allocation for Mobile Code. In *First International Workshop on Mobile Agents, MA'97 Berlin*, April 1997.

36. Christian Frederic Tschudin. The Messenger Environment M0 – A Condensed Description. In Jan Vitek and Christian Frederic Tschudin, editors, *Mobile Object Systems: Towards the Programmable Internet (MOS'96)*, volume 1222 of *LNCS*, pages 149–156. Springer-Verlag, Berlin, Germany, 1997.

37. Christian Frederic Tschudin. Mobile agent security. In Matthias Klusch, editor, *Intelligent Information Agents*. Springer, July 1999.

38. Ian Welch and Robert J. Stroud. Dalang - A Reflective Java Extension. In *OOPSLA'98 Workshop on Reflective Programming in C++ and Java*, Vancouver, Canada, October 1998.

39. Ian Welch and Robert J. Stroud. From Dalang to Kava - The Evolution of a Reflective Java Extension. In Pierre Cointe, editor, *Meta-Level Architectures and Reflection, Second International Conference, Reflection'99*, volume 1616 of *LNCS*, Saint-Malo, France, July 1999.

40. David J. Wetherall, John Guttag, and David L. Tennenhouse. ANTS: A Toolkit for Building and Dynamically Deploying Network Protocols. In *IEEE OPE-NARCH'98, San Francisco, CA*, April 1998.

OpenJava: A Class-Based Macro System for Java

Michiaki Tatsubori[1], Shigeru Chiba[2], Marc-Olivier Killijian[3], and Kozo Itano[2]

[1] Doctoral Program in Engineering, University of Tsukuba,
Tennohdai 1-1-1, Tsukuba, Ibaraki, Japan,
`mt@is.tsukuba.ac.jp`

[2] Department of Information Science and Electronics,
University of Tsukuba

[3] LAAS-CNRS, 7, Avenue du Colonel Roche,
31077 Toulouse cedex 04, France

Abstract This paper presents OpenJava, which is a macro system that we have developed for Java. With traditional macro systems designed for non object-oriented languages, it is difficult to write a number of macros typical in object-oriented programming since they require the ability to access a logical structure of programs. One of the drawbacks of traditional macro systems is that abstract syntax trees are used for representing source programs. This paper first points out this problem and then shows how OpenJava addresses this problem. A key idea of OpenJava is to use metaobjects, which was originally developed for reflective computing, for representing source programs.

1 Introduction

Reflection is a technique for changing the program behavior according to another program. From software engineering viewpoint, reflection is a tool for separation of concerns and thus it can be used for letting programmers write a program with higher-level abstraction and with good modularity. For example, a number of reflective systems provide metaobjects for intercepting object behavior, that is, method invocations and field accesses. Those metaobjects can be used for *weaving* several programs separately written from distinct aspects, such as an application algorithm, distribution, resource allocation, and user interface, into a single executable program.

However, previous reflective systems do not satisfy all the requirements in software engineering. Although the abstraction provided by the metaobjects for intercepting object behavior is easy to understand and use, they can be used for implementing only limited kinds of separation of concerns. Moreover, this type of reflection often involves runtime penalties. Reflective systems should enable more fine-grained program weaving and perform as much reflective computation as possible at compile time for avoiding runtime penalties.

On the other hand, a typical tool for manipulating a program at compile time has been a macro system. It performs textual substitution so that a particular aspect of a program is separated from the rest of that program. For example, the

W. Cazzola et al. (Eds.): Reflection and Software Engineering, LNCS 1826, pp. 117–133, 2000.

C/C++ macro system allows to separate the definition of a constant value from the rest of a program, in which that constant value is used in a number of distinct lines. The Lisp macro system provides programmable macros, which enables more powerful program manipulation than the C/C++ one. Also, since macro expansion is done at compile time, the use of macros does not imply any runtime penalties. However, the abstraction provided by traditional macro systems is not sophisticated; since macros can deal with only textual representation of a program, program manipulation depending on the semantic contexts of the program cannot be implemented with macros.

This paper proposes a macro system integrating good features of the reflective approach, in other words, a compile-time reflective system for not only behavioral reflection but also structural reflection. A key idea of our macro system, called *OpenJava*, is that macros (meta programs) deal with class metaobjects representing logical entities of a program instead of a sequence of tokens or abstract syntax trees (ASTs). Since the class metaobjects abstract both textual and semantic aspects of a program, macros in OpenJava can implement more fine-grained program weaving than in previous reflective systems. They can also access semantic contexts if they are needed for macro expansion. This paper presents that OpenJava can be used to implement macros for helping complex programmings with a few design patterns.

In the rest of this paper, section 2 presents a problem of ordinary macro systems and section 3 discusses the design and implementation of OpenJava, which addresses this problem. We compare OpenJava with related work in section 4. Finally, section 5 concludes this paper.

2   Problems with Ordinary Macros

Macro systems have been typical language-extension mechanisms. With C/C++'s #define macro system, programmers can specify a symbol or a function call to be replaced with another expression, although this replacement is simple token-based substitution. In Common Lisp, programmers can write more powerful macros. However, even such powerful macros do not cover all requirements of OO languages programming.

2.1   Programmable Macros

Macros in Common Lisp are programmable macros. They specify how to replace an original expression in Common Lisp itself. A macro function receives an AST (abstract syntax tree) and substitutes it for the original expression. Since this macro system is powerful, the object system of Common Lisp (CLOS) is implemented with this macro system.

Programmable macros have been developed for languages with more complex syntax like C. MS^2[19] is one of those macro systems for C. Macro functions are written in an extended C language providing special data structure representing ASTs. The users of MS^2 can define a new syntax and how it is expanded into a regular C syntax. The parameter that a macro function receives is an AST of the code processed by that macro function.

One of the essential issue in designing a programmable macro system is a data structure representing an original source program. Another essential issue is how to specify where to apply each macro in a source program. For the former, most systems employed ASTs. For the latter, several mechanisms were proposed.

In Common Lisp and MS[2], a macro is applied to expressions or statements beginning with the trigger word specified by the macro. For example, if the trigger word is unless, all expressions beginning with unless are expanded by that macro. In this way, they cannot use macros without the trigger words. For instance, it is impossible to selectively apply a macro to only + expressions for adding string objects.

Some macro systems provide fine-grained control of where to apply a macro. In A^* [14], a macro is applied to expressions or statements matching a pattern specified in the BNF. In EPP [9], macros are applied to a specified syntax elements like if statements or + expressions. There's no need to put any trigger word in front of these statements or expressions.

2.2 Representation of Object-Oriented Programs

Although most of macro systems have been using ASTs for representing a source program, ASTs are not the best representation for all macros: some macros typical in OO programming require a different kind of representation. ASTs are purely textual representation and independent of logical or contextual information of the program. For example, if an AST represents a binary expression, the AST tells us what the operator and the operands are but it never tells us the types of the operands. Therefore, writing a macro is not possible with ASTs if the macro expansion depends on logical and contextual information of that binary expression.

There is a great demand for the macros depending on logical and contextual information in OO programming. For example, some of design patterns [6] require relatively complicated programming. They often require programmers to repeatedly write similar code [1]. To help this programming, several researchers have proposed to extend a language to provide new language constructs specialized for particular patterns [1,7]. Those constructs should be implemented with macros although they have been implemented so far by a custom preprocessor. This is because macros implementing those constructs depend on the logical and contextual information of programs and thus they are not implementable on top of the traditional AST-based macro systems.

Suppose that we write a macro for helping programming with the OB-SERVER [6] pattern, which is for describing one-to-many dependency among objects. This pattern is found in the Java standard library although it is called the event-and-listener model. For example, a Java program displays a menu bar must define a listener object notified of menu-select events. The listener object is an instance of a class MyMenuListener implementing interface MenuListener:

```
class MyMenuListener implements MenuListener {
    void menuSelected(MenuEvent e) { .. }
    void menuDeselected(MenuEvent e) { return; }
    void menuCanceled(MenuEvent e) { return; }
}
```

This class must declare all the methods for event handling even though some events, such as the menu cancel event, are simply ignored.

We write a macro for automating declaration of methods for handling ignored events. If this macro is used, the definition of MyMenuListener should be rewritten into:

```
class MyMenuListener follows ObserverPattern
    implements MenuListener
{
    void menuSelected(MenuEvent e) { .. }
}
```

The `follows` clauses specifies that our macro ObserverPattern is applied to this class definition. The declarations of `menuDeselected()` and `menuCanceled()` are automated. This macro first inspects which methods declared in the interface MenuListener are not implemented in the class MyMenuListener. Then it inserts the declarations of these methods in the class MyMenuListener.

Writing this macro is difficult with traditional AST-based macro systems since it depends on the logical information of the definition of the class MyMenuListener. If a class definition is given as a large AST, the macro program must interpret the AST and recognize methods declared in MenuListener and MyMenuListener. The macro program must also construct ASTs representing the inserted methods and modify the original large AST to include these ASTs. Manipulating a large AST is another difficult task. To reduce these difficulties, macro systems should provide logical and contextual information of programs for macro programs. There are only a few macro systems providing the logical information. For example, XL [15] is one of those systems although it is for a functional language but not for an OO language.

3   OpenJava

OpenJava is our advanced macro system for Java. In OpenJava, macro programs can access the data structures representing a logical structure of the programs. We call these data structure class metaobjects. This section presents the design of OpenJava.

3.1   Macro Programming in OpenJava

OpenJava produces an object representing a logical structure of class definition for each class in the source code. This object is called a class metaobject. A class metaobject also manages macro expansion related to the class it represents. Programmers customize the definition of the class metaobjects for describing macro expansion. We call the class for the class metaobject *metaclass*. In OpenJava, the metaprogram of a macro is described as a metaclass. Macro expansion by OpenJava is divided into two: the first one is macro expansion of class declarations (callee-side), and the second one is that of expressions accessing classes (caller-side).

Applying Macros Fig. 1 shows a sample using a macro in OpenJava. By adding a clause `instantiates` M in just after the class name in a class declaration, the programmer can specify that the class metaobject for the class is an instance of the metaclass M. In this sample program, the class metaobject for MyMenuListener is an instance of ObserverClass. This metaobject controls macro expansion involved with MyMenuListener. The declaration of ObserverClass is described in regular Java as shown in Fig. 2.

```
class MyMenuListener
    instantiates ObserverClass
    extends MyObject
    implements MenuListener
{ .... }
```

Fig. 1. Application of a macro in OpenJava.

```
class ObserverClass
    extends OJClass
{
    void translateDefinition() { ... }
    ....
}
```

Fig. 2. A macro in OpenJava.

Every metaclass must inherit from the metaclass OJClass, which is a built-in class of OpenJava. The `translateDefinition()` in Fig. 2 is a method inherited from OJClass, which is invoked by the system to make macro expansion. If an `instantiates` clause in a class declaration is found, OpenJava creates an instance of the metaclass indicated by that `instantiates` clause, and assigns this instance to the class metaobject representing that declared class. Then OpenJava invokes `translateDefinition()` on the created class metaobject for macro expansion on the class declaration later.

Since the `translateDefinition()` declared in OJClass does not perform any translation, a subclass of OJClass must override this method for the desired macro expansion. For example, `translateDefinition()` can add new member methods to the class by calling other member methods in OJClass. Modifications are reflected on the source program at the final stage of the macro processing.

Describing a Metaprogram The method `translateDefinition()` implementing the macro for the OBSERVER pattern in section 2.2 is shown in Fig. 3. This metaprogram first obtains all the member methods (including inherited ones) defined in the class by invoking `getMethods()` on the class metaobject. Then, if a member method declared in interfaces is not implemented in the class, it generates a new member method doing nothing and adds it to the class by invoking `addMethod()` on the class metaobject.

```
void translateDefinition() {
    OJMethod[] m = this.getMethods(this);
    for (int i = 0; i < m.length; ++i) {
        OJModifier modif = m[i].getModifiers();
        if (modif.isAbstract()) {
            OJMethod n = new OJMethod(this,
                m[i].getModifiers().removeAbstract(),
                m[i].getReturnType(), m[i].getName(),
                m[i].getParameterTypes(),
                m[i].getExceptionTypes(),
                makeStatementList("return;"));
            this.addMethod(n);
        }
    }
}
```

Fig. 3. `translateDefinition()` in ObserverClass.

As a class is represented by a class metaobjects, a member method is also represented by a method metaobjects. In OpenJava, classes, member methods, member fields, and constructors are represented by instances of the class OJClass, OJMethod, OJField, and OJConstructor, respectively. These metaobject represent logical structures of class and member definitions. They are easy to handle, compared to directly handling large ASTs representing class declarations and collecting information scattered in these ASTs.

3.2   Class Metaobjects

As shown in section 2, a problem of ordinary macro systems is that their primary data structure is ASTs (abstract syntax trees) but they are far from logical structures of programs in OO languages. In OO languages like Java, class definitions play an important role as a logical structure of programs. Therefore, OpenJava employs the class metaobjects model, which was originally developed for reflective computing, for representing a logical structure of a program. The class metaobjects make it easy for meta programs to access a logical structure of program.

Hiding Syntactical Information In Java, programmers can use various syntax for describing the logically same thing. These syntactical differences are absorbed by the metaobjects. For instance, there are two notations for declaring a String array member field:

```
String[] a;
String b[];
```

Both a and b are String array fields. It would be awkward to write a metaprogram if the syntactical differences of the two member fields had to be considered. Thus OJField provides only two member methods getType() and setType() for handling the type of a member field. getType() on the OJField metaobjects representing a and b returns a class metaobject representing the array type of the class String.

Additionally, some elements in the grammar represent the same element in a logical structure of the language. If one of these element is edited, the others are also edited. For instance, the member method setName() in OJClass for modifying the name of the class changes not only the class name after the class keyword in the class declaration but also changes the name of the constructors.

Logically Structured Class Representation Simple ASTs, even arranged and abstracted well, cannot properly represent a logical structure of a class definition. The data structure must be carefully designed to corresponded not only to the grammar of the language but also to the logical constructs of the language like classes and member methods. Especially, it makes it easy to handle the logical information of program including association between names and types.

For instance, the member method getMethods() in OJClass returns all the member methods defined in the class which are not only the methods immediately declared in the class but also the inherited methods. The class metaobjects contain type information so that the definition of the super class can be accessible.

3.3   Class Metaobjects in Details

The root class for class metaobjects is OJClass. The member methods of OJClass for obtaining information about a class are shown in Tab. 1 and Tab. 2. They cover all the attributes of the class. In OpenJava, all the types, including array types and primitive types like int, have corresponding class metaobjects. Using the member methods shown in Tab. 1, metaprograms can inspect whether a given type is an ordinary class or not.

Tab. 3 gives methods for modifying the definition of the class. Metaprograms can override translateDefinition() in OJClass so that it calls these methods for executing desired modifications. For instance, the example shown in Fig. 3 adds newly generated member methods to the class with addMethod().

Table 1. Member methods in OJClass. for non-class types.

---

boolean isInterface()
    Tests if this represents an interface type.

boolean isArray()
    Tests if this represents an array type.

boolean isPrimitive()
    Tests if this represents a primitive type.

OJClass getComponentType()
    Returns a class metaobject for the type of array components.

Table 2. Member methods in OJClass for introspection (1).

String getPackageName()
    Returns the package name this class belongs to.

String getSimpleName()
    Returns the unqualified name of this class.

OJModifier getModifiers()
    Returns the modifiers for this class.

OJClass getSuperclass()
    Returns the superclass declared explicitly or implicitly.

OJClass[] getDeclaredInterfaces()
    Returns all the declared superinterfaces.

StatementList getInitializer()
    Returns all the static initializer statements.

OJField[] getDeclaredFields()
    Returns all the declared fields.

OJMethod[] getDeclaredMethods()
    Returns all the declared methods.

OJConstructor[] getDeclaredConstructors()
    Returns all the constructors declared explicitly or implicitly.

OJClass[] getDeclaredClasses()
    Returns all the member classes (inner classes).

OJClass getDeclaringClass()
    Returns the class declaring this class (outer class).

Table 3. Member methods in OJClass for modifying the class.

`String setSimplename(String name)`
  Sets the unqualified name of this class.

`OJModifier setModifiers(OJModifier modifs)`
  Sets the class modifiers.

`OJClass setSuperclass(OJClass clazz)`
  Sets the superclass.

`OJClass[] setInterfaces(OJClass[] faces)`
  Sets the superinterfaces to be declared.

`OJField removeField(OJField field)`
  Removes the given field from this class declaration.

`OJMethod removeMethod(OJMethod method)`
  Removes the given method from this class declaration.

`OJConstructor removeConstructor(OJConstructor constr)`
  Removes the given constructor from this class declaration.

`OJField addField(OJField field)`
  Adds the given field to this class declaration.

`OJMethod addMethod(OJMethod method)`
  Adds the given method to this class declaration.

`OJConstructor addConstructor(OJConstructor constr)`
  Adds the given constructor to this class declaration.

Metaobjects Obtained through Class Metaobjects

The method `getSuperclass()` in OJClass, which is used to obtain the superclass of the class, returns a class metaobject instead of the class name (as a string). As the result, metaprogram can use the returned class metaobject to directly obtain information about the superclass. OpenJava automatically generates class metaobjects on demand, even for classes declared in another source file or for classes available only in the form of bytecode, that is, classes whose source code is not available.

The returned value of the member method `getModifiers()` in Tab. 2 is an instance of the class OJModifier. This class represents a set of class modifiers such as `public`, `abstract` or `final`. Metaprograms do not have to care about the order of class modifiers because OJModifier hides such useless information.

The class OJMethod, which is the return type of `getDeclaredMethods()` in OJClass, represents a logical structure of a method. Thus, similarly to the class OJClass, this class has member methods for examining or modifying the attributes of the method. Some basic member methods in OJMethod are shown in Tab. 4. Any type information obtained from these methods is also represented by a class metaobject. For instance, `getReturnType()` returns a class metaobject as the return type of the method. This feature of OJMethod is also found in

Table 4. Basic methods in OJMethod.

`String getName()`
  Returns the name of this method.
`OJModifier getModifiers()`
  Returns the modifiers for this method.
`OJClass getReturnType()`
  Returns the return type.
`OJClass[] getParameterTypes()`
  Returns the parameter types in declaration order.
`OJClass[] getExceptionTypes()`
  Returns the types of the exceptions declared to be thrown.
`String[] getParameterVariables()`
  Returns the parameter variable names in declaration order.
`StatementList getBody()`
  Returns the statements of the method body.
`String setName(String name)`
  Sets the name of this method.
`OJModifier setModifiers(OJModifier modifs)`
  Sets the method modifiers.
`OJClass setReturnType()`
  Sets the return type.
`OJClass[] setParameterTypes()`
  Sets the parameter types in declaration order.
`OJClass[] setExceptionTypes()`
  Sets the types of the exceptions declared to be thrown.
`String[] setParameterVariables()`
  Sets the parameter variable names in declaration order.
`StatementList setBody()`
  Sets the statements of the method body.

OJField and OJConstructor, which respectively represent a member field and a constructor.

The class StatementList, which is the return type of the member method getBody() in the class OJMethod, represents the statements in a method body. An instance of StatementList consists of objects representing either expressions or statements. StatementList objects are AST-like data structures although they contain type information. This is because we thought that the logical structure of statements and expressions in Java can be well represented with ASTs.

Logical Structure of a Class Tab. 5 shows the member methods in OJClass handling a logical structure of a class. Using these methods, metaprograms can obtain information considering class inheritance and member hiding. Although these member methods can be implemented by combining the member methods in Tab.2, they are provided for convenience. We think that providing these methods is significant from the viewpoint that class metaobjects represent a logical structure of a program.

Table 5. Member methods in OJClass for introspection (2).

OJClass[] getInterfaces()
> Returns all the interfaces implemented by this class or the all the superinterfaces of this interface.

boolean isAssignableFrom(OJClass clazz)
> Determines if this class/interface is either the same as, or is a superclass or superinterface of, the given class/interface.

OJMethod[] getMethods(OJClass situation)
> Returns all the class available from the given situation, including those declared and those inherited from superclasses/superinterfaces.

OJMethod getMethod(String name, OJClass[] types, OJClass situation)
> Returns the specified method available from the given situation.

OJMethod getInvokedMethod(String name, OJClass[] types, OJClass situation)
> Returns the method, of the given name, invoked by the given arguments types, and available from the given situation.

In considering the class inheritance mechanism, the member methods defined in a given class are not only the member methods described in that class declaration but also the inherited ones. Thus, method metaobjects obtained by invoking getMethods() on a class metaobject include the methods explicitly declared in its class declaration but also the methods inherited from its superclass or superinterfaces.

Moreover, accessibility of class members is restricted in Java by member modifiers like public, protected or private. Thus, getMethods() returns only the member methods available from the class specified by the argument. For instance, if the specified class is not a subclass or in the same package, getMethods() returns only the member methods with public modifier. In Fig. 3, since the metaprogram passes this to getMethods(), it obtains all the member methods defined in that class.

3.4 Type-Driven Translation

As macro expansion in OpenJava is managed by metaobjects corresponding to each class (type), this translation is said to be type-driven. In the above example, only the member method translateDefinition() of OJClass is overridden to translate the class declarations of specified classes (callee-side translation).

In addition to the callee-side translation, OJClass provides a framework to translate the code related to the corresponding class spread over whole program selectively (caller-side translation). The parts related to a certain class is, for example, instance creation expressions or field access expressions.

Here, we take up an example of a macro that enables programming with the FLYWEIGHT [6] pattern to explain this mechanism. This design pattern is applied to use objects-sharing to support large numbers of fine-grained objects efficiently. An example of macro supporting uses of this pattern would need to translate an instance creation expression of a class Glyph:

```
new Glyph('c')
```

into a class method call expression:

```
GlyphFactory.createCharacter('c')
```

The class method createCharacter() returns an object of Glyph correspondent to the given argument if it was already generated, otherwise it creates a new object to return. This way, the program using Glyph objects automatically shares an object of Glyph representing a font for a letter c without generating several objects for the same letter. In ordinary programming using Glyph objects with the FLYWEIGHT pattern, programmers must explicitly write createCharacter() in their program with creations of Glyph objects. With a support of this macro, instance creations can be written in the regular new syntax and the pattern is used automatically.

In OpenJava, this kind of macro expansions are implemented by defining a metaclass FlyweightClass to be applied to the class Glyph. This metaclass overrides the member method expandAllocation() of OJClass as in Fig.4. This method receives a class instance creation expression and returns a translated expression. The system of OpenJava examines the whole source code and apply this member method to each Glyph instance creation expression to perform the macro expansion.

```
Expression expandAllocation(AllocationExpression expr, Environment env) {
    ExpressionList args = expr.getArguments();
    return new MethodCall(this, "createCharacter", args);
}
```

Fig. 4. Replacement of class instance expressions.

The member method expandAllocation() receives an AllocationExpression object representing a class instance creation expression and an Environment object representing the environment of this expression. The Environment object holds name binding information such as type of variable in the scope of this expression.

OpenJava uses type-driven translation to enable the comprehensive macro expansion of partial code spread over various places in program. In macro systems

for OO programming languages, it is not only needed to translate a class declaration simply but translating expressions using the class together is also needed.
In OpenJava, by defining a methods like `expandAllocation()`, metaprogrammers can selectively apply macro expansion to the limited expressions related
to classes controlled by the metaclass. This kind of mechanism has not been
seen in most of ordinary macro systems except some systems like OpenC++ [3].
Tab. 6 shows the primary member methods of OJClass which can be overridden
for macro expansion at caller-side.

Table 6. Member methods for each place applied the macro-expansion to.

Member method	Place applied the macro expansion to
translateDefinition()	Class declaration
expandAllocation()	Class instance allocation expression
expandArrayAllocation()	Array allocation expression
expandTypeName()	Class name
expandMethodCall()	Method class expression
expandFieldRead()	Field-read expression
expandFieldWrite()	Field-write expression
expandCastedExpression()	Casted expression from this type
expandCastExpression()	Casted expression to this type

3.5   Translation Mechanism

Given a source program, the processor of OpenJava:

1. Analyzes the source program to generate a class metaobject for each
   class.
2. Invokes the member methods of class metaobjects to perform macro
   expansion.
3. Generates the regular Java source program reflecting the modification made by the class metaobjects.
4. Executes the regular Java compiler to generate the corresponding
   byte code.

The Order of Translations Those methods of OJClass whose name start from
`expand` performs caller-side translation, and they affect expressions in source
program declaring another class C. Such expressions may also be translated by
`translateDefinition()` of the class metaobject of C as callee-side translation.
Thus different class metaobjects affect the same part of source program.

In OpenJava, to resolve this ambiguousness of several macro expansion,
the system always invokes `translateDefinition()` first as callee-side translation, then it apply caller-side translation to source code of class declarations
which was already applied callee-side translation. Metaprogrammers can design metaprogram considering this specified order of translation. In this rule,
if `translateDefinition()` changes an instance creation expression of class X
into Y's, `expandAllocation()` defined in the metaclass of X is not performed.

Moreover, the OpenJava system always performs `translateDefinition()` for superclasses first, i.e. the system performs it for subclasses after superclasses. As a class definition strongly depends on the definition of its superclass, the translation of a class often varies depending on the definition of its superclass. To settle the definition of superclasses, the system first translates the source program declaring superclasses. Additionally, there are some cases where the definition of a class D affects the result of translation of a class E. In Open-Java, from `translateDefinition()` for E, metaprogrammer can explicitly specify that `translateDefinition()` for D must be performed before.

In the case there are dependency relationships of translation among several macro expansions, consistent order of translation is specified to address this ambiguousness of translation results.

Dealing with Separate Compilation In Java, classes can be used in program only if they exist as source code or byte code (.class file). If there is no source code for a class C, the system cannot specify the metaclass of C, as is. Then, for instance, it cannot perform the appropriate `expandAllocation()` on instance creation expressions of C.

Therefore, OpenJava automatically preserves metalevel information such as the metaclass name for a class when it processes the callee-side translation of each class. These preservation are implemented by translating these information into a string held in a field of a special class, which is to be compiled into byte code. The system uses this byte code to obtain necessary metalevel information in another process without source code of that class. Additionally, metaprogrammers can request the system to preserve customized metalevel information of a class.

Metalevel information can be preserved as special attributes of byte code. In OpenJava, such information is used only at compile-time but not at runtime. Thus, in order to save runtime overhead, we chose to preserve such information in separated byte code which is not to be loaded by JVM at runtime.

3.6   Syntax Extension

With OpenJava macros, a metaclass can introduce new class/member modifiers and clauses starting with the special word at some limited positions of the regular Java grammar. The newly introduced clauses are valid only in the parts related to instances of the metaclass.

In a class declaration (callee-side), the positions allowed to introduce new clauses are:

- before the block of member declarations,
- before the block of method body in each method declaration,
- after the field variable in each field declaration.

And in other class declarations (caller-side), the allowed position is:

- after the name of the class.

Thanks to the limited positions of new clauses, the system can parse source programs without conflicts of extended grammars. Thus, metaprogrammers do not have to care about conflicts between clauses.

```
class VectorStack instantiates AdapterClass
    adapts Vector in v to Stack
{
    ....
}
```

Fig. 5. An example of syntax extension in OpenJava.

Fig. 5 shows an example source program using a macro, a metaclass Adapter-Class, supporting programming with the ADAPTER pattern [6]. The metaclass introduces a special clause beginning with `adapts` to make programmers to write special description for the ADAPTER pattern in the class declaration. The `adapts` clause in the Fig. 5 VectorStack is the adapter to a class Stack for a class Vector. The information by this clause is used only when the class metaobjects representing VectorStack performs macro expansion. Thus, for other class metaobjects, semantical information added by the new clause is recognized as a regular Java source code.

```
static SyntaxRule getDeclSuffix(String keyword) {
    if (keyword.equals("adapts")) {
        return new CompositeRule(
            new TypeNameRule(),
            new PrepPhraseRule("in", new IdentifierRule()),
            new PrepPhraseRule("to", new TypeNameRule()) );
    }
    return null;
}
```

Fig. 6. A meta-program for a customized suffix.

To introduce this `adapts` clause, metaprogrammers implement a member method `getDeclSuffix()` in the metaclass AdapterClass as shown in Fig. 6. The member method `getDeclSuffix()` is invoked by the system when needed, and returns a SyntaxRule object representing the syntax grammar beginning with the given special word. An instance of the class SyntaxRule implements a recursive descendant parser of LL(k), and analyzes a given token series to generate an appropriate AST. The system uses SyntaxRule objects obtained by invoking `getDeclSuffix()` to complete the parsing.

For metaprogrammers of such SyntaxRule objects, OpenJava provides a class library of subclasses of SyntaxRule, such as parsers of regular Java syntax elements and synthesizing parser for tying, repeating or selecting other SyntaxRule objects. Metaprogrammers can define their desired clauses by using this library or by implementing a new subclass of SyntaxRule.

3.7 Metaclass Model of OpenJava

A class must be managed by a single metaclass in OpenJava. Though it would be useful if programmers could apply several metaclasses to a class, we did not implement such a feature because there is a problem of conflict of translation between metaclasses. And, a metaclass for a class A does not manage a subclass A' of A, that is, the metaclass of A does not perform the callee-side and caller-side translation of A' it is not specified to be the metaclass of A' in the source program declaring A'.

For innerclasses such as member classes, local classes, anonymous classes in the Java language, each of them are also an instance of a metaclass in OpenJava. Thus programmers may apply a desired metaclass to such classes.

4   Related Work

There are a number of systems using the class metaobjects model for representing a logical structure of a program: 3-KRS [16], ObjVlisp [5], CLOS MOP [13], Smalltalk-80 [8], and so on. The reflection API [11] of the Java language also uses this model although the reflection API does not allow to change class metaobjects; it only allows to inspect them. Furthermore, the reflection API uses class metaobjects for making class definition accessible at runtime. On the other hand, OpenJava uses class metaobjects for macro expansion at compile-time.

OpenC++ [3] also uses the class metaobject model. OpenJava inherits several features, such as the type-driven translation mechanism, from OpenC++. However, the data structure mainly used in OpenC++ is still an AST (abstract syntax tree). MPC++ [10] and EPP [9] are similar to OpenC++ with respect to the data structure. As mentioned in section 2, an AST is not an appropriate abstraction for some macros frequently used in OO programming.

5   Conclusion

This paper describes OpenJava, which is a macro system for Java providing a data structure called class metaobjects. A number of research activities have been done for enhancing expressive power of macro systems. This research is also in this stream. OpenJava is a macro system with a data structure representing a logical structure of an OO program. This made it easier to describe typical macros for OO programming which was difficult to describe with ordinary macro systems.

To show the effectiveness of OpenJava, we implemented some macros in OpenJava for supporting programming with design patterns. Although we saw that class metaobjects are useful for describing those macros, we also found limitations of OpenJava. Since a single design pattern usually contains several classes, a macro system should be able to deal with those classes as a single entity [17]. However it is not easy for OpenJava to do that because macros are applied to each class. It is future work to address this problem by incorporate OpenJava with techniques like aspect-oriented programming [12].

References

1. Jan Bosch. Design Patterns as Language Constructs. *Journal of Object Oriented Programming*, 1997.
2. Peter J. Brown. *Macro Processors and Techniques for Portable Software*. Wiley, 1974.
3. Shigeru Chiba. A Metaobject Protocol for C++. *SIGPLAN Notices*, 30(10):285–299, 1995.
4. Shigeru Chiba. Macro Processing in Object-Oriented Languages. In *Proceedings of TOOLS Pacific '98*, Australia, November 1998. IEEE, IEEE Press.
5. Pierre Cointe. Metaclasses are First Class : the ObjVlisp Model. *SIGPLAN Notices*, 22(12):156–162, December 1987.
6. Erich Gamma, Richard Helm, Ralph Johnson, and John Vlissides. *Design Patterns - Elements of Reusable Object-Oriented Software*. Addison-Wesley, 1994.
7. Joseph Gil and David H. Lorenz. Design Patterns and Language Design. *IEEE Computer*, 31(3):118–120, March 1998.
8. Adele Goldberg and Dave Robson. *Smalltalk-80: The Language*. Addison Wesley, 1989.
9. Yuji Ichisugi and Yves Roudier. Extensible Java Preprocessor Kit and Tiny Data-Parallel Java. In *Proceedings of ISCOPE'97*, California, December 1997.
10. Yutaka Ishikawa, Atsushi Hori, Mitsuhisa Sato, Motohiko Matsuda, Jörg Nolte, Hiroshi Tezuka, Hiroki Konaka, and Kazuto Kubota. Design and Implementation of Metalevel Architecture in C++ - MPC++ Approach -. In *Proceedings of Reflection'96*, pages 153–166, 1996.
11. JavaSoft. Java Core Reflection API and Specification. online publishing, January 1997.
12. Gregor Kiczales, John Lamping, Anurag Mendhekar, Chris Maeda, Cristina Videira Lopes, Jean Marc Loingtier, and John Irwin. Aspect-Oriented Programming. *LNCS 1241*, pages 220–242, June 1997.
13. Gregor Kiczales, Jim Rivières, and Daniel G. Bobrow. *The Art of the Metaobject Protocol*. The MIT Press, 1991.
14. David A. Ladd and J. Christopher Ramming. A* : A Language for Implementing Language Processors. *IEEE Transactions on Software Engineering*, 21(11):894–901, November 1995.
15. William Maddox. Semantically-Sensitive Macroprocessing. Master's thesis, University of California, Berkeley, 1989. ucb/csd 89/545.
16. Pattie Maes. Concepts and Experiments in Computational Reflection. *SIGPLAN Notices*, 22(12):147–155, October 1987.
17. Jiri Soukup. Implementing Patterns. In *Pattern Languages of Program Design*, chapter 20, pages 395–412. Addison-Wesley, 1995.
18. Guy L. Steel Jr. *Common Lisp: The Language*. Digital Press, 2nd edition, 1990.
19. Daniel Weise and Roger Crew. Programmable Syntax Macros. *SIGPLAN Notices*, 28(6):156–165, 1993.

OpenJIT Frontend System: An Implementation of the Reflective JIT Compiler Frontend

Hirotaka Ogawa[1], Kouya Shimura[2], Satoshi Matsuoka[1], Fuyuhiko Maruyama[1], Yukihiko Sohda[1], and Yasunori Kimura[2]

[1] Tokyo Institute of Technology
{ogawa,matsu,Fuyuhiko.Maruyama,sohda}@is.titech.ac.jp
[2] Fujitsu Laboratories Limited
{kouya,ykimura}@flab.fujitsu.co.jp

Abstract OpenJIT is an open-ended, reflective JIT compiler framework for Java being researched and developed in a joint project by Tokyo Inst. Tech. and Fujitsu Ltd. Although in general self-descriptive systems have been studied in various contexts such as reflection and interpreter/compiler bootstrapping, OpenJIT is a first system we know to date that offers a stable, full-fledged Java JIT compiler that plugs into existing monolithic JVMs, and offer competitive performance to JITs typically written in C or C++. We propose an architecture for a reflective JIT compiler on a monolithic VM, and describe the details of its frontend system. And we demonstrate how reflective JITs could be useful class- or application specific customization and optimization by providing an important reflective "hook" into a Java system. We will focus on the Frontend portion of the OpenJIT system for this article; the details of the backend is described in [20].

1 Introduction

Programming Languages with high-degree of portability, such as Java, typically employ portable intermediate program representations such as bytecodes, and utilize *Just-In-Time compilers (JITs)*, which compile (parts of) programs into native code at runtime. However, all the Java JITs today as well as those for other languages such as Lisp, Smalltalk, and Self, only largely focuses on standard platforms such as Workstations and PCs, merely stress optimizing for speeding up single-threaded execution of general programs, usually at the expense of memory for space-time tradeoff. This is not appropriate, for example, for embedded systems where the tradeoff should be shifted more to memory rather than speed. Moreover, we claim that JITs could be utilized and exploited more opportunely in the following situations:

- **Platform-specific optimizations:** Execution platforms could be from embedded systems and hand-held devices all the way up to large servers and massive parallel processors (MPPs). There, requirements for optimizations differ considerably, not only for space-time tradeoffs, but also for particular

W. Cazzola et al. (Eds.): Reflection and Software Engineering, LNCS 1826, pp. 135–154, 2000.

class of applications that the platform is targeted to execute. JITs could be made to adapt to different platforms if it could be customized in a flexible way.

- **Platform-specific compilations:** On related terms, some platforms require assistance of compilers to generate platform- specific codes for execution. For example, DSM (Distributed-Shared Memory) systems and persistent object systems require specific compilations to emit code to detect remote or persistent reference operations. Thus, if one were to implement such systems on Java, one not only needs to modify the JVM, but also the JIT compiler. We note that, as far as we know, representative work on Java DSM (cJVM [2] by IBM) and persistent objects (PJama [3] at University of Glasgow) lack JIT compiler support for this very reason.

- **Application-specific optimizations:** One could be more opportunistic by performing optimizations that are specific to a particular application or a data set. This includes techniques such as selection of compilation strategies, runtime partial evaluation, as well as application-specific idiom recognition. By utilizing application-specific as well as run-time information, the compiled code could be made to execute substantially faster, or with less space, etc. compared to traditional, generalized optimizations. Although such techniques have been proposed in the past, it could become a generally-applied scheme and also an exciting research area if efficient and easily customizable JITs were available.

- **Language-extending compilations:** Some work stresses on extending Java for adding new language features and abstractions. Such extensions could be implemented as source-level or byte-code level transformations, but some low-level implementations are very difficult or inefficient to support with such higher-level transformations in Java. The abovementioned DSM is a good example: Some DSMs permit users to add control directives or storage classifiers at a program level to control the memory coherency protocols, and thus such a change must be done at JVM and native code level. One could facilitate this by encoding such extensions in bytecodes or classfile attributes, and customizing the JIT compilers accordingly to understand such extensions.

- **Environment- or Usage-specific compilations and optimizations:** Other environmental or usage factors could be considered during compilation, such as adding profiling code for performance instrumentation, debugging etc.[1]

Moreover, with Java, we would like these customizations to occur within an easy framework of portable, security-checked code downloaded across the network. That is to say, just as applets and libraries are downloadable on-the-fly, we would like the JIT compiler customization to be downloaded on-the-fly as well, depending on the specific platform, application, and environment. For

---

[1] In fact we do exactly that in the benchmarking we will show in [20], which for the first time characterizes the behavior of a self-descriptive JIT compiler.

example, if a user wants to instrument his code, he will want to download the (trusted) instrumentation component from the network on-the-fly to customize the generated code accordingly.

Unfortunately, most JITs today, especially those for Java, are designed to be closed and monolithic, and do not facilitate interfaces, frameworks, nor patterns as a means of customization. Moreover, JIT compilers are usually written in C or C++, and live in a completely separate scope from normal Java programs, without enjoying any of the language/systems benefits that Java provides, such as ease of programming and debugging, code safety, portability and mobility, etc. In other words, current Java JIT compilers are "black boxes", being in a sense against the principle of modular, open-ended, portable design ideals that Java itself represents.

In order to resolve such a situation, the collaborative group between Tokyo Institute of Technology and Fujitsu Limited have been working on a project OpenJIT [19] for almost the past two years. OpenJIT itself is a "reflective" Just-In-Time open compiler framework for Java written almost entirely in Java itself, and plugs into the standard JDK 1.1.x and 1.2 JVMs. All compiler objects coexist in the same heap space as the application objects, and are subject to execution by the same Java machinery, including having to be compiled by itself, and subject to static and dynamic customizations. At the same time, it is a fully-fledged, JCK (Java Compatibility Kit) compliant JIT compiler, able to run production Java code. In fact, as far as we know, it is the ONLY Java JIT compiler whose source code is available in public, and is JCK compliant other than that of Sun's. And, as the benchmarks will show, although being constrained by the limitations of the "classic" JVMs, and still being in development stage lacking sophisticated high-level optimizations, it is nonetheless equal to or superior to the Sun's (classic) JIT compiler on SpecJVM benchmarks, and attains about half the speed of the fastest JIT compilers that are much more complex, closed, and requires a specialized JVM. At the same time, OpenJIT is designed to be a compiler framework in the sense of Stanford SUIF [28], in that it facilitates high-level and low-level program analysis and transformation framework for the users to customize.

OpenJIT is still in active development, and we have just started distributing it for free for non-commercial purposes from http://www.openjit.org/. It has shown to be quite portable, thanks in part to being written in Java—the Sparc version of OpenJIT runs on Solaris, and the x86 version runs on different breeds of Unix including Linux, FreeBSD, and Solaris. We are hoping that it will stem and cultivate interesting and new research in the field of compiler development, reflection, portable code, language design, dynamic optimization, and other areas.

The purpose of the paper is to describe our experiences in building OpenJIT, as well as presenting the following technical contributions:

1. We propose an architecture for a reflective JIT compiler framework on a monolithic "classic" JVM, and identify the technical challenges as well as the techniques employed. The challenges exist for several reasons, that the

JIT compiler is reflective, and also the characteristics of Java, such as its pointer-safe execution model, built-in multi-threading, etc.

2. We demonstrate how reflective JITs could be useful class- or application specific customization and optimization by providing an important reflective "hook" into a Java system, with the notion of *compilets*. Although the current examples are small, we nevertheless present a possibility of larger-scale deployment of OpenJIT for uses in the abovementioned situations.

2   Overview of the OpenJIT Framework

Although there have been reflective compilers and OO compiler frameworks, OpenJIT has some characteristic requirements and technical challenges that were previously not seen in traditional reflective systems as well as JIT compilers. In order to better describe the technical challenges, we will first overview the OpenJIT framework.

2.1   OpenJIT: The Conceptual Overview

OpenJIT is a JIT compiler written in Java to be executed on "classic" VM systems such as Sun JDK 1.1.x and 1.2. OpenJIT allows a given Java code to be portable and maintainable with compiler customization. With standard Java, the portability of Java is effective insofar as the capabilities and features provided by the JVM (Java Virtual Machine); thus, any new features that has to be transparent from the Java source code, but which JVM does not provide, could only be implemented via non-portable means. For example, if one wishes to write a portable parallel application under multi-threaded, shared memory model, then some form of distributed shared memory (DSM) would be required for execution under MPP and cluster platforms. However, JVM itself does not facilitate any DSM functionalities, nor provide any software 'hooks' for incorporating the necessary read/write barriers for user-level DSM implementation. As a result, one must either modify the JVM, or employ some ad-hoc preprocessor solution, neither of which are satisfactory in terms of portability and/or performance. With OpenJIT, the DSM class library implementor can write a set of compiler metaclasses so that necessary read/write barriers, etc., would be appropriately inserted into critical parts of code.

Also, with OpenJIT, one could incorporate platform-, application-, or usage-specific compilation or optimization. For example, one could perform various numerical optimizations such as loop restructuring, cache blocking, etc. which have been well-studied in Fortran and C, but have not been well adopted into JITs for excessive runtime compilation cost. OpenJIT allows application of such optimizations to critical parts of code in a pinpointed fashion, specified by either the class-library builder, application writer, or the user of the program. Furthermore, it allows optimizations that are too application and/or domain specific to be incorporated as a general optimization technique for standard compilers, as has been reported by [15].

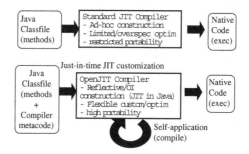

Fig. 1. Comparison of traditional JITs and OpenJIT.

In this manner, OpenJIT allows a new style of programming for optimizations, portability, and maintainability, compared to traditional JIT compilers, by providing separations of concerns with respect to optimization and code-generation for new features. That is to say, with traditional JIT compilers, we see in the upper half of Figure 1, the JIT compilers would largely be transparent from the user, and users would have to maintain code which might not be tangled to achieve portability and performance. OpenJIT, on the other hand, will allow the users to write clean code describing the base algorithm and features, and by selecting the appropriate compiler metaclasses, or even by writing his own separately, one could achieve optimization while maintaining appropriate separation of concerns. Furthermore, compared to previous open compiler efforts, OpenJIT could achieve better portability and performance, as source code is not necessary, and late binding at run-time allows exploitation of run-time values, as is with run-time code generators.

2.2 Architectural Overview of OpenJIT

The OpenJIT architecture is largely divided into the frontend and the backend processors. The frontend takes the Java bytecodes as input, performs higher-level optimizations involving source-to-source transformations, and passes on the intermediate code to the backend, or outputs the transformed bytecode. The backend is effectively a small JIT compiler in itself, and takes either the bytecode or the intermediate code from the frontend as input, performs lower-level optimizations including transformation to register code, and outputs the native code for direct execution. The reason why there is a separate frontend and the backend is largely due to modularity and ease of development, especially for higher-level transformations, as well as defaulting to the backend when execution speed is not of premium concern. In particular, we strive for the possibility of the two modules being able to run as independent components.

OpenJIT will be invoked just as a standard Java JIT compiler would, using the standard JIT API on each method invocation. A small OpenJIT C runtime is dynamically linked onto the JVM, disguised as a full-fledged C-based JIT compiler. Upon initialization, it will have set the `CompiledCodeLinkVector` within the JVM so that it calls the necessary OpenJIT C stub routines. In particular, when a class is loaded, JVM calls the `OpenJIT_InitializeForCompiler()` C function, which redirects the invoker functions for each method within the loaded class to to `OpenJIT_invoke()`. `OpenJIT_invoke`, in turn upcalls the appropriate Java `compile()` method in the `org.OpenJIT.Compile` class, transferring the necessary information for compilation of the specific method. It is possible to specify, for each method, exactly which portion of the compiler is to be called; by default, it is the OpenJIT backend compiler, but for sophisticated compilation OpenJIT frontend is called. After compilation, the upcall returns to `OpenJIT_invoke()`, which calls the just compiled code through `mb->invoker` (`mb` = method block). Thus, the heart of OpenJIT compiler is written in Java, and the C runtime routines merely serve to "glue" the JVM and the Java portion of OpenJIT. The details will be presented in [20].

Upon invocation, the *OpenJIT frontend* system processes the bytecode of the method in the following way: The *decompiler* recovers the AST of the original Java source from the bytecode, by recreating the control-flow graph of the source program. At the same time, the *annotation analysis module* will obtain any annotating info on the class file, which will be recorded as attribute info on the AST[2].

Next, the obtained AST will be subject to optimization by the *(higher-level) optimization module*. Based on the AST and control-flow information, we compute the data & control dependency graphs, etc., and perform program transformation in a standard way with modules such as *flowgraph construction module*, *program analysis module*, and *program transformation module* using template matching. The result from the OpenJIT frontend will be a new bytecode stream, which would be output to a file for later usage, or an intermediate representation to be used directly by the OpenJIT backend.

The *OpenJIT backend* system, in turn, performs lower-level optimization over the output from the frontend system, or the bytecodes directly, and generates native code. It is in essence a small JIT compiler in itself.

Firstly, when invoked as an independent JIT compiler bypassing the frontend, the *low-level IL translator* analyzes and translates the bytecode instruction streams to low-level intermediate code representation using stacks. Otherwise the IL from the frontend is utilized. Then, the *RTL Translator* translates the stack-based code to intermediate code using registers (RTL). Here, the bytecode is analyzed to divide the instruction stream into basic blocks, and by calculating the depth of the stack for each bytecode instruction, the operands are generated with assumption that we have infinite number of registers. Then, the *peephole optimizer* would eliminate redundant instructions from the RTL instruction stream, and finally, the *native code generator* would generate the target code of the CPU,

---

[2] In the current implementation, the existence of annotation is a prerequisite for frontend processing; otherwise, the frontend is bypassed, and the backend is invoked immediately.

allocating physical registers. Currently, OpenJIT supports the SPARC and the x86 processors as the target, but could be easily ported to other machines. The generated native code will be then invoked by the Java VM, as described earlier.

3   Overview of the OpenJIT Backend System

As a JIT compiler, the high-level overview of the workings of OpenJIT backend is standard. The heart of the low-level IL translator is the `parseBytecode()` method of the `ParseBytecode` class, which parses the bytecode and produces an IL stream. The IL we defined is basically an RISC-based, 3-operand instruction set, but is tailored for high affinity with direct translation of Java instructions into IL instruction set with stack manipulations for later optimizations. There are 36 IL instructions, to which each bytecode is translated into possibly a sequence of these instructions. Some complex instructions are translated into calls into run-time routines. We note that the IL translator is only executed when the OpenJIT backend is used in a standalone fashion; when used in conjunction with the frontend, the frontend directly emits IL code of the backend.

Then, RTL converter translates the stack-based IL code to register based RTL code. The same IL is used, but the code is restructured to be register-based rather than encoded stack operations. Here, a dataflow analyzer is then run to determine the type and the offset of the stack operands. We assume that there are infinite number of registers in this process. In practice, we have found that 24–32 registers are sufficient for executing large Java code without spills when no aggressive optimizations are performed [24]. Then, the *peephole optimizer* would eliminate redundant instructions from the RTL instruction stream.

Finally, the *native code generator* would generate the target code of the CPU. It first converts IL restricting the number of registers, inserting appropriate spill code. Then the IL sequence is translated into native code sequence, and ISA-specific peephole optimizations are performed. Currently, OpenJIT supports the SPARC and x86 processors as the target, but could be easily ported to other machines[3]. The generated native code will be then invoked by the Java VM, upon which the *OpenJIT runtime module* will be called in a supplemental way, mostly to handle Java-level exceptions.

The architectural outline of the OpenJIT backend is illustrated in Figure 2. Further details of the backend system can be found in [23].

4   Details of the OpenJIT Frontend System

As described in Section 2, the OpenJIT frontend system provides a Java class framework for higher-level, abstract analysis, transformation, and specialization

---

[3] Our experience has been that it has not been too difficult to port from SPARC to x86, save for its slight peculiarities and small number of registers, due in part being able to program in Java. We expect that porting amongst RISC processors to be quite easy.

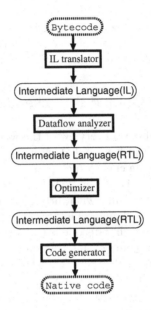

Fig. 2. Overview of the OpenJIT backend system.

of Java programs which had already been compiled by `javac`: (1) The decompiler translates the bytecode into augmented AST, (2) analysis, optimizations, and specialization are performed on the tree, and (3) the AST is converted into the low-level IL of the backend system, or optionally, a stream of bytecodes is generated.

Transformation over AST is done in a similar manner to Stanford SUIF, in that there is a method which traverses the tree and performs update on a node or a subtree when necessary. There are a set of abstract methods that are invoked as a hook. The OpenJIT frontend system, in order to utilize such a hook functionality according to user requirements, extends the class file (albeit in a conformable way so that it is compatible with other Java platforms) by adding annotation info to the classfile. Such an info is called "classfile annotation".

The overall architecture of the OpenJIT frontend system is as illustrated in Fig. 3, and consists of the following four modules:

1. **OpenJIT Bytecode Decompiler**
   Translates the bytecode stream into augmented AST. It utilizes a new algorithm for systematic AST reconstruction using dominator trees.
2. **OpenJIT Class Annotation Analyzer**
   Extracts classfile annotation information, and adds the annotation info onto the AST.
3. **OpenJIT High-level Optimizer Toolkit**
   The toolkit to construct "compilets", which are modules to specialize the OpenJIT frontend for performing customized compilation and optimizations.

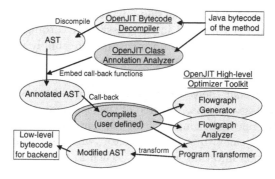

Fig. 3. Overview of OpenJIT frontend system.

4. **Abstract Syntax Tree Package**
   Provides construction of the AST as well as rewrite utilities.

We first describe the classfile annotation, which is a special feature of OpenJIT, followed by descriptions of the four modules.

4.1   Classfile Annotation

Classfile annotation in OpenJIT is additional info or directive added to the classfile to direct OpenJIT to perform classfile-specific (or application-specific, platform-specific) optimization and customization. Here are examples of directives possible with classfile annotations:

– Support for User-defined Optimizers and Specializers
– Support for Memory Models e.g., DSM
– Optimizing Numerical Code

Support for User-defined Optimizers and Specializers.   OpenJIT permits user-level definitions and customizations of its optimizer and specializer classes in the frontend. The classfile annotation allows the user to specify which of the classes the user-defined compiler classes to employ, by means of naming the class directly, or encoding the classfile itself as an annotation.

Support for Memory Models e.g., DSM.   As mentioned in Section 1, the support for various memory models including DSM requires insertion of appropriate Read/Write barriers for access to shared objects. However, there are algorithms to statically determine that objects are immutable or do not escape such as [8,4,5,32], which allow such barriers to be compiled away, eliminating runtime overhead.

Optimizing Numerical Optimizations.   Numerical performance of Java is known to suffer due to array bounds checks, non-rectangular multidimensional storage allocation, etc. By marking the loops that can be statically determined to use the array in regular ways, we can apply traditional Fortran-style optimizations such as loop transformation, cache blocking, etc.

In order to implement the classfile annotation feature, we employ the attribute region of of each method in the classfile. According to the JVM specs, any attributes that the JVM does not recognize are simply ignored; thus, classfiles with OpenJIT annotations can be executed on platforms without OpenJIT, achieving high portability (save for the programs that do not work without OpenJIT). One caveat is that there is no simple way to add extra information in the attribute field of classes themselves, due to the lack of appropriate JIT interface in the JVM; thus, one must employ some convention, say, defining a "dummy" null method that is called by the constructor, whose sole purpose is to supply class-wide annotation info that would be cached in the OpenJIT compiler.

In order to create a classfile with annotation information, we either employ an extended version of source-to-bytecode compilers such as javac; for classfiles without source, we could use a tool to add such annotation in an automated way; in fact the tool we are currently testing is a modified version of the OpenJIT frontend system.

4.2   OpenJIT Bytecode Decompiler Module

OpenJIT Bytecode Decompiler inputs the bytecode stream from the classfile, and converts it into an augmented AST. The module processes the the bytecode in the following way:

1. Converts the bytecode stream into an internal representation of JVM instruction, and marks the instructions that become the leading instruction of basic blocks.
2. Construct a control flow graph (CFG) with basic block nodes.
3. Construct a dominator tree that corresponds to the CFG.
4. Reconstruct the Java AST by symbolic execution of the instructions within the basic block.
5. Discover the control flow that originated from the short-circuit optimizations of the Java conditional expressions such as && or || and (x ? a * b), and recover the expressions.
6. Reconstruct the Java control structure using the algorithm described in [16].
7. Output the result as an AST, augmented with control-flow and dominator information.

All the above steps except (6) are either simple, or could be done with existing techniques, such as that described in [21]. Step (6), is quite difficult; most previous techniques published so far analyzed the CFG directly, and used pattern matching to extract valid Java control structures [21,27]. Instead, we have proposed an algorithm which walks over the dominator tree, and enumerates over every possible patterns of dominance relation, which has a corresponding Java control structure. Compared to existing techniques such as Krakatoa [27], our method was shown to be faster, and more robust to code obfuscation. Some preliminary details can be found in [16].

4.3   OpenJIT Class Annotation Analyzer Module

The OpenJIT Class Annotation Analyzer module extracts the class annotation from a classfile, and adds the annotation info to the AST. The added annotations are typically *compilets* that modify the compiler more concretely, it processes the annotation in the following way:

1. First, it access the attribute region of the method. This is done by parsing the method block region extracted from the JVM.
2. We process this byte array assuming that the annotation object has been serialized with `writeObject()`, constructing an annotation object.
3. we attach the annotation object to the AST as annotation information.

Because what kind of information is to be embodied in the classfile annotation differs according to its usage, the `OpenJIT_Annotation` is actually an abstract class, and the user is to subclass a concrete annotation class. The abstract superclass embodies the identifier of the annotation, and the AST node where it is to be attached. This is similar in principle to SUIF, except that the annotation must be extracted from the classfile instead of being given a priori by the user.

4.4   OpenJIT High-Level Optimizer Toolkit

OpenJIT High-level Optimizer Toolkit is used to construct OpenJIT *compilets*, that are a set of classes that customizes the compiler. The toolkit provides means of utilizing the augmented AST for implementing traditional compiler optimizations, and is largely composed of the following three submodules:[4]

1. Flowgraph Constructor
   Flowgraph Constructor creates various (flow) graphs from the augmented AST, such as dataflow graph, FUD chains, control dependence graph, etc. The Flowgraph class is an abstract class, and Factory Method pattern is employed to construct user-defined flowgraphs.
2. Flowgraph Analyzer
   The Flowgraph Analyzer performs general computation over the flowgraph, i.e., dataflow equation solving, handling merges, fix point calculation, etc. We employ the Command Pattern to subclass the `Analyzer` class for each algorithm, and each subclass triggers its own algorithm with the `execute()` method. The user can subclass the `Analyzer` class to add his own flowgraph algorithm.

---

[4] In the current version, compilets are not downloadable; this is primarily due to the fact OpenJIT itself is not yet entirely downloadable due to a few restrictions in the JVM. We are currently working to circumvent the restrictions, and a prototype is almost working. Meanwhile, the Toolkit itself is available, and a custom version of OpenJIT can be created with "static" compilets using standard inheritance.

3. Program Transformer

The Program Transformer employs declarative pattern matching and rewrite rules to transform the augmented AST. One registers the rule using the following API:

- register_pattern(Expression src, Expression dst)
- register_pattern(Statement src, Statement dst)

  Registers the transformation rule that transforms the src pattern to the dst pattern. The pattern can be constructed using the Abstract Syntax Tree Package described next.

- substitution(Expression root)
- substitution(Statement root)

  Searches the subtree with the designated root node depth-first, and if a match is found with the registered patterns, we perform the transformation.

Initial use of the current pattern matching technique proved to be somewhat too low-level; in particular, generation and registration of the transformation rule is still cumbersome. The next version of OpenJIT will have APIs to generate patterns and transformation rules from higher-level specifications, in particular for well-known program transformations (such as code motion, loop transformation, etc.)

4.5   Abstract Syntax Tree Package

The Abstract Syntax Tree Package is a utility package called from other parts of the OpenJIT frontend to implement low-level construction of the augmented AST, patterns for transformation rules, etc. The AST essentially implements the entire syntactic entities of the Java programming language. Each node of the AST corresponds to the expression or a statement in Java. The class hierarchy for the package is organized with appropriate subclassing of over 100 classes: (Fig. 4). We show typical Expression and Statement classes in Fig. 5 and Fig. 6, respectively.

A typical **Expression** subclass for a binary operator (**MultiplyExpression** in the example) consists of the operator ID, left-hand and right-hand expressions, and reference to an annotation object. The **code()** method either generates the low-level IL for the backend, or a Java bytecode stream. The **code()** method walks over the left- and right-hand expressions in a recursive manner, generating code. When a node has non-null reference to an annotation object, it calls the **execute()** method of the annotation, enabling customized transformations and compilations to occur.

As a typical **Statement** subclass, **IfStatement** recursively generates code for the conditional in a similar manner to **Expressions**.

As such, the current OpenJIT is structured in a similar manner to OpenC++ [6], in that syntactic entities are recursively compiled. The difference is that we provide annotation objects that abstracts out the necessary hook to the particular syntax node, in addition to customization of the syntax node themselves.

- Node
  - Expression
    - BinaryExpression
      · AddExpression
      · SubtractExpression
      · MultiplyExpression
      · ...
    - UnaryExpression
    - ConstantExpression
    - ...
  - Statement
    - IfStatement
    - ForStatement
    - WhileStatement
    - CaseStatement
    - ...

Fig. 4. Class hierarchy of the abstract syntax tree package.

Thus, it is possible to perform similar reflective extensions as OpenC++ in an encapsulated way. On the other hand, experience has shown that some traditional optimizations are better handled using SSA, such as dataflow analysis, constant propagation, CSE, loop transformation, code motion. In the next version of OpenJIT, we plan to support SSA directly by translating the augmented AST into SSA, and providing the necessary support packages.

```
public class MultiplyExpression extends BinaryExpression {
    int op;                        // Construct ID
    Expression left;               // LHS expression
    Expression right;              // RHS expression
    Type type;                     // Type of this expression
    Annotation ann;                // Embedded Annotation (default: null)

    void code() {                  // Convert AST to backend-IR form
                                   // (or bytecodes)
        if (ann) ann.execute(this); // call-back for metacomputation
        left.code();               // generate code for LHS
        right.code();              // generate code for RHS
        add(op);                   // generate code for "operator"
    }

    Expression simplify() {}       // Simplify expression form
                                   // (e.g. convert "a * 1" to "a")
    ...
}
```

Fig. 5. An expression class for a typical binary expression (multiply).

```
public class IfStatement extends Statement {
    int op;                        // Construct ID
    Expression cond;               // Condition expression
    Statement ifTrue;              // Statement of Then-part
    Statement ifFalse;             // Statement of Else-part
    Annotation ann;                // Embedded Annotation (default: null)

    void code() {                  // Convert AST to backend-IR form
                                   // (or bytecodes)
        if (ann) ann.execute(this); // call-back for metacomputation
        codeBranch(cond);          // generate code for Condition
        ifTrue.code();             // generate code for Then-part
        ifFalse.code();            // generate code for Else-part
        addLabel();                // add label for "Break" statement
    }

    Statement simplify() {}        // Simplify statement form
                                   // (e.g. if (true) S1 S2 => S1)
    ...
}
```

Fig. 6. A example statement class for the "If" statement.

5   Reflective Programming with OpenJIT—A Preliminary Example

As a preliminary example, we tested loop transformation of the program in Fig. 8 into an equivalent one as shown in Fig. 9[5]. In this example, we have added a compilet called **LoopTransformer** using the class annotation mechanism in the attribute region of the **matmul()** method by using a tool mentioned in Section 4.1. The **execute()** method of the **LoopTransformer** class searches the AST of the method it is attached to for the innermost loop of the perfect tri-nested loop. There, if it finds a a 2-dimensional array whose primary index is only bound to the loop variable of the outermost loop, it performs the necessary transformation. The overview of the **LoopTransformer** is shown in Fig. 7; the real program is actually about 200 lines, and is still not necessarily easy to program due to relatively low level of abstraction that the tree package provides, as mentioned earlier. We are working to provide a higher level API by communizing some of the operations as a compilet class library.

Also, one caveat is that the IL translator is still incomplete, and as such we have generated the bytecode directly, which is fed into the OpenJIT backend. Thus we are not achieving the best performance, due to the compilation over-head, and the information present in the frontend is not utilized in the backend. Nevertheless, we do demonstrate the effectiveness to some degree.

For OpenJIT, we compared the results of executing Fig. 8 directly, and also transforming at runtime using the OpenJIT frontend into Fig. 9. For sunwjit, we performed the transformation offline at source level, and compiled both programs with javac. The size of the matrices (SIZE) are set to 200×200 and 600×600.

---

[5] Note that although we are using the Java source to represent the program, in reality the program is in bytecode form, and transformation is done at the AST level.

```
public class LoopTransformer extends Annotation {
  int loop_nest = 0;
  LocalField index;
  LoopTransformer() {}
  boolean isRegularForm(Statement init, Expression cond, Expression inc) {
    // Check the initializer and the conditions of the For statement
    // to verify that it is in a normal form.
  }
  void execute(Node root) {
    if (root instanceof CompoundStatement) {
      for (int i = 0; i < root.args.length; i++) { execute(root.args[i]); }
    }
    // Test whether the loop is a perfect tri-nested loop
    else if (root instanceof ForStatement &&
             root.body instanceof ForStatement &&
             root.body.body instanceof ForStatement) {
      if (isRegularForm(root.init, root.cond, root.inc) &&
          isRegularForm(root.body.init, root.body.cond, root.body.inc) &&
          isRegularForm(root.body.body.init, root.body.body.cond, root.body.body.inc)) {
        // Record the loop variable of the root
        // Verify that root.body.body does not include a ForStatement
        // If it doesn't then scan the RHS for a 2-dimensional
        //    array of the form ([] ([] index) _)
        // If found then perform the appropriate transformation

} } }
    else return;
} }
```

Fig. 7. Overview of LoopTransformer.

```
public int[][] matmul(int[][] m1, int[][] m2) {
  for (int i = 0; i < SIZE; ++i) {
    for (int j = 0; j < SIZE; j++) {
      for (int k = 0; k < SIZE; k++) {
        T[i][j] += m1[i][k] * m2[k][j];
      }
    }
  }
  return T;
}
```

Fig. 8. Matrix multiply method (original).

```
public int[][] matmul(int[][] m1, int[][] m2) {
  for (int i = 0; i < SIZE; ++i) {
    int tmp[] = m1[i];
    for (int j = 0; j < SIZE; j++) {
      for (int k = 0; k < SIZE; k++) {
        T[i][j] += tmp[k] * m2[k][j];
      }
    }
  }
  return T;
}
```

Fig. 9. Matrix multiply method (transformed).

Table 1. Results of OpenJIT frontend optimization (all times are seconds).

matrix size	200		600	
	before	after	before	after
OpenJIT	2.52	2.26	85.22	77.74
OpenJIT setup-time	1.09	2.68	1.09	2.67
sunwjit	2.34	2.06	80.19	73.55
sunwjit setup-time	0.49	0.49	0.49	0.49

Table 1 shows the results, before and after the transformation, and the setup time required for JIT compilation. (The overhead of for sunwjit is zero as it had been done offline.)

We see that the execution time of OpenJIT and sunwjit are within 10% of each other. This similar to SpecJVM98 where OpenJIT and sunwjit for SPARCs. So, for the purposes of this benchmark, we can regard both systems to be essentially equivalent, and thus the benefits of reflection can be judged in a straightforward way.

The setup time for OpenJIT without frontend transformation is approximately 1.09 seconds, compared to 0.49 seconds for sunwjit. This verifies our benchmarks in the previous section where the compiler bootstrap overhead was quite small. The 1.59 seconds difference between the original and transformed is the overhead of frontend execution. The overhead consists of the process described in Section 4. We believe we can improve this overhead substantially, as the frontend has not been tuned as much as the backend, especially regarding generation of numerous small objects.

Still we see that, although when the matrix size is small (200 × 200), the overhead of frontend processing with a compilet exceeds that of the speed gain, for larger problem (600 × 600) this overhead is amortized for 7% improvement. Moreover, we expect to further amortize this as the transformation is done only once, and as a result, multiple execution of the same method will not pay the overhead allowing us to essentially ignore the setup overhead for 9% gain.

We are in the process of running larger benchmarks, with more interesting compilet examples. Still, we have been able to some preliminary demonstration that run-time reflective customization of OpenJIT frontend with compilets can be beneficial for compute-intensive tasks, by achieving more gains than the overhead added to the JIT compilation process.

6   Related Work

We know of only two other related efforts paralleling our research, namely MetaXa [11] and Jalapeño [1]. Metaxa overall is a comprehensive Java reflective system, constructing a fully reflective system whereby many language features could be reified, including method invocations, variable access, and locking. MetaXa has built its own VM and a JIT compiler; as far as we have communicated with the MetaXa group, their JIT compiler is not full-fledged, and is specific to their own reflective JVM. Moreover, their JIT is not robust enough to compile itself[6].

Jalapeño [1] is a major IBM effort in implementing a self-descriptive Java system. In fact, Jalapeño is an aggressive effort in building not only the JIT compiler, but the entire JVM in Java. The fundamental difference stems from the fact that Jalapeño rests on *its own customized JVM with completely shared address space*, much the same way the C-based JIT compilers are with C-based JVMs. Thus, there is little notion of separation of the JIT compiler and the VM for achieving portability. For example, the JIT compilers in Jalapeño can access the internal objects of the JVM freely, whereas this is not possible with OpenJIT. So, although OpenJIT did not face the challenges of JVM bootstrapping, this gave rise to investigation of an effective and efficient way of interfacing with a monolithic, existing JVMs, resulting in very different technical issues as have been described in [20].

OpenJIT is architected to be a compiler framework, supporting features such as decompilation, various frontend libraries, whereas it is not with Jalapeño. No performance benchmarks have been made public for Jalapeño, whereas we present detailed studies of execution performance validating the effectiveness of reflective JITs, in particular memory profiling technique which directly exploits the 'openness' of OpenJIT.

Still, the Jalapeño work is quite impressive, as it has a sophisticated three-level compiler system, and their integrated usage is definitely worth investigating. Moreover, there is a possibility of optimizing the the application together with the runtime system in the VM. This is akin to optimization of reflective systems using the First Futamura projection in object oriented languages, as has been demonstrated by one of the author's older work in [17] and also in [18], but could produce much more practical and interesting results. Such an optimization is more difficult with OpenJIT, although some parts of JVM could be supplanted with Java equivalents, resulting in a hybrid system.

There have been a number of work in practical reflective systems that target Java, such as OpenJava [26], Javassist [7], jContractor [14] , EPP [13], Kava [30], just to name a few. Welch and Stroud present a comprehensive survey of Java reflective systems, discussing differences and tradeoffs of where in the Java's execution process reflection should occur [30].

Although a number of work in the context of open compilers have stressed the possibility of optimization using reflection such as OpenC++ [6], our work is the first to propose a system and a framework in the context of a dynamic (JIT) compiler, where run-time information could be exploited. A related work is Welsh's Jaguar system [31], where a JIT compiler is employed to optimize VIA-based communication at runtime in a parallel cluster.

From such a perspective, another related area is dynamic code generation and specialization such as [9,12,10]. Their intent is to mostly provide a form of run-time partial evaluation and code specialization based on runtime data and environment. They are typically not structured as a generalized compiler,

---

[6] In fact, we are considering collaborative porting of OpenJIT to their system.

but have specific libraries to manipulate source structure, and generate code in a "quick" fashion. In this sense they have high commonalities with the Open-JIT frontend system, sans decompilation and being able to handle generalized compilation. It is interesting to investigate whether specialization done with a full-fledged JIT compiler such as OpenJIT would be either be more or less beneficial compared to such specific systems. This not only includes execution times, but also ease of programming for customized compilation. Consel et. al. have investigated a hybrid compile-time and run-time specialization techniques with their Tempo/Harrisa system [29,22], which are source-level Java specialization system written in C; techniques in their systems could be applicable for OpenJIT with some translator to add annotation info for predicated specializations.

7   Conclusion and Future Work

We have described our research and experience of designing and implementing OpenJIT, an open-ended reflective JIT compiler framework for Java. In particular, we proposed an architecture for a reflective JIT compiler framework on a monolithic VM, and demonstrate a small example of how reflective JITs could be useful class- or application specific customization and optimization by defining a compilet which allowed us to achieve 8-9% performance gain without changing the base-level code.

Numerous future work exists for OpenJIT. We are currently redesigning the backend so that it will be substantially extensible, and better performing. We are also investigating the port of OpenJIT to other systems, including more modern VMs such as Sun's research JVM (formerly EVM). In the due process we are investigating the high-level, generic API for portable interface to VMs. The frontend requires substantial work, including speeding up its various parts as well as adding higher-level programming interfaces. Dynamic loading of not only the compilets, but also the entire OpenJIT system, is also a major goal, for live update and live customization of the OpenJIT. We are also working on several projects using OpenJIT, including a portable DSM system [25], numerical optimizer, and a memory profiler whose early prototype we employed in this work. There are numerous other projects that other people have hinted; we hope to support those projects and keep the development going for the coming years, as open-ended JIT compilers have provided us with more challenges and applications than we had initially foreseen when we started this project two years ago.

Acknowledgments. Many acknowledgments are in order, too many to name here. We especially thank Matt Welsh, who coded parts of OpenJIT during his summer job at Fujitsu. Ole Agesen for discussing various technical issues, etc.

References

1. Bowen Alpern, Dick Attanasio, Anthony Cocchi, Derek Lieber, Stephen E. Smith, Ton Ngo, and John J. Barton. Implementing Jalapeño in Java. In *Proceedings of OOPSLA'99*, 1999.

 2. Yariv Aridor, Michael Factor, and Avi Teperman. cJVM: a Single System Image of a JVM on a Cluster. In *Proceedings of ICPP'99*, September 1999.
 3. Malcolm Atkinson, Laurent Daynes, Mick Jordan, Tony Printezis, and Susan Spence. An Orthogonally Persistent Java. *ACM SIGMOD Record*, 25(4), December 1996.
 4. Bruno Blanchet. Escape Analysis for Object-Oriented Languages. Application to Java. In *Proceedings of OOPSLA'99*, pages 20–34, November 1999.
 5. Jeff Bogda and Urs Holzle. Removing Unnecessary Synchronization in Java. In *Proceedings of OOPSLA'99*, pages 35–46, November 1999.
 6. Shigeru Chiba. A Metaobject Protocol for C++. In *Proceedings of OOPSLA'95*, pages 285–299, 1995.
 7. Shigeru Chiba. Javassist — A Reflection-based Programming Wizard for Java. In *Proceedings of OOPSLA'98 Workshop on Reflective Programming in C++ and Java*, October 1998.
 8. Jong-Deok Choi, Manish Gupta, Mauricio Serrano, Vugranam C. Sreedhar, and Sam Midkiff. Escape Analysis for Java. In *Proceedings of OOPSLA'99*, pages 1–19, November 1999.
 9. Dawson R. Engler and Todd A. Proebsting. Vcode: a Retargetable, Extensible, Very Fast Dynamic Code Generation System. In *Proceedings of PLDI '96*, 1996.
10. Nobuhisa Fujinami. Automatic and Efficient Run-Time Code Generation Using Object-Oriented Languages. In *Proceedings of ISCOPE '97*, December 1997.
11. Michael Gölm. metaXa and the Future of Reflection. In *Proceedings of OOPSLA'98 Workshop on Reflective Programming in C++ and Java*, October 1998.
12. Brian Grant, Matthai Philipose, Markus Mock, Craig Chambers, and Susan J. Eggers. An Evaluation of Staged Run-time Optimization in DyC. In *Proceedings of PLDI '99*, 1999.
13. Yuuji Ichisugi and Yves Roudier. Extensible Java Preprocessor Kit and Tiny Data-Parallel Java. In *Proceedings of ISCOPE '97*, December 1997.
14. Murat Karaorman, Urs Holzle, and John Bruno. jContractor: A Reflective Java Library to Support Design by Contract. In *Proceedings of Reflection'99*, pages 175–196, July 1999.
15. Gregor Kiczales, John Lamping, Anurag Mendhekar, Chris Maeda, Cristina Videira Lopes, Jean-Marc Loingtier, and John Irwin. Aspect-Oriented Programming. In *Proceedings of ECOOP'97*, pages 220–242, 1997.
16. Fuyuhiko Maruyama, Hirotaka Ogawa, and Satoshi Matsuoka. An Effective Decompilation Algorithm for Java Bytecodes. *IPSJ Journal PRO (written in Japanese)*, 1999.
17. Hidehiko Masuhara, Satoshi Matsuoka, Keinichi Asai, and Akinori Yonezawa. Compiling Away the Meta-Level in Object-Oriented Concurrent Reflective Languages Using Partial Evaluation. In *Proceedings of OOPSLA'95*, pages 57–64, October 1995.
18. Hidehiko Masuhara and Akinori Yonezawa. Design and Partial Evaluation of Meta-objects for a Concurrent Reflective Language. In *Proceedings of ECOOP'98*, pages 418–439, July 1998.
19. Satoshi Matsuoka, Hirotaka Ogawa, Kouya Shimura, Yasunori Kimura, and Koichiro Hotta. OpenJIT — A Reflective Java JIT Compiler. In *Proceedings of OOPSLA'98 Workshop on Reflective Programming in C++ and Java*, October 1998.
20. Hirotaka Ogawa, Kouya Shimura, Satoshi Matsuoka, Fuyuhiko Maruyama, Yukihiko Sohda, and Yasunori Kimura. OpenJIT: An Open-Ended, Reflective JIT Compiler Framework for Java. In *Proceedings of ECOOP'2000*, June 2000.

21. Ole Agesen. Design and Implementation of Pep, a Java Just-In-Time Translator. *Theory and Practice of Object Systems*, 3(2):127–155, 1997.
22. Ulrik Pagh Schultz, Julia L. Lawall, Charles Consel, and Gilles Muller. Towards Automatic Specialization of Java Programs. In *Proceedings of ECOOP'99*, June 1999.
23. Kouya   Shimura.   OpenJIT   Backend   Compiler. http://www.openjit.org/docs/backend-compiler/openjit-shimura-doc-1.pdf, June 1998.
24. Kouya Shimura and Yasunori Kimura. Experimental Development of Java JIT Compiler. In *IPSJ SIG Notes 96-ARC-120*, pages 37–42, 1996.
25. Yukihiko Sohda, Hirotaka Ogawa, and Satoshi Matsuoka. OMPC++ — A Portable High-Performance Implementation of DSM using OpenC++ Reflection. In *Proceedings of Reflection'99*, pages 215–234, July 1999.
26. Michiaki Tatsubori and Shigeru Chiba. Programming Support of Design Patterns with Compile-time Reflection. In *Proceedings of OOPSLA'98 Workshop on Reflective Programming in C++ and Java*, October 1998.
27. Todd A. Proebsting and Scott A. Watterson. Krakatoa: Decompilation in Java. In *Proceedings of COOTS'97*, June 1997.
28. Stanford University. SUIF Homepage. http://www-suif.stanford.edu/.
29. Eugen-Nicolae Volanschi, Charles Consel, and Crispin Cowan. Declarative Specialization of Object-Oriented Programs. In *Proceedings of OOPSLA'97*, pages 286–300, October 1997.
30. Ian Welch and Robert J. Stroud. From Dalang to Kava - the Evolution of a Reflective Java Extention. In *Proceedings of Reflection'99*, pages 2–21, July 1999.
31. Matt Welsh and David E. Culler. Jaguar: Enabling Efficient Communication and I/O from Java. *Concurrency: Practice and Experience*, December 1999. Special Issue on Java for High-Performance Applications.
32. John Whaley and Martin Rinard. Compositional Pointer and Escape Analysis for Java Programs. In *Proceedings of OOPSLA'99*, pages 187–206, November 1999.

Kava - A Reflective Java Based on Bytecode Rewriting

Ian Welch and Robert J. Stroud

University of Newcastle-upon-Tyne, United Kingdom NE1 7RU
{I.S.Welch, R.J.Stroud}@ncl.ac.uk,
{I.S.Welch,R.J.Stroud} http://www.cs.ncl.ac.uk/people/

Abstract Current implementations of reflective Java typically either require access to source code, or require a modified Java platform. This makes them unsuitable for applying reflection to Commercial-off-the-Shelf (COTS) systems. The high level nature of Java bytecode makes on-the-fly rewritings of class files feasible and this has been exploited by a number of authors. However, in practice working at bytecode level is error prone and leads to fragile code. We propose using metaobject protocols in order to specify behavioural changes and use standard bytecode rewritings to implement the changes. We have developed a reflective Java called *Kava* that provides behavioural runtime reflection through the use of bytecode rewriting of Java classes. In this paper we discuss the binary rewriting approach, provide an overview of the *Kava* system and provide an example of an application of *Kava*.

1 Introduction

We are interested in the problems of applying non-functional requirements to Commercial Off-the-Shelf (COTS) software components. In an environment such as Java, components are usually supplied in a compiled form without source code, and can be integrated into a system at runtime.

Metaobject protocols [12] offer a principled way of extending the behaviour of these components. Metaobjects can encapsulate the behavioural adaptations necessary to satisfy desirable non-functional requirements (NFRs) such as fault tolerance or application level security [1,2,18,19] transparently at the metalevel. Ideally we want to apply these metaobjects to compiled code that executes on a standard Java platform.

The Java 2 Reflection package `java.lang.reflect` provides introspection, dynamic dispatch and the ability to generate proxies for classes on-the-fly. However, this is not sufficient to build a rich metaobject protocol that can be applied transparently. There are a number of alternative extensions for Java that provide more powerful and more transparent reflection. However, they all have flaws that do not make them applicable to the problem of adapting components. These flaws include the requirement for customised Java Virtual Machines (JVMs), limited reflective capabilities, or weak non-bypassability. The term non-bypassability refers to the binding between the base level and the meta level. For a number of

W. Cazzola et al. (Eds.): Reflection and Software Engineering, LNCS 1826, pp. 155–167, 2000.
© Springer-Verlag Berlin Heidelberg 2000

NFRs such as security the meta level should never be able to be bypassed. This is what we term strong non-bypassability. However, in a number of implementations the techniques used to implement the bindings are easily bypassed. We refer to this as weak non-bypassability.

We have produced our own implementation of a reflective extension for Java called *Kava* that provides a rich metaobject protocol, requires only a standard JVM and provides strong non-bypassability. *Kava* implements a runtime behavioural metaobject protocol through the application of standard byte code rewritings, and behavioural adaptation is implemented using Java metaobject classes. This is to be distinguished from structural reflection where a metaobject protocol provides an interface for a programmer who wants to change the actual structure of an object.

The rest of the paper is organized as follows. In section two we provide a review of different approaches to implementing reflection in Java. Section three introduces the *Kava* metaobject protocol. Section four explains the byte code rewriting approach. Section five gives an example of an application of *Kava*. Finally section six provides some conclusions about the general approach.

A prototype implementation of *Kava* has been completed and is available from http://www.cs.ncl.ac.uk/people/i.s.welch/kava.

2   Review of Reflective Java Implementations

In this section we briefly review a number of reflective Java implementations and attempt to categorize them according to the point in the Java class lifecycle that reflection is implemented.

The Java class lifecycle is as follows. A Java class starts as source code that is compiled into byte code, it is then loaded by a class loader into the JVM for execution, where the byte code is further compiled by a Just-In-Time compiler into platform specific machine code for efficient execution.

Different reflective Java implementations introduce reflection at different points in the lifecycle. The point at which they introduce reflection characterizes the scope of their capabilities. In order to realise reflective control by a metalevel the baselevel system is modified through the addition of traps on operations. These traps are known as metalevel interceptions [26]. For example, in *Reflective Java* method calls sent to the base object are brought under control of an associated meta object by trapping each method call to the base object. These traps are added at the source code stage of the lifecycle making it necessary to have access to the source code. In contrast *MetaXa* adds the traps into the JVM, here the implementation of the dispatch mechanism of the JVM is changed in order to take control over method calls. As the traps are added to the runtime system source code is no longer required. The drawback of this approach is that unlike *Reflective Java* a specialized JVM must be used.

Table 1 summarizes the features of the different reflective Java implementations.

Table 1. Comparison of reflective Java implementations.

Point in Lifecycle	Reflective Java	Description	Capabilities	Restrictions
Source Code	Reflective Java [25]	Preprocessor.	Dynamic switching of metaobjects. Intercept method invocations.	Can't make a compiled class reflective, requires access to source code.
Compile Time	OpenJava [21]	Compile-time metaobject protocol.	Can intercept wide range of operations, and extends language syntax.	Requires access to source code.
Byte Code	Bean Extender [9]	Byte code preprocessor.	No need to have access to source code.	Restricted to Java Beans, requires offline preprocessing.
	Dalang [22][23]	Byte code rewriting as late. as loadtime	No need to have access to source code.	Suffers from known problems with class wrapper approach - delegation, identity, weak encapsulation etc.
	Javassist [4]	Byte code rewriting as late. as loadtime.	No need to have access to source code.	Focus on metaobject protocol for structural adaptation. Weak encapsulation.
Runtime	MetaXa [7]	Reflective JVM.	Can intercept wide range of operations, Can be dynamically applied.	Custom JVM.
	Rjava [8]	Wrapper based reflection allowing dynamic binding.	Intercepts method invocations, and allows dynamic extension of classes.	Custom JVM - addition of new byte code.
	Guarana [15]	Reflective kernel supported by modified JVM.	Interception of message sends, state access and supports metaobject composition.	Custom JVM.
	java.lang.reflect [20]	Reflective capabilities part of the standard Java development kit.	Runtime introspection, dynamic dispatch, and on-the-fly generation of proxies.	Overall introspection rather than behavioural or structural reflection.
Just-in-time Compilation	OpenJIT [14]	Compile-time metaobject protocol for compilation to machine language.	Can take advantage of facilities present in the native platform. No need for access to source code.	No behavioural metaobject protocol.

All these implementations have drawbacks that make them unsuitable for use with compiled components or in a standard Java environment where the purpose is to add security. Some require access to source code, others are non-standard because they make use of a modified Java platform, and none of the portable approaches support strong non-bypassability.

In contrast, *Kava* does not require access to source code because it is based on bytecode rewriting, doesn't require a non standard Java environment and provides a rich set of capabilities. It also provides strong non-bypassability. Most implementations add traps through renaming of classes, or of methods which means that it may be possible to call the original methods and therefore bypass the meta layer. However, *Kava* actually adds the traps directly into the method bodies avoiding this problem.

Recently a new reflective Java called *Javassist* has been developed that provides a metaobject protocol for structural modification of Java classes and supports a simple metaobject protocol for behavioural reflection. It is the most similar in character to *Kava* of all the reflective Java implementations. However, it uses method renaming to implement the trapping of method calls and therefore doesn't support strong non-bypassability. It also currently doesn't support the same range of reflective capabilities of *Kava*.

3   Kava Metaobject Protocol

The *Kava* metaobject protocol provides an interface to the Java runtime object model that gives programmers the ability to modify a Java application's behaviour safely and incrementally. Each object is causally connected with a unique metaobject. The metaobject provides a representation of the structure of the object, and of the behaviour of the object. Metaobjects are implemented in the Java language in the same way that objects are implemented. However, bytecode rewriting techniques are used to create the causal connection between the meta and base levels. This approach allows *Kava* is be used in a standard Java environment, means that it can be applied to compiled Java classes and allows for a rich metaobject protocol. The idea of bytecode rewriting is not new but using it to implement behavioural reflection is a new idea.

When *Kava* creates a reflective Java class then a binding is created between the class and a metaobject class (or metaclass). In *Kava* a metaobject class is a Java class that implements the interface `Metaobject`. Whenever an instance of the class is created then a unique instance of the metaobject implementation is also created. By creating different metaobject implementations the programmer can create standard redefinitions of the Java runtime object model. These different implementations are bound to base level objects in order to customize the behaviour of the base level objects.

In the following sections we first look at the aspects of base level behaviour under the control of the metaobject protocol, and then at how the binding between objects and metaobjects is specified.

3.1   Scope of Metaobject Protocol

The aspects of base level behaviour that can be redefined in *Kava* are:

- Method calls to base objects.
- Method calls from base objects.
- State access by base objects.

- Creation of new instances by base objects.
- Initialisation of base objects.
- Finalization of base objects.

The metaobject associated with the base object traps the base level behaviours and specifies what will happen before the behaviour and what will happen after the behaviour. For example, when a base object makes a call to method then the method beforeSendMethod is invoked. By redefining before-SendMethod behaviour to take place before the call is dispatched can be defined. An example is shown below. In this example the target of the call, the method itself and the arguments on the call stack are reified respectively as a Reference, Method and array of Value.

```
import kava.*;
public boolean beforeSendMethod(
   Reference target, Method method, Value[] arguments)
{
  System.out.println("invoking " + method.getName());
  return Constants.INVOKE_BASELEVEL;
}
```

Here a tracing message is displayed - the name of the method being invoked. The metalevel then allows the base level behaviour to take place. This is indicated by returning Constants.INVOKE_BASELEVEL from the method.

Kava also supports extended introspection on the structure of the object. The following aspects of the structure can be determined and manipulated using Kava :

- Binding between Metaobject and Object.
- State of the Object.

The implementor of the metaobject can choose to make the metalevel visible to the baselevel by implementing the getMeta method and returning a pointer to the metaobject. The default implementation should be to raise a runtime exception if the base level attempts to access the metalevel directly. In the case of implementing security using metaobject protocols we would not want the metalevel to be visible. However, if we were implementing distribution then we may want to access the metalevel in order to adjust parameters such as timeout.

The implementor may also choose to allow the binding between the metaobject and object to be changed. Again the default implementation should be to raise a runtime exception. However, the implementor can define the method setMeta to allow the binding to be changed from one metaobject to another metaobject.

The Kava metaobject protocol also supports extended introspection. It allows access to and adjustment of base level state. This is under the control of the Java 2 security model so a security administrator can allow or prevent reflective access to state.

3.2 Binding Specification

Kava uses a simple binding language to specify which metaobjects are bound
to which base level objects or classes. This allows binding information to be
removed from the metaobject implementation and reasoned about separately.
This adds to the separation of concerns and promotes reuse. It is also more
appropriate for situations where source code may not be available, for example
with COTS components.

A metaclass definition defines what aspects of the Java object model a metaclass redefines. Only those aspects redefined in the binding specification will be
redefined at the metalevel irrespective of whether the metaclass implementation
has defined methods for handling other aspects of the base level. This allows a
fine granularity for the late binding between the meta and base level. For example, a tracing metaobject may be interested in all method invocations made by
an object or only specific method invocations. The binding specification allows
the method to be specified by name, or a wildcard to be used (any-method for
any method, any-class for any class and any-desc for any parameter list) to
indicate that all methods are of interest. An example of a binding between the
MetaTrace class and the methods notify and setObserver of the class Test
is given below. This means that each instance of Trace will be bound to an
instance of MetaTrace.

```
metaclass kava.MetaTrace {
  INTERCEPT SEND_METHOD( any-class, "notify" , any-desc );
  INTERCEPT SEND_METHOD( any-class, "setObserver" , any-desc );
}
class Test metaclass-is kava.MetaTrace;
```

4 Bytecode Rewriting

The *Kava* metaobject protocol is implemented using the technique of byte code
rewriting. Byte code rewriting has become an established technique for extending Java both syntactically and behaviourally. For example it has been used to
support parametric types [3] and add resource consumption controls to classes
[6]. Generic frameworks for transforming byte code such as *JOIE* [5] and *Binary Component Adaptation* [10] have been developed to make coding byte code
rewriting easier. However, as pointed out by the authors of *JOIE*, most of these
frameworks lack a high-level abstraction for describing the behavioural adaptations. This makes coding adaptations difficult as it requires a detailed knowledge
of byte code instructions and of the structure of class files. Binary Component
Adaptation does support a form of a higher-level abstraction in that it has the
concept of *deltaClasses* that describe structural changes to a class file in terms of
methods for renaming methods, mixin type methods, etc. However, the purpose
of the framework is to support software evolution rather than behavioural adaptation. This means that the focus is on adding, renaming or removing methods
and manipulating the type hierarchy in order to adapt ill-fitting components to
work together rather than describing behavioural adaptation.

The *Kava* metaobject protocol provides a high-level abstraction for adaptation of component behaviour that specifies the change to behaviour in terms of the Java object model and is implemented using byte code rewriting. We exploit the *JOIE* framework to simplify the implementation of this metaobject protocol. The framework frees us from dealing with technical details such as maintaining relative addressing when new byte codes are inserted into a method, or determining the number of arguments a method supports before it has been instantiated as part of a class.

As byte code instructions and the structure of the class file preserve most of the semantics of the source code we can use byte code rewriting to implement metalevel interceptions for a wide range of aspects of the Java Object model such as caller and receiver method invocation, state access, object formalization, object initialisation and some aspects of exception handling. Like compile-time reflection we reflect upon the structure of the code in order to implement reflection. However, we work at a level much closer to the Java machine than most compile-time approaches that deal with the higher-level language. Although this means we cannot extend the syntax of the higher-level language it does mean that we can implement some kinds of reflection more easily than in a traditional compile-time MOP. For example, in the application of *OpenC++ version 2* to adding fault tolerance in the form of checkpointing *CORBA* applications [11] data flow analysis is performed on the source code to determine when the state of the object is updated. With *Kava* no such analysis would be necessary; all that would be required is to intercept the update of state of an object by changing the behaviour of the update field operation in the Java runtime object model. When an update was done a flag could be set indicating that the current state should be checkpointed.

Also since we are often dealing with compiled classes we do not have access to the source code in order to annotate it. There is also an argument that source code annotations are not necessarily a good idea especially when different annotation schemes are used together.

By transforming the class itself we address the problems introduced by the separation of base class and class wrapper (see earlier paper). Instead, standard byte code rewritings are used to wrap individual methods and even bytecode instructions. These micro-wrappers will switch control from the baselevel to metalevel when the methods or byte code instructions are executed at runtime. The metalevel is programmed using standard Java classes. The metalevel allows the customisation of the Java object model at runtime. The scope of the customisation is be determined by which methods and byte code instructions are wrapped at load time, but the exact nature of the customisation is adjustable at runtime.

Byte code rewriting can either be applied at loadtime through the use of an application level classloader [13] or prior to loadtime by directly rewriting class files.

To provide a flavour of this approach we provide an example of the wrapping of access to a field of a base level class. Due to space constraints we present this at a high level using source code instead of byte code. Consider the following field access:

```
myGreeting = "Hello " + name;
```

At the byte code level this is rewritten to:

```
import kava.*;

Reference target = new Reference(this);
Field field = newField("myGreeting");
Value fieldValue = Value.newValue("Hello " + name);

if (meta.beforePutField(target, field, fieldValue)
      == Constants.INVOKE_BASELEVEL)
{
   helloWorld = (String)fieldValue.getObject();
}
meta.afterPutField(target, field, fieldValue);
```

In this example the first line of code specifies that the field belongs to this instance of the base class, the second line specifies the field being updated, and the third line specifies the value the field is being updated with. Then beforePutField method of the associated metaobject is invoked with parameters representing the field ("helloWorld"), and the marshalled value. At the metalevel the value may be modified in order to adjust the final value that is stored in the field. Alternatively the update of field could be suppressed by returning a Constants.SUPPRESS_BASE in which case the base level action does not take place. The last line calls the afterPutField method of the associated metaobject with the same parameters as the initial call to the metalevel.

5   Application of Kava

Kava has wide application potential and should prove well suited to the customising the behaviour of COTS applications that are built from dynamically loaded components. It provides a high-level abstraction for implementing behavioural adaptations that are expressed as bytecode rewritings. This means that it can be used to reimplement in a principled way behavioural adaptations that have already been implemented through byte code rewriting e.g. enforcing resource controls on applications, instrumentation of applications, visualization support etc. The advantage of using *Kava* would be that these adaptations could be combined as required since they have been built using a common abstraction.

In this section we provide an example application of *Kava* : to prevent downloaded applets from mounting a particular class of denial-of-service attack.

In [16] examples of using bytecode rewriting techniques for protecting against malicious attacks are discussed. In particular the authors provide an example of how bytecode rewriting can be used to protect against denial-of-service caused by a window consuming attack.

The basic idea is that an applet can crash the host system by creating more windows than the windowing system can handle. In order to protect against this attack the system should track the number of windows created and either block or throw an exception when a predetermined limit is exceeded. The class used to generate the top-level windows is the Java library class **Frame**.

The solution provided in [16] is to prevent an applet from invoking the constructor methods of the **Frame** class more than a predefined number of times. They achieve this by subclassing **Frame** to create **Safe$Frame**. **Safe$Frame** is implemented in such a way that it counts the number of top-level windows created and blocks further creation of windows if the predefined limit is exceeded. Then every application class downloaded with the applet is checked for references to **Frame**. When a reference is found then it is replaced by a reference to **Safe$Frame**. The bytecode rewriting is done within a proxy server that intercepts requests for applets.

This approach has the advantage that it is transparent and can work with COTS browsers. The main drawback to the technique that it is difficult to generalize to other classes. For example, another denial-of-service attack might rely upon the applet creating more threads than the system can handle. This would require the creation by hand of a **Safe$Thread** class that monitored and controlled the creation of **Thread** instances.

Kava provides a higher level approach to applying such safety mechanisms. The high level approach is to describe a mechanism for limiting the creation of new instances of monitored classes such as **Frame** or **Thread**. Using *Kava* this is done by creating an implementation of a **Metaobject** that performs the resource monitoring. A simplified implementation is shown below:

```
import kava.*;

public class ResourceMonitor implements Metaobject {
  public void beforeCreation(Reference target, Value[] arguments) {
    incrementUsage(target);
    if (exceededMaximum(target) {
      throw new RuntimeException("resource count exceeded by " +
                                 target.getClass());
    }
  }
  ...
}
```

The method **beforeCreation** redefines how new instances are created. First, it calls a method **incrementUsage** that increments a global count of the number of instances of the that class and its superclasses. We count superclasses as an instance of a subclass of a monitored class might be created. Then it calls a method **exceededMaximum** that checks if the maximum limit for the number of instances of any monitored class has been exceeded. If the limit has been exceeded then a runtime exception is thrown and the execution of the applet halts.

The advantage of this approach over the original approach is more general and doesn't require manual generation of new classes if a new class is to be monitored. In [24] we propose a even more general reflective security model for resource consumption control.

6 Conclusions

Ideally, a reflective extension for Java that is intended to be used to adapt the runtime behaviour of COTS components should not require access to source code, or modifications to the Java platform, and should provide strong non-bypassability. Unfortunately, existing reflective extensions that we have reviewed do not meet these requirements and provide the scope of control required.

We have implemented a system called *Kava* that overcomes these problems by using bytecode rewriting in order to establish a causal connection between metaobjects and objects. It provides a higher level abstraction for specifying changes to the behaviour of objects than is provided by currently available byte-code rewriting toolkits. It addresses some reflective capabilities not handled by some extensions such as the ability to redefine how base level objects call other base level objects, and offers strong non-bypassability.

To the best of our knowledge *Kava* was the first reflective Java extension to make use of bytecode rewriting in order to implement behavioural reflection. Subsequently there have been similar developments such as *Javassist* although these lack some of the capabilities of *Kava* and do not support strong non-bypassability.

We are currently using the *Kava* prototype to implement a reflective security metalevel for Java applications. Current versions of *Kava* are available from `http://www.cs.ncl.ac.uk/people/i.s.welch/kava`.

Acknowledgements. This work has been supported by the UK Defence Evaluation Research Agency, grant number CSM/547/UA.

References

1. Massimo Ancona, Walter Cazzola, and Eduardo B. Fernandez. Reflective Authorization Systems: Possibilities, Benefits and Drawbacks. In Jan Vitek and Christian Jensen, editors, *Secure Internet Programming: Security Issues for Mobile and Distributed Objects*, Lecture Notes in Computer Science 1603, pages 35–51. Springer-Verlag, July 1999.
2. Messaoud Benantar, Bob Blakley and Anthony J. Nadalin. Approach to Object Security in Distributed SOM. *IBM Systems Journal*, 35(2):204-226, 1996.
3. Ole Agesen, Stephen N. Freund and John C. Mitchell. Adding Type Parameterization. In *Proceedings of OOPSLA'97*. Atlanta, Georgia. 1997.
4. Shigeru Chiba. Load-time Structural Reflection in Java. In *Proceedings of ECOOP'2000*. June 2000.
5. Geoff A. Cohen and Jeff Chase. Automatic Program Transformation with JOIE. In *Proceedings of USENIX Annual Technical Symposium*. 1998.

6. Grzegorz Czaijkowski and Thorsten von Eicken. JRes: A Resource Accounting Interface for Java. In *Proceedings of OOPSLA'98*. 1998.
7. Michael Gölm. Design and Implementation of a Meta Architecture for Java. Master's thesis, University of Erlangen-Nurnberg, Germany, January 1997.
8. Joao Guimarães. Reflection for Statically Typed Languages. In *Proceedings of ECOOP'98*. July 1998.
9. IBM. Bean Extender Documentation, version 2.0. 1997.
10. Ralph Keller and Urs Holzle. Binary Component Adaptation. In *Proceedings of ECOOP'98*. July 1998.
11. Ruiz-Garcia Marc-Olivier Killijian, Jean-Charles Fabre and Shigeru Chiba. A Metaobject Protocol for Fault-Tolerant CORBA Applications. In *Proceedings of the 17th Symposium on Reliable Distributed Systems (SRDS'98)*, pages 127–134, 1998.
12. Gregor Kickzales, Jim des Rivières, and Daniel G. Bobrow. *The Art of the Metaobject Protocol*. MIT Press, Cambridge, Massachusetts, 1991.
13. Sheng Liang and Gilad Bracha. Dynamic Class Loading in the Java™ Virtual Machine. In *Proceedings of OOPSLA'98*, Vancouver, Canada, October 1998.
14. Satoshi Matsuoka, Hirotaka Ogawa, Kouya Shimura, Yasunori Kimura, Koichiro Hotta, and Hiromitsu Takagi. OpenJIT A Reflective Java JIT Compiler. In *Proceedings of OOPSLA'98 Workshop on Reflective Programming in C++ and Java*, November 1998.
15. Alexandre Olivia, Luis Eduardo Buzato, and Calciolari Islene. The Reflective Architecture of Guaraná. http://www.dcc.unicamp.br/ oliva.
16. Insik Shin and John C. Mitchell. Java Bytecode Modification and Applet Security. Stanford CS Tech Report. 1998.
17. Robert J. Stroud. Transparency and Reflection in Distributed Systems. *ACM Operating System Review*, 22:99–103, April 1992.
18. Robert J. Stroud and Zhixue Wu. Using Metaobject Protocols to Satisfy Non-Functional Requirements. In Chris Zimmerman, editor, *Advances in Object-Oriented Metalevel Architectures and Reflection*, chapter 3, pages 31–52. CRC Press, Inc., 2000 Corporate Blvd.,N.W., Boca Raton, Florida 33431, 1996.
19. Robert J. Stroud and Zhixue Wu. Using Meta-Object Protocol to Implement Atomic Data Types. In Walter Olthoff, editor, *Proceedings of the 9th Conference on Object-Oriented Programming (ECOOP'95)*, LNCS 952, pages 168–189, Aarhus, Denmark, August 1995. Springer-Verlag.
20. Sun Microsystems, Inc. Java Development Kit version 1.3.0 Documentation. 2000.
21. Michiaki Tatsubori and Shigeru Chiba. Support of Design Patterns with Compile-time Reflection. In Shigeru Chiba and Jean-Charles Fabre, editors, *Proceedings of OOPSLA Workshop on Reflective Programming in C++ and Java*, Vancouver, Canada, November 1998.
22. Ian Welch and Robert J. Stroud. Dalang - A Reflective Extension for Java. Computing Science Technical Report CS-TR-672, University of Newcastle upon Tyne. 1999.
23. Ian Welch and Robert J. Stroud. From Dalang to Kava - The Evolution of a Reflective Java Extension. In *Proceedings of Meta-Level Architectures and Reflection, Second International Conference, Reflection 1999*, page 19-21. Saint-Malo, France. LNCS 1616, Springer. July 1999.
24. Ian Welch and Robert J. Stroud. Supporting Real World Security Models in Java. In *Proceedings of 7th IEEE International Workshop on Future Treads of Distributed Computing Systems*, pages 20-22. Cape Town, South Africa. IEEE Computer Society. December 1999.

25. Zhixue Wu and Scarlet Schwiderski. Reflective Java - Making Java Even More Flexible. FTP: Architecture Projects Management Limited (apm@ansa.co.uk), Cambridge, UK. 1997.
26. Chris Zimmerman. Metalevels, MOPs and What all the Fuzz is All about. In Chris Zimmerman, editor, *Advances in Object-Oriented Metalevel Architectures and Reflection*, chapter 1, pages 3–24. CRC Press, Inc., 2000 Corporate Blvd.,N.W., Boca Raton, Florida 33431, 1996.

Appendix A - Full Metaobject Protocol

```
public interface MetaObject {

// behavioural - can override base action
 public boolean beforeGetField(Reference target, Field field);
 public void afterGetField(Reference target, Field field,
                           Value value);
 public boolean beforePutField(Reference target, Field field,
                           Value value);
 public void afterPutField(Reference target, Field field,
                           Value value);
 public boolean beforeReceiveMethod(Method method, Value[] arguments);
 public void afterReceiveMethod(Method method, Value[] arguments,
                           Value result);
 public boolean beforeSendMethod(Reference target, Method method,
                           Value[] arguments);
 public void afterSendMethod(Reference target, Method method,
                           Value[] arguments, Value result);

// behavioural - can only modify arguments of base action
//               or throw a runtime exception
 public void beforeInitialisation(Reference target, Value[] arguments);
 public void afterInitialisation(Reference target, Value[] arguments);
 public void beforeFinalization(Reference target);
 public void afterFinalization(Reference target);
 public void beforeCreation(Reference target, Value[] arguments);
 public void afterCreation(Reference target, Value[] arguments);

 // introspection
 public Object getMeta();
 public Value getFieldValue(Field field);
 public void setFieldValue(Field field, Value value);
 }
```

Appendix B - Grammar for Binding Language

```
configuration ::= metaclass_defn class_binding_list ;
class_binding_list ::= class_binding_list class_binding_part
 | class_binding_part ;
```

```
class_binding_part ::= CLASS class_name METACLASS_IS
 metaclass_name [RECURSIVE] EOS;
metaclass_defn ::= METACLASS metaclass_name (meta_expr_list);
meta_expr_list ::= meta_expr_list meta_expr_part
 | meta_expr_part;
meta_expr_part ::=
 INTERCEPT RECEIVE_METHOD (class, method , params) EOS |
 INTERCEPT SEND_METHOD (class, method , params) EOS |
 INTERCEPT GET_FIELD (class, field_name, method, params) EOS |
 INTERCEPT PUT_FIELD (class, field_name, method, params) EOS |
 INTERCEPT INITIALISE_INSTANCE (class) EOS |
 INTERCEPT INITIALISE_CLASS (class) EOS |
 INTERCEPT FINALIZE_INSTANCE (class) EOS |
 INTERCEPT FINALIZE_CLASS (class) EOS |
 INTERCEPT CREATION (class, method, params} EOS
}
```

Using Reflection to Support Dynamic Adaptation of System Software: A Case Study Driven Evaluation

Jim Dowling, Tilman Schäfer, Vinny Cahill, Peter Haraszti, and
Barry Redmond

Distributed Systems Group,
Department of Computer Science,
Trinity College Dublin
{jpdowlin, schaefet, vinny.cahill, harasztp, redmondb}@cs.tcd.ie

Abstract A number of researchers have recently suggested the use of reflection as a means of supporting dynamic adaptation of object-oriented software especially systems software including both middleware and operating systems. In order to evaluate the use of reflection in this context we have implemented a resource manager that can be adapted to use different resource management strategies on behalf of its clients using three distinct technologies: design patterns, dynamic link libraries, and reflection. In this paper we report on this experiment and compare the three approaches under performance, ability to separate functional code from code concerned with adaptation, and programming effort. We conclude that although the overhead of using reflection may be high, reflection offers significant advantages in terms of the ability to separate functional and adaptation code.

1 Introduction

The ability to design software that can be tailored, whether statically or dynamically, to the requirements of specific users presents an opportunity to optimise the performance of the software based on application-specific knowledge. This is particularly important in the context of systems software such as middleware and operating systems that are characterised by the need to support a wide range of applications, each with different requirements, simultaneously and on behalf of different users. In [4], Draves identified a number of problems that can be addressed by making operating systems adaptable and similar problems arise in the context of other forms of system software:

- feature deficiency: the operating system does not provide some feature required by the application;
- performance: (some) operating system services do not provide performance that is acceptable to the application;
- version skew: the application is dependent on a different version of the operating system for its correct operation.

W. Cazzola et al. (Eds.): Reflection and Software Engineering, LNCS 1826, pp. 169–188, 2000.
© Springer-Verlag Berlin Heidelberg 2000

Clearly, adaptability should allow operating systems to be more easily tailored to provide (only) the features required by the currently executing applications. It is perhaps not so obvious how adaptability might improve performance. The essential observation is that every software system embodies particular trade-offs concerning the way in which the services that it provides are implemented. Typically, in general-purpose operating systems, these trade-offs are made to suit the requirements of what are perceived to be typical applications. The resulting trade-offs will certainly not be the right ones for every application resulting in sub-optimal performance for some. There is a substantial body of evidence showing that, for some applications at least, exploiting knowledge of the application in making these trade-offs can substantially improve performance. Kiczales et al. [10] use the term mapping dilemma to refer to these trade-offs and characterise a mapping dilemma as a "crucial strategy issue whose resolution will invariably bias the performance of the resulting implementation". Decisions as to how to resolve mapping dilemmas are called mapping decisions and a mapping conflict occurs when the application performs poorly as a result of an inappropriate mapping decision. Increased adaptability is intended to allow mapping decisions to be more easily made on an application-specific basis.

Following this rationale, a number of designers of operating systems and middleware have proposed architectures for supporting dynamic adaptation in their systems [1,9]. For the most part these systems have been implemented from scratch in an ad hoc manner with little or no specific language support for dynamic adaptation. A number of other researchers have suggested using reflection as a "principled" [2] approach to supporting dynamic adaptation particularly in the context of middleware [2,12,13]. However, little practical experience exists on the relative merits and demerit of using reflection versus more traditional and ad hoc methods of supporting dynamic adaptation of system software. With this in mind, this paper reports on a case study driven evaluation of the use of reflection to support dynamic adaptation versus the use of design patterns and the more or less ad hoc use of dynamic link libraries (DLLs). While design patterns represent a best-practice approach to the structuring of an object-oriented system that is intended to be adaptable, DLLs represent a more traditional approach that is not specific to the use of object-orientation. Doubtless other approaches are possible. However, our intent was solely to get some real experience with the likely tradeoffs involved in choosing between different approaches. We choose three of many possible evaluation criteria. Firstly, we looked at the effect of the chosen approach on system performance as well as the cost of dynamic adaptation. We expected that supporting dynamic adaptation would imply some overhead that would hopefully be compensated for by the ability to choose more appropriate algorithms for a particular client or mix of clients. Our study only assesses the relative overhead due to the different approaches and not the benefits of supporting dynamic adaptation per se.

In the long term, we are particularly interested in being able to retrofit support for dynamic adaptation to existing or legacy software as well as in what sort of language support for dynamic adaptation might be useful. To this end we were interested in the degree to which we could separate functional code from code concerned with dynamic adaptation as well as in what effort is need to add support for dynamic adaptation to a system.

2   Dimensions of Dynamic Adaptation

In considering the inclusion of support for dynamic adaptation in a software system a wide variety of issues need to be addressed. These range from how adaptation is to be triggered, through how system consistency is maintained in the face of adaptation, through issues of authorisation and protection. We categorise these issues under eight dimensions:

1. The interface dimension

A key question concerns the design of the interface via which adaptation is triggered since this largely determines the kind of adaptations that can be supported. A typical system may provide an interface towards its clients allowing them to trigger adaptation either declaratively (e.g., based on the specification of Quality of Service parameter) or procedurally (e.g., by providing hooks to which client code can be bound). A system may also provide an interface towards its environment, allowing environmental changes to trigger adaptations (e.g., a change in network connectivity or bandwidth). Other issues related to the interface dimension include determining the scope [10] of requested adaptations.

2. The authorisation dimension

A separate issue is the question of who is authorised to trigger an adaptation and when, along with the means for making this determination.

3. The admission dimension

Even if a requested adaptation is authorised, there remains the question of whether the adaptation is possible under the current system load taking into account the presence of concurrent applications and the availability of required resources.

4. The extension dimension

Given that an adaptation is to take place, another question is where does the required code come from? Typically, it will loaded from disk or over the network or may be provided directly as part of a client application.

5. The safety dimension

A related question concerns how system security is ensured in the face of loaded code. This is in part determined by the nature of the adaptation interface exposed by the system and may involve the use of mechanisms such as software sandboxing or hardware isolation of untrusted code that is provided by an application. It also addresses questions such as what execution rights this code may have.

6. *The binding model*

When a new component is loaded into a running system, there needs to be a mechanism to allow that code to be activated in response to client request. This may involve the use of a name or trading service or other discovery mechanism, or where a higher degree of transparency is required some redirection mechanism or the use of an anonymous (perhaps event-based) communication mechanism [1].

7. *State transfer dimension*

Where an existing component is being replaced with a new or upgraded implementation, it will often be necessary to transfer state between the old and new components for which a standardised state transfer mechanism must be defined.

8. *Dependency management model*

The software components comprising a software system often have complex interdependencies. Adapting a single component may have implications for other components that need to be explicitly considered in performing adaptation [17].

In our on-going work we are addressing each of these dimensions. We are particularly interested in the degree to which these issues can be tackled independently of the system to be adapted, the degree to which adaptation can be transparent to client applications (where appropriate) and the level of language support that might be useful in supporting dynamic adaptation.

In this experiment we consider the impact of using design patterns, DLLs, and reflection in addressing the extension, binding and state transfer dimensions in the context of an adaptable resource manager.

3   The Buffer Manager Case Study

As a canonical (and easily understood) example of a resource manager we choose a memory allocator. Given a memory pool, i.e., a region of contiguous memory, the role of a memory allocator is simply to allocate non-overlapping subregions of the available memory to its client(s) on request. For historical reasons, we tend to refer to our memory allocator as "the buffer manager". The buffer manager supports two basic operations - allocate and release. The allocate operation locates a contiguous region of unused memory of a specified size in the memory pool and returns a pointer to that region. The release operation returns a region of allocated memory to the pool. Contiguous regions of unused memory are stored in a linear list called the free list.

The objective of a buffer manager implementation is to minimise the execution times of the allocate and release operations, ideally with both operations running in near constant time. In implementing a buffer manager it is very difficult to predict its performance when subjected to a typical sequence of allocate and release operations generated by some application. A typical application calls the allocate operation periodically, uses the allocated memory for a certain amount of time, and then calls the release operation to free up the memory. Depending on the pattern of memory usage by the application, it is difficult, if not impossible, to implement an allocation strategy that the buffer manager can use to minimise the execution times of allocate and release in all cases. Sequences of allocate and release operations are very much application-specific and, as such, a single allocation strategy will have to trade-off performance for generality.

Examples of potential strategies for the buffer manager's allocate and release operations are the *first-fit*, *best-fit* and *worst-fit* [15]. The first-fit allocation strategy always allocates storage in the first free area in the memory pool that is large enough to satisfy a request. The best- fit allocation strategy always allocates storage from the free area that most closely matches the requested size. The worst-fit allocation strategy always allocates storage from the largest free area. The choice of strategy dictates how the buffer manager keeps track of free memory, i.e., whether the list of free memory regions is ordered by size or address. For example, for fastest execution time with low memory usage, first-fit is the optimal allocation strategy, but under certain circumstances it may cause excessive fragmentation and best-fit would be a more appropriate strategy.

Given these observations, we believe that the buffer manager is a good example of a manager of a shared resource that could benefit from dynamic adaptation depending on the mix of clients in the system at any time and their memory usage patterns. Moreover, the buffer manager exhibits the classic requirement to synchronise operations on behalf of possibly multiple clients although we note that an optimised implementation of the buffer manager could be used where there is only a single client in the system. Moreover, since the buffer manager necessarily maintains state describing the status of the memory pool, there may be a requirement to transfer that state between buffer manager implementations if and when dynamic adaptation takes place. In fact, we have considered three different usage scenarios for an adaptable buffer manager as follows:

- the simplest implementation supports a single client allowing the client to change memory allocation strategy at will;
- a multi-client buffer manager supports synchronisation between multiple clients - any client can change the memory allocation strategy but all clients share the same strategy;
- the final version supports per-client memory allocation strategies.

Starting from a minimal single-client, non-adaptable buffer manager (section 2.1 below), we have implemented each of the scenarios described above using design patterns, DLLs, and a reflective language and assessed the impact of each implementation approach in terms of

- performance overhead;
- the degree of separation of concerns between the functional (i.e., implementation of allocate and release) and non-functional aspects (i.e., support for synchronisation and dynamic adaptation);
- the programming effort required to add support for the non- functional aspects given the minimal implementation.

It should be noted that, where supported, adaptation is triggered by a meta-interface that allows clients to request their desired buffer management strategy from among those available. While this interface is semantically the same in each of the usage scenarios, it may be differ syntactically.

The Minimal Buffer Manager

In its minimal form, the public interface of the buffer manager provides operations for allocating and releasing regions of memory as depicted in Figure 1. Internally, the buffer manager maintains a linked list of free blocks of memory. The actual policy employed by the buffer manager for managing the memory is embedded in the implementation of its methods and cannot be changed. This minimal implementation could of course support multiple clients if the necessary synchronisation code were included in its methods; our implementation doesn't.

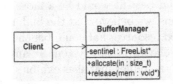

Fig. 1. The minimal buffer manager.

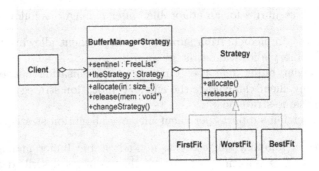

Fig. 2. The buffer manager with the strategy pattern.

Buffer Manager Implementation Using Design Patterns

The strategy pattern is an object-oriented design pattern [6] and has been used previously in the design of dynamically adaptable systems such as TAO [16]. The strategy pattern describes how the buffer manager can delegate the implementation of its exported operations to methods in a replaceable strategy object. In the case of the buffer manager, the strategy objects implement the methods in the Strategy interface shown in Figure 2. Strategy objects are able to access the buffer manager's state (free list) by binding to a reference to that state. The strategy objects themselves are stateless. For the system programmer to provide multiple strategies requires that corresponding implementations of Strategy be provided and compiled into the system.

As depicted in Figure 2., the strategy pattern also specifies an interface that allows clients to request a change of implementation strategy by giving the name of the required strategy as an argument. The changeStrategy operation represents a declarative meta-interface [10] to the buffer manager. At any time, a client can use knowledge of its own memory access patterns to select the most appropriate allocation strategy from those available by invoking changeStrategy. changeStrategy operates by swapping the buffer manager's old strategy object reference with a substitute reference to a new strategy object. When any client calls changeStrategy, the allocation strategy is changed for all clients of the buffer manager.

Supporting Synchronisation between Multiple Clients

Synchronisation is clearly required to ensure that the buffer manager's state does not become inconsistent under concurrent usage by many clients. Moreover, where dynamic adaptation is supported, any change in strategy should be both transparent to other clients as well as atomic. Other clients being serviced by the previous strategy object should be able to complete their execution while clients that issue requests while the strategy is being replaced should be blocked until the update completes.

To synchronise access to the buffer manager's state, synchronisation code has to be added to the allocate, release, and
changeStrategy operations. Broadly speaking, there are two possible ways in which this synchronisation code can be added:

1. One possible approach is to use a mutual exclusion lock to serialise all operations on the buffer manager. In this case code to acquire and release the lock can be inserted before and after the buffer manager dispatches the operations to the allocate, release, and changeStrategy methods.
2. An alternative approach might be to allow multiple clients to execute operations on the buffer manager concurrently with synchronisation taking place at a finer level of granularity. In this case the synchronisation code is embedded in the implementation of the allocate, release, and changeStrategy methods.

For both options, we have to recompile and rebuild our buffer manager implementation to add synchronisation code. In the case of the second approach we would also need to keep track of how many clients are executing in the buffer manager in order to allow us to determine when changeStrategy can be safely executed. For simplicity, our implementation uses the first approach.

Supporting per Client Allocation Strategies

Since different clients have different patterns of memory access and it is difficult to provide an optimal allocation strategy for all of them, it makes sense to allow each client have its own allocation strategy policy.

Employing the abstract factory pattern [6], Figure 3, each client can request a client-specific buffer manager from a factory of type BMFactory. A BMFactory is a singleton factory object that supports the creation of client-specific buffer managers as well as managing how the global memory pool is shared between these competing buffer managers. Two different implementation strategies are possible depending on whether or not the factory returns a minimal buffer manager or one that implements the strategy pattern, i.e., whether changing allocation strategy requires the client to bind to a different buffer manager or not.

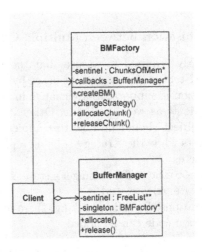

Fig. 3. Supporting per-client buffer managers with the abstract factory pattern.

In the first case, clients request the creation of a buffer manager that provides a specific allocation strategy using the createBufferManager operation. The returned buffer manager object is then responsible for:

- handling allocate and release operations from that client;
- requesting (potentially non-contiguous) chunks of memory from the BMFactory if needed to service client requests.

The buffer manager should be able to satisfy client allocate and release operations by allocating and releasing memory from the chunk(s) of memory it has been allocated by the BMFactory. If a buffer manager does not have a contiguous memory area available to satisfy a client's allocate request, the buffer manager then calls the BMFactory allocateChunk operation to request a new chunk of free memory. This requires synchronised access to the BMFactory's memory pool. The number of these requests for chunks of memory from competing buffer managers should be small compared to the number of requests from clients. Moreover, since chunks can be of the same size, a single policy can be chosen for the factory.

If the client wants to change its allocation strategy, it calls the BMFactory changeStrategy operation, passing a reference to its old buffer manager and a string representing a new allocation strategy. When changing a client's buffer manager object, the BMFactory does the following:

1. it locates an appropriate buffer manager object to implement the requested allocation strategy
2. creates the new buffer manager object
3. transfers the state from the old buffer manager object to its replacement
4. reorders the list of free memory areas if appropriate

The most obvious way to transfer the state of the old buffer manager object to its replacement is to use a copy constructor. Where the buffer manager objects represent non-substitutable types, specialised mappings could also be employed.

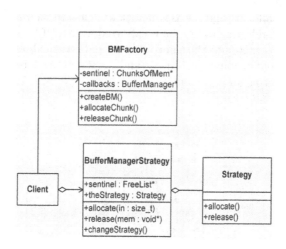

Fig. 4. Supporting per-client buffer managers with the abstract factory and strategy patterns.

An alternative implementation could have the BMFactory create per-client buffer manager objects that implement the strategy pattern. The buffer manager objects that implement the strategy pattern are now responsible for

- handling the allocate and release operations from that client
- requesting (potentially non-contiguous) chunks of memory from the BMFactory
- changing the client's allocation strategy

This framework provides the same meta-interface to clients as the original strategy pattern based implementation, but still provides per-client buffer manager objects. Moreover, synchronisation is only required in the implementation of the BMFactory and not in the single-client buffer managers. However, this implementation will not perform as well as the previous implementation unless the strategy changes frequently.

Buffer Manager Implementation Using DLLs

An obvious limitation of designs based on the strategy pattern per se is that the set of supported policies must be predetermined. This limitation of the strategy pattern can be overcome using an ad hoc combination of dynamic linking, function pointers and customised method dispatching. Support for dynamic linking of client-specific strategies at runtime has been used before in dynamically adaptable systems such as SPIN [1] and 2K [12].

In this design, calls to the buffer manager allocate and release operations use a level of indirection similar to the virtual function table in C++. The buffer manager's allocate and release operations delegate their implementation to function pointers, referring to functions exported from a DLL. Since the functions in the DLL are mapped into the same address space as the buffer manager, they can bind to the buffer manager object (and its state) via a reference passed to the original object as an argument.

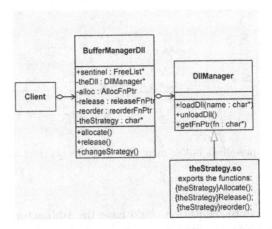

Fig. 5. The buffer manager using DLLs to load strategies.

Using the changeStrategy operation on the buffer manager, the allocate and release operations can be redirected to different functions. The new functions can be loaded at runtime from a different DLL specified by the client, while the old functions can either be left in memory or unloaded. This means that there is no limit on the number of potential allocation strategies a buffer manager can provide and more importantly that clients can develop client-specific allocation strategies as extension code (DLLs here) and link them in at runtime. In this sense, the client no longer has a declarative meta-interface to the buffer manager, but rather a procedural meta-interface instead.

Supporting Synchronisation between Multiple Clients

As for the strategy pattern, there are two possible places where synchronisation code can be added:

1. before and after the buffer manager dispatches the operations to the allocate, release, and changeStrategy implementation methods
2. in the implementation of the allocate, release and changeStrategy methods

In either case we still have to recompile and rebuild our buffer manager implementation to add support for synchronisation. Even in the second case, were we to provide new implementations of the allocate and release functions with support for synchronisation from a DLL we would still need to support a reference count to ensure that changeStrategy can be executed atomically.

Supporting per Client Allocation Strategies

As with the strategy pattern, the use of DLLs can be combined with the BMFactory object to provide per-client buffer managers. The buffer manager objects are responsible for

- handling the allocate and release operations from that client
- requesting (potentially non-contiguous) chunks of memory from the BMFactory
- changing the client's allocation strategy using the DllManager object

Reflective Implementation

The reflective version of our dynamically adaptable buffer manager is implemented using the Iguana/C++ reflective programming language [7]. Iguana allows the selective reification of language constructs such as object creation/deletion, method invocation, and state access. Important design goals of Iguana included support for transparent addition of reflection to existing software and the provision of language support for building dynamically adaptable systems. The implementation of Iguana/C++ is based on the use of a pre-processor: the application's source code is augmented with meta-level directives that declare one or more metaobject protocols (MOPs) and make the association between classes or individual objects and particular MOPs. The annotated code is then translated into standard C++.

In the case of the buffer manager, adaptation is introduced by reifying invocations on the original buffer manager class and by providing a meta-interface that allows the code of the allocate/release methods to be rebound to code provided at run-time, for example, in the form of a DLL. Using Iguana, the steps involved in making the buffer manager adaptive consist of :

1. defining a MOP that reifies all structural information (class, method and attribute) and reifies method invocation;
2. associating the appropriate classes with that MOP (specifically classes Buffer-Manager and Hole); and
3. defining an extension protocol, i.e. a meta-interface, that allows clients to request that a different strategy be used by the buffer manager.

The syntax for defining a MOP in Iguana consists of the keyword protocol followed by an enumeration of the selected reification categories as outlined in Figure 6. Each reification category is followed by the name of a class implementing that reification category, for example objects of type DefaultInvocation reify Invocation. Classes are associated with a MOP using the selection operator ($==¿$).

```
protocol DefaultMOP {
   reify Class      : MClass;
   reify Method     : MMethod;
   reify Attribute  : MAttribute;
   reify Invocation : DefaultInvocation;
};
class Hole            ==> Defaul tMOP {..};
class BufferManager==> DefaultMOP {..};
class AdaptationProtocol {
  public:
  void changePolicy(Mobject *bufman, char *strategy);
};
```

Fig. 6. Sample MOP definition and protocol selection in Iguana.

An *extension protocol* is simply a class definition that encapsulates the necessary steps for carrying out meta-level computations, in this case switching to a new strategy. The purpose of an extension protocol is to separate meta-level code from the actual MOPs, allowing the same extension protocol to be used for multiple, compatible MOPs. In the case of AdaptationProtocol, the name of the new strategy is used to identify a DLL containing the object code. No further modifications to the source are necessary and the annotated code is then pre-processed into standard C++.

When a client binds to a buffer manager object in the first place, it is provided with a default strategy, the strategy employed by the original buffer manager class. Invocation is not reified as long as the client does not request a different strategy, implying that the standard C++ invocation mechanism is used for calling methods. Only in the event that adaptation take place is invocation reified. We achieve this by inserting run-time checks into the application code, guarding all invocations to the buffer manager object. This has the advantage of reducing the overhead that is paid in the case that a client doesn't use the adaptation mechanism.

New strategies can be provided on the fly by subclassing the annotated buffer manager class, redefining the allocate/release methods and by compiling the code into a DLL. Clients can now request a different strategy by simply invoking the meta-interface and providing the name of the DLL. It is worth mentioning that the original interface of the buffer manager class has not been altered, the additional functionality to support adaptation is completely encapsulated in the extension protocol and is orthogonal to the base-level program.

The meta-level code of the extension protocol responsible for rebinding the allocate/release methods performs the following tasks:

1. open a DLL as specified by the strategy parameter;
2. rebind the code of the allocate/release methods;
3. transfer state (if necessary);
4. reify invocation for the client.

Figure 7 shows the conceptual view of the resulting meta-level architecture. Invocations on the buffer manager are reified and diverted to the meta-level. Rebinding the methods is done by updating the method metaobjects: each method metaobject contains a function pointer that points to the actual function code. As we mentioned earlier, all invocations to the buffer manager object are guarded allowing the reification of method invocations to be switched on/off dynamically. Once new code is loaded from the DLL, all further invocations are trapped and redirected to the new implementation.

Supporting Synchronisation between Multiple Clients

Synchronisation can be achieved in Iguana by defining a MOP that intercedes in all method invocations on the buffer manager and executes the additional synchronisation code before and after a method gets executed. The corresponding meta-level architecture is shown in figure 8: calls are trapped by the buffer-manager's class metaobject and synchronously dispatched to the allocate/release

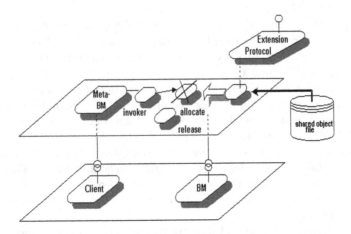

Fig. 7. Meta-level architecture allowing the dynamic rebinding of methods with state transfer.

methods. By reifying creation, we are able to modify the semantics of object creation in that successive calls of the new operator always return a reference to a single, global buffer manager object. Switching to a new strategy in this scenario can only be done when there are no pending requests, i.e. the extension protocol needs to synchronise with the method dispatcher of the buffer manager. As a consequence, the MOP that implements synchronisation and the extension protocol are no longer independent from each other, but still independent of the base-level code.

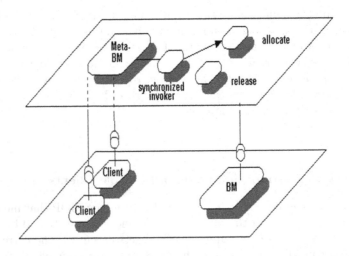

Fig. 8. Method calls are trapped and synchronised at the meta-level.

Supporting per Client Allocation Strategies

Iguana distinguishes between local and shared metaobjects: local metaobjects are associated with a single instance of a (base-level) class whereas shared metaobjects are shared between all instances of a class. This feature is particularly useful in order to allow multiple clients to choose a strategy of their own preference without affecting competing clients. In this scenario, we allow a client to bind to an individual instance of the buffer-manager class with its own, local metaobjects. In other words, each buffer manager object now maintains a private set of metaobjects representing its class definition. This allows much more fine-grained adaptation to take place, affecting only individual objects rather than whole classes. A buffer manager object can now autonomously switch to a different strategy on behalf of its client using the same meta-interface and MOP as described before.

We still have to link the per-client buffer managers to a global memory manager object and have to forward a request if necessary. We decided in this case to hard code the delegation mechanism into the allocate/release methods. An alternative would have been to reify state access for the class representing the free memory blocks (class Hole) and to delegate all accesses to the global memory manager. This can only be done by exploiting application specific knowledge (the meta-level code would no longer be application independent) and would also introduce significant run-time overhead.

4   Evaluation

As we explained in section 1, we were interested in evaluating the different approaches to supporting dynamic adaptation under three criteria:

- **Performance:** what overhead does support for dynamic adaptation introduce and what is the cost of performing adaptation?
- **Separation of concerns:** how far can the design and implementation of an adaptable system be separated from its application domain, i.e., to what extent is existing application code affected by adding support for dynamic adaptation?
- **Thinking adaptively - ease of programming:** what effort is involved in adding support for dynamic adaptation and how well does the framework/language support programmers in thinking in terms of building adaptable systems?

4.1   Performance

In this section, we compare how the different design strategies affect the performance of the running system. Specifically, we are interested in

- the relative overhead incurred in handing client requests;
- the cost of performing adaptation, i.e., switching between strategies.

Experimental setup The measurements were conducted on a 350 MHz Pentium II PC with 64 MB of RAM running the Linux operating system. The programs are written in C++ and were compiled using GNU C++ 2.8. The reflective version also uses the Iguana/C++ pre-processor.

Experiment 1 - Adaptation overhead

Intent This experiment evaluates the cost of method dispatching for the different adaptation techniques and the relative overhead they introduce in a typical usage scenario.

Description The cost of a null method call is measured to determine the relative overhead of method dispatching for the different adaptation approaches. The performance of the buffer manager under a simulated load is measured. The simulated load consists of a fixed number of time-stepped non-interleaved allocate and release operations with varying sizes.

Results The overhead for a null method invocation is summarised in table 1. In Iguana, a reified method invocation costs about 12-times a C++ virtual function invocation. In table 2, the No Sync. column represents the case of a single client performing the allocate and release operations with no synchronisation code. In Iguana, we measured the overhead solely introduced by the additional run-time checks that guard all accesses to the buffer-manager object, and the costs of both run-time check and reified method invocations. The former scenario represents the case when the system hasn't been adapted yet and carries out the default strategy, the latter scenario represents the case after the system switched to a new strategy and invocations are redirected. The Sync. column represents the case where a synchronisation lock is acquired before method execution and released after completion. We only measured the effective time spent for a single client thus only measuring the overhead introduced by the synchronisation code.

Evaluation As expected, using a reflective language for building an adaptable system introduces the most overhead to the application compared to the object-oriented implementations. Although the relative overhead for a reflective method invocation is high, its effective runtime overhead in the context of this experiment does not seriously impact on its performance. We expect that a real application that infrequently uses the buffer manager could yield enough performance gain from adapting its strategy to warrant its usage.

Experiment 2 - Cost of adaptation

Intent This experiment evaluates the cost of dynamically loading an adaptation strategy at runtime.

Description The dynamic adaptation of the buffer manager's allocation strategy requires the loading of new strategy code from a DLL at runtime and is triggered when an application changes its pattern of memory usage. Application-specific knowledge is used to know when to change the strategy.

Table 1. Relative null method call overhead.

Null method call	Relative execution time
C++ method invocation	1
Strategy pattern	1.38
DLL	1.45
Iguana (check)	1.10
Iguana (check + reified Invocation)	16.50

Table 2. Relative overall execution time.

Overall execution time	No Sync.	Sync.
C++ method invocation	1	1
Strategy pattern	1.07	1.09
DLL	1.05	1.06
Iguana (check)	1.54	N/A
Iguana (check + reified Invocation)	1.58	1.64

Results The results are given in table 3 and show the absolute time spent (in ms) carrying out 3000 switches from best-fit to first-fit to worst-fit strategies.

Evaluation The overhead of loading code from a DLL at runtime is made up primarily of time taken to swap the code from disk into memory and to map the code into the application's address space. System calls to open the DLL and acquire references to its exported functions make up the rest of the overhead. Lazy relocation of symbols is used throughout the measurements. The costs of loading and unloading a DLL are largely dependent on the memory footprint of the DLL. In the strategy pattern version only two functions were compiled into the DLL, whereas in Iguana we compiled a complete class hierarchy (all classes are embedded into the Iguana meta-level class hierarchy) into object code resulting in a considerably larger DLL. When client-specific strategies are supported (rightmost column in table 3), the adaptation time is significantly faster as the DLL implementing the requested strategy might already be in use by a different client. The DLL only gets unloaded when there are no existing references to symbols in that DLL.

Table 3. Loading code at runtime (MC = Multiple Clients, SS = Single Strategy, MS = Multiple Strategies).

Technique	Single Client	MC, SS	MC, MS
Reflection using Iguana	2280	2150	1310
Standard DLL Loading	840	840	620

4.2   Separation of Concerns

The addition of the strategy pattern to the buffer manager to support dynamic adaptation necessitated the complete restructuring of the buffer manager class, thus leading to a tangling of the code that implements dynamic adaptation and the original code. Delegating the implementation of the buffer manager's methods to a strategy object also had the undesirable side-effect of having to make its state visible to the strategy object, either by making the object's state public or by using friends. The reflective version neither required the modification of the original buffer manager class nor did it have any undesired side-effects, apart from its impact on performance.

The addition of the abstract factory pattern to support per-client buffer managers required changing the interface used to bind to a buffer manager. This change is not transparent to clients of the buffer manager and required rewriting the client code used to bind to the buffer manager. The reflective buffer manager overcomes this problem, however, due to its ability to intercede in object creation and re-direct the request to a meta-level factory object. With the reflective programming language our experiences have shown that building a framework to support dynamic adaptation of an existing application can often be achieved independently from the application's domain.

4.3   Ease of Programming

Here we compare the steps required by an application programmer to add the adaptation functionality to the buffer manager class, first using patterns, then with Iguana.

Strategy Pattern

1. Rewrite the original class' implementation and make its state visible to the strategy class;
2. Add the change strategy interface to the original class;
3. Write the different strategy classes.

Iguana

1. Write a MOP that reifies method invocation;
2. Write a separate extension protocol for changing strategy by reifying method invocation;
3. Implement the different strategies as subclasses of the buffer manager.

Abstract Factory Pattern:

1. Write the factory class and instantiate the factory object;
2. Rewrite the buffer manager class to request memory chunks from the factory object;
3. Rewrite all client code that is used to bind to a buffer manager.

Iguana

1. Write a MOP that reifies object creation and implement the factory as a meta-object;
2. Write a subclass of the buffer manager class to request memory chunks from the factory.

A problem with writing meta-level code in Iguana is that it is not always intuitive: concepts such as "reification" and "meta-object protocols" are inherently abstract and not targeted at solving everyday problems. However, a major benefit of using a reflective programming language is that there are many patterns of adaptation that can be encapsulated in meta-level code, even though some patterns require application-specific knowledge. For example, the strategy pattern can be encapsulated in a MOP, while the per-client buffer manager code requires a hybrid solution.

We conclude that it therefore appears to be possible to build an adaptation framework that is orthogonal to its application domain, although this is likely to constrain the types of adaptation that are possible.

5   Summary and Conclusion

Using a reflective programming language our experiences have shown that building a framework to support dynamic adaptation of an application can be achieved independently of the application's domain. The addition of dynamic adaptation functionality to an application does not necessarily require changing the static class structure of the application. The additional functionality to support adaptation can be completely encapsulated in an extension protocol and is orthogonal to the application's static class structure.

Performance remains the main disadvantage of using a reflective programming language to build systems software. This aside, we believe that a reflective programming language adds valuable intercessive features required for designing and building adaptable systems, most notably the provision of a general infrastructure (consisting of a MOP and an extension protocol) that can be used to make existing software adaptable. Future work will include the identification and application of other design patterns to existing code using Iguana/C++, as well as ongoing work on implementing our reflective programming language more efficiently.

Acknowledgements. The work is supported by Enterprise Ireland under Basic Research Grant SC/97/618.

References

1. Brian Bershad, Przemyslaw Pardyak, and et. Al. Language Support for Extensible Operating Systems. In *Workshop on Compiler Support for System Software*, 1996.

2. Gordon Blair, Fabio Costa, Geoff Coulson, Fabien Delpiano, Hector Duran, Bruno Dumant, Francois Horn, Nikos Parlavantzas, and Jean-Bernard Stefani. The Design of a Resource-Aware Reflective Middleware Architecture. In *Proceedings of Meta-Level Architectures and Reflection'99*, pages 115–134, 1999.

3. Vinny Cahill. The Iguana Reflective Programming Model. Technical report, Dept. of Computer Science, Trinity College Dublin, 1998.

4. Richard P. Draves. The Case for Run-Time Replaceable Kernel Modules. In *In Procceedings of the 4th Workshop on Workstation Operating Systems*, pages 160–164, 1993.

5. Roy Campbell et al. Designing and Implementing Choices: an Object-Oriented System in C++. In *Communications of the ACM, Sept. 1993*, 1993.

6. Erich Gamma, Richard Helm, Ralph Johnson, and John Vlissides. *Design Patterns: Elements of Reusable Object-Oriented Software*. Addison Wesley, 1995.

7. Brendan Gowing. *A Reflective Programming Model and Language for Dynamically Modifying Compiled Software*. PhD thesis, Department of Computer Science, University of Dublin, Trinity College, 1997.

8. Brendan Gowing and Vinny Cahill. Meta-Object Protocols for C++: The Iguana Approach. In , editor, *Proceedings of Reflection'96*, pages 137–152. XEROX Palo Alto Research Center, April 1996.

9. Graham Hamilton, Michael L. Powell, and James G. Mitchell. Subcontract: A Flexible Base for Distributed Programming. In *Proceedings of the 14th Symposium on Operating Systems Principles*, pages 69–79. ACM Special Interest Group on Operating Systems, December 1993. Also Operating Systems Review, 27(5).

10. Gregor Kiczales, John Lamping, Christina Lopes, Chris Maeda, and Anurag Mendhekar. Open Implementation Guidelines. In *19th International Conference on Software Engineering (ICSE)*. ACM Press, 1997.

11. Gregor Kiczales, John Lamping, Chris Maeda, David Keppel, and Dylan McNamee. The Need for Customisable Operating Systems. In *Proceedings of the 4th Workshop on Workstation Operating Systems*, pages 165–169. IEEE Computer Society, IEEE Computer Society Press, October 1993.

12. Fabio Kon, Roy Campbell, and Manual Roman. Design and Implementation of Runtime Reflection in Communication Middleware: the dynamicTAO case. In *ICDCS'99 Workshop on Middleware*, 1999.

13. Thomas Ledoux. Implementing Proxy Objects in a Reflective ORB. In *CORBA Workshop ECOOP*, 1997.

14. Scott Mitchell, Hani Naguib, George Colouris, and Tim Kinberg. Dynamically Reconfiguring Multimedia Components: A Model-based Approach. In *SIGOPS European Workshop on Support for Composing Distributed Applications*, 1998.

15. Bruno R. Preiss. *Data Structures and Algorithms with Object-Oriented Design Patterns in C++*. John Wiley & Sons, 1999.

16. Douglas C. Schmidt and Chris Cleeland. Applying Patterns to Develop Extensible and Maintainable ORB Middleware. In *IEEE Communications Magazine Special Issue on Design Patterns*, April 1999.

17. Ashish Singhai, Aamod Sane, and Roy Campbell. Quarterware for Middleware. In *18th IEEE International Conference on Distributed Computing Systems (ICDCS 1998)*, pages 192–201, 1998.

On the Integration of Configuration and Meta-level Programming Approaches

Orlando Loques[1], Alexandre Sztajnberg[2], Julius Leite[1], and Marcelo Lobosco[1]

[1] Instituto de Computação, Universidade Federal Fluminense,
Niterói, RJ, Brazil
{loques,julius,lobosco}@ic.uff.br
[2] Instituto de Matemática e Estatística/UERJ, RJ, Brazil
Grupo de Teleinformática e Automação/COPPE/UFRJ, RJ, Brazil
alexszt@uerj.br

Abstract Configuration Programming, based on Architecture Description Languages, and Meta-Level Programming are considered promising approaches in the software engineering field. This paper shows that there is an immediate correspondence between some key concepts of Configuration and Meta-Level Programming approaches and that some of the main issues to be solved for their deployment in real systems are quite similar. The main result is that the integration of both approaches in a single configuration programming framework can assist in employing meta-level programming in order to achieve separation of concerns and improve software reuse. In addition, the capability of supporting dynamic configuration and flexibility on component programming language choice are potentially improved. A prototype of a configuration programming centered environment and some application examples are presented in order to demonstrate the useful features of the combined approach.

1 Introduction

Modern computer applications must be developed rapidly in order to meet increased market demands and fierce manufacturer competition. In many cases, different variants of a basic functional system have to be delivered in a short time, in order to cater to specific consumer requirements and particular operational environments.

Two extra requirements complete the current software engineering scene: (i) the components of these systems can be independently designed and may be implemented using different programming languages; (ii) many applications of interest have to change their component makeup during their operational life, i.e., they have dynamic architectures.

In the previously described context, software reuse becomes mandatory and compositional system development and separation of concerns are two key concepts that have been proposed to attain this goal. Another desirable characteristic is the capacity to support dynamic architectures and include components programmed in diverse languages in these architectures.

W. Cazzola et al. (Eds.): Reflection and Software Engineering, LNCS 1826, pp. 189–208, 2000.

Architecture Description Languages (ADLs) are a convenient way of specifying a software architecture, either textually or graphically. This consists of the composition or configuration of the system in terms of a set of *modules* (components), which desirably encapsulate functional computation, and a set of *connectors*, which primarily describe how the modules are glued into and may interact within the architecture [1,23,31]. Using an ADL, a system designer can specify the functional composition of the system , through module selection, and attach to it particular module interaction styles or contracts (in communication contexts they are called protocols) through the connectors. For convenience, we call this activity Configuration Programming (CP).

Meta-Level Programming (MLP) in its different versions, such as computational reflection [6,11], compositional filters [3] and aspect-oriented programming [13,21], is being proposed as an approach that helps to achieve separation of concerns. MLP facilitates concentrating application concerns related to particular system requirements, that are in principle (hopefully) orthogonal to the pure functional behavior of the application, in explicit pieces of code, that together define the so-called meta-level architecture of the system. Reification, the switching process between the normal program (base-level) and the extra program (meta-level), can be implemented in several ways, depending on the particular MLP environment being considered. For example, in a procedural language context, specific procedure calls can be intercepted in order to transfer the control flow to the extra code. This is quite similar to the code control transfer that happens between a module and a connector in configuration programming contexts. This fact paves the way for integrating both paradigms in order to benefit from their intrinsic advantages.

Like other researchers, we are investigating techniques that may facilitate the combined use of the best of both concepts, CP and MLP, by system designers. This goal entails some simple insights and in the future may allow the construction of very powerful tools and integrated support environments to design, build, document, verify, operate and maintain software architectures. This happens mainly because Configuration Programming, based on ADLs, allows us to describe many static and dynamic system characteristics in very explicit forms that map naturally to the actual system software structure. This exposition makes it easier for the designer to understand the system architecture and to make the interventions required for customization, either at the application development stage or during its operational life, in order to cater to evolutionary requirements.

The remainder of this paper is organized as follows. Initially, in section 2, we present basic ADL/CP concepts and in the following section some of their implementation details in a specific environment. In section 4 a set of examples is used to illustrate our proposition. In sections 5 and 6 we discuss some related proposals and issues that are common in the context of both (MLP and CP) approaches, respectively. Finally, in Section 6, we draw some conclusions.

2   Basic Concepts

Software architecture is an emerging field still without a universally accepted terminology; in order to describe our proposition, we define some basic concepts on the ADL/CP area.

Module: A single or structured component with an independent existence, e.g., a process, object or procedure, a set of processes, objects or procedures, or any identifiable composition of code or data. A module functions as a type or class when used as a template to create execution units, and, as an execution unit it is called a module or class instance, or simply an object.

Port: A typed object that identifies a logical point of interaction of a module and its environment. The set of ports of a module defines its interface. Port type definitions can be reused in different modules to define their particular interfaces. A port instance is named and referenced in the context of its owner module (interface definition and code); this provides configuration-level port-naming independence. We distinguish ports that are active and can initiate interactions, called outports, from ports that are passive in the interaction, called inports; outports can be mapped to method calls and inports can be mapped to method entry points in an object code. Ports are similar to reification points used in MLP approaches and, similarly, can be associated with different code boundary transfer mechanisms, e.g., method, procedure or messaging passing primitive invocations.

Connector: an object that is used to relate ports or module interfaces. Besides this the connector encapsulates the contracts [12] used for module interaction. Connectors have properties similar to modules and can either be implemented by modules written in a particular programming language, or by run-time facilities of a particular operating system, or by any mix of resources available in the supporting environment. Protocols used in distributed systems and pipes used in Unix systems are immediate example of specialized connector implementations.

As mentioned in [31], the architecture of a software system defines that system in terms of modules and of interactions among these modules; these interactions are expressed and implemented by connectors. In addition to specifying the structure and topology of the system, the architecture shows the intended correspondence between system requirements and the elements of the constructed system. In this context, we can look a non-functional requirement (and many other particular types of requirements) as an aspect or concern, and by an agreed self-discipline map its corresponding implementation into a specific connector type. In this way connectors can be seen as meta-objects in MLP based contexts. According to our proposal, Table 1 summarizes the correspondences between the MLP and ADL/CP abstractions.

With the help of ADL constructs, modules and connectors can be composed in order to define new aggregated components that can be reused in different application systems. For example, some system requirements can be described at higher levels of abstraction, and specified through composite connectors that encapsulate the meta-configurations required for the support of these requirements, e.g., fault-tolerance support connectors [22].

Table 1. Correspondence between ADL/CP and MLP abstractions.

MLP abstraction		ADL/CP abstraction
base-level components	<->	modules
reification points	<->	ports
meta-level components	<->	connectors

The ADL itself may be extensible in order to allow the addition of new connectors and at the same time let the configuration programming environment get to know their semantic properties and configuration rules. This is required for formal reasoning and verification of architecture specifications, and, in addition, it may help to simplify the syntax required to use some connector types, e.g., connectors that implement communication protocols. Achieving ADL extension capability while retaining such properties is a non-trivial task [1].

3   R-RIO

In this section we describe some details of R-RIO (Reflective-Reconfigurable Interconnectable Objects), a distributed configuration programming environment, based on Java, that we are currently developing [19,32].

3.1   Implementation

As described in the previous section, the mapping of modules, ports and connectors to an implementation depends on the particular environment. In our prototype environment, primitive module types are defined by Java classes, and composite modules can be composed by arbitrary configurations of primitive modules (it is also possible to compose modules using Java's inheritance features, but this would imply losing the capability of reconfiguring the individual composite modules). Ports are associated with Java method declarations (signatures) at the configuration level and to method invocations at the code level. It is important to note that only the methods explicitly associated with ports are configurable through connectors and directly visible at the configuration level; the remaining methods use normal Java referencing and binding mechanisms. Connector types are currently defined and composed as modules, but they have a special implementation and are specially treated by the configuration tools. Module and connector types (mapped to Java classes) are associated with module and connector instances through R-RIO's ADL declarations. At configuration time, module and connector instances are created as Java objects. Table 2 summarizes the Java to R-RIO mappings.

R-RIO's connectors are context-reflective (Figure 1) in the sense that, when plugged into modules, they can be automatically and dynamically (at configuration time) adapted to mediate interactions between ports using any method

Table 2. R-RIO to Java mapping.

R-RIO		Java
modules / module instances	->	classes / objects
connectors	->	Encapsulated in classes / objects or mapped to native support mechanisms
ports	->	method signatures / invocations

A/B & C/D: pairs of modules with different interface signatures

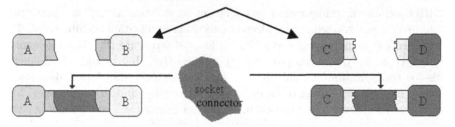

Fig. 1. Context-reflective connectors.

signature, including the exception-handling definitions associated with each particular method. This capability is achieved using information provided by the Java Structural Reflection Interface to adapt, at run-time, the particular connector type to the context of signatures defined by the port interfaces of the set of modules for which it is mediating interactions. Specifically, for each specified port-to-port connection, the connector automatically acquires the structural information required for the manipulation of the parameters of the associated method and provides the support machinery required for its invocation. This approach makes it unnecessary statically to generate and keep either stubs or connector executable code for each specific pair of connectable ports in a repository. We took advantage of this capability to provide generic connectors in order to support common communication styles (Java RMI, sockets, multicast, etc) used in distributed applications. This same technique, could be used to make generic connectors to encapsulate mechanisms to support functions such as, e.g., encryption / decryption, compression / decompression, state saving, transactions support, and fault-tolerance achieved through replicated servers [22]. An application of context-reflective connectors is presented in sub-section 4.4.

The structure of R-RIO's connectors follows a standard pattern and can be programmed according to a well-defined procedure, whose implementation could be supported by a tool. Basically, on the invoker side, after identifying the method, its invocation is serialized. In the sequel, on the target object side a dynamic invocation of the concerned method is performed; in a distributed environment the serialized data is transmitted over the network. It is worth to point out that our connectors are implemented using the standard Java virtual machine. Also, we have not put much effort in optimizing our connector implementation. However, we have made a set of measurements that show that the overhead is small when compared to the cost associated with the basic machinery required to perform dynamic method invocations in Java, which is considerably greater than the cost of normal method invocation. The connector's performance can be optimized either using precompiled stubs (losing the dynamic context-reflective capability) or using a customized JVM (losing portability).

3.2 Configuration Management

R-RIO includes a configuration management service that is used to create running images and to reconfigure already executing application architectures. The configuration management service has a layered structure that is implemented by two types of system components: (i) an executive, that provides basic methods for configuration control: module and connector instantiation/deletion as well as binding/unbinding of modules and connectors; and (ii) a manager, that provides higher level configuration management functions. The manager is based on an interpreter that takes architecture specifications (ADL scripts) and generates the basic executive method invocations to create a running image of the specified architecture. R-RIO also supports configuration changes in a running architecture (see sub-sections 4.3 and 6.2 for related points).

Currently, the configuration management service has a centralized implementation (i.e. there is only one manager component) and the basic configuration executive component is replicated in every processing node included in an R-RIO context. However, the configurator service could have a more distributed implementation, i.e., separated managers can be used to take care of different parts of a running architecture.

4   Examples

In its origins, our research had a distributed systems orientation. Most of the previously mentioned examples of connectors are well suited to the message communication area. However, we came to believe that connectors can be used to mediate general concerns related to module interactions. A similar view of connectors is presented in [31] where a scheduling connector is used to mediate real-time requirements of a set of modules. In our project, as exemplified in this section, we were able to express through connectors coordination (synchronization and concurrency) requirements similar to those expressed using the aspect-oriented language for coordination proposed in [20]. We also managed to encapsulate into connectors the machinery required to support fault-tolerance through server replication (see section 5.1), and found that diverse general purpose module interaction patterns can be mapped to connectors.

In this section we also outline additional points of our proposal. Initially, we customize a simple producer-consumer buffer application, that is also presented in other related works, e.g., [3,20]. Finally, we show how the contextual-reflection capability of our connectors can be used for improving reuse. For clarity, in the examples, we avoided using configuration parameters, and ignore the error handling issue. CBabel, R-RIO's ADL, is described in [25] and [32].

4.1   Basic Buffer Architecture

The graphical and textual representations of this producer-consumer buffer architecture are presented in Figure 2. This basic version uses as connectors the standard Java method invocation support, that is the default in R-RIO; they are represented by dashed lines. The signature of the ports Put and Get are

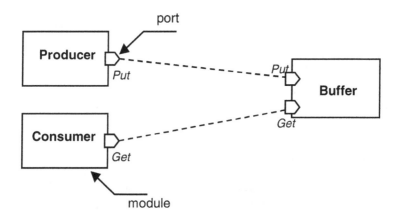

```
module   BufferApplication {
   port Put (Any Item) (void);
   port Get (void) (Any Item);
   module   BufferType{
        inport Put;
        inport Get;
   } Buffer;
   module   ProducerType {
        outport Put;
   } Producer;
   module   ConsumerType {
        outport Get;
   } Consumer;
   install   Buffer, Producer, Consumer;
   link Producer, Consumer to Buffer;
} Example;
start Example;
```

Fig. 2. Producer-consumer buffer architecture.

defined independently; they can be reused to define the interfaces of the application modules that compose the architecture. `BufferType`, `ProducerType` and `ConsumerType` are module type declarations; `Buffer`, `Producer` and `Consumer` declare respectively instances of these modules. `Inport` and `outport` designate the effective directions of the flow of data arguments through the ports; they also allow a port to be renamed, e.g., `outport Put Store`, when required to identify different ports for configuration naming purposes. Install declares the module instances that will be created in the running system.

A map directive is available to specify the module instance programming language and to designate a specific code implementation for it; here it is omitted and Java is considered the default language. The module's port linkage concludes the architecture specification. The final start declaration tells the configurator to create an instance called `Example` of the `BufferApplication` type.

4.2   Introducing Coordination

The basic buffer assumes standard Java semantics for method invocation and may not work well in the presence of concurrency even in the simplest case (one producer and one consumer). In Figure 3, we present the configuration description of a coordination connector that can be used to extend the buffer, adding mutual exclusion and flow control for the buffer access operations, allowing the inclusion and safe operation of multiple concurrent producers and consumers.

The configuration description uses standard declarations of R-RIO that may be used to implement similar requirements in other applications. `Exclusive` specifies that method invocations through enclosed ports (`Put` and `Get`) are mutually exclusive. Guards (`empty` and `full`) are used to control the flow of method invocations; if the guard is false the associated method invocation is deferred. The state variable `n_items` has to be acquired in the buffer data space. This was done through a method coded by hand; however it could also be automatically generated. One instance of this connector can be included in the configuration using primitive configuration language constructs. However, when the interfaces of the connectors and of the involved modules are paired and context compatible a simplified notation may be used:

```
link  Producer, Consumer to Buffer by Guard_Mutex;
```

4.3   Introducing Distribution and Encryption/Decryption

Here a distributed environment (producer, consumer and buffer are in different nodes) is considered. The distributed architecture and part of its configuration specification in R-RIO are represented in Figure 4. An `at` directive is available to specify the module's location (this could be parameterized); the shaded areas represent different nodes. As a default communication protocol R-RIO offers a Java-RMI connector; in this example we chose to use a connector that directly implements socket communication. Note that socket is a composite connector, with a distributed implementation. In principle, at the application code level,

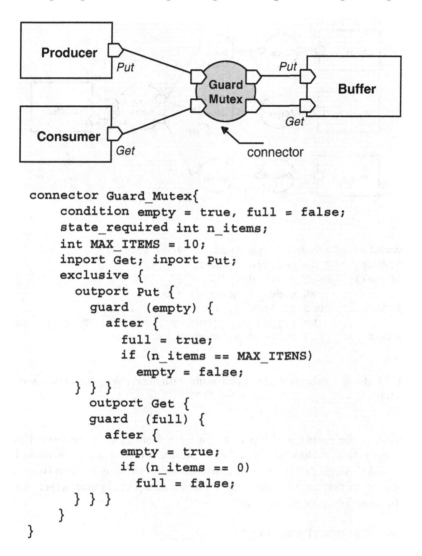

```
connector Guard_Mutex{
    condition empty = true, full = false;
    state_required int n_items;
    int MAX_ITEMS = 10;
    inport Get; inport Put;
    exclusive {
      outport Put {
        guard  (empty) {
          after {
             full = true;
             if (n_items == MAX_ITENS)
                empty = false;
    } } }
         outport Get {
         guard  (full) {
           after {
             empty = true;
             if (n_items == 0)
                full = false;
      } } }
     }
  }
}
```

Fig. 3. Producer-consumer buffer architecture with a coordination connector.

the introduction of the module distribution aspect is invisible; see the related
discussion in section 5.4. At this stage we could also add encryption/decryption
support to the architecture.

   In general, the capability to perform dynamic reconfiguration requires special system or application programming in order to ensure overall application
state consistency [15]. For example, in the previously presented architectures,
the removal of producer or consumer instances could lead the application to an
inconsistent state, e.g., an item value could be lost. Also, in the architecture presented in figure 4, the initial introduction of encryption/decryption would require

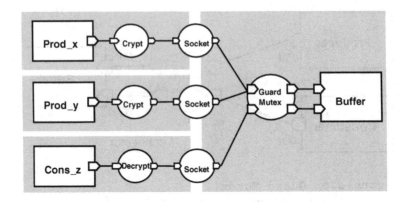

```
...
module    ProducerType Prod_x, Prod_y;
module    ConsumerType Cons_z;
install   Prod_x, Prod_y, Cons_z;
             at node_i, node_j, node_k;
link      Prod_x, Prod_y, Cons_z to Buffer
             by Crypt|Crypt|Decrypt, Socket, Guard_Mutex;
start     Prod_x, Prod_y, Cons_z;
...
```

Fig. 4. Producer-consumer buffer architecture with encryption/decryption and socket connectors.

the buffer to be empty and has to be in force from system start-up. However, during operation, an arbitrary number of producer or consumer instances can be introduced through dynamic reconfiguration of the running architecture without causing any buffer state inconsistency. The following configuration script can be used to introduce a new consumer:

```
module   ConsumerType Cons_t;
install  Cons_t at node_l;
link     Cons_t to Buffer
            by Decrypt, Socket, Guard_Mutex;
start    Cons_t;
```

We further discuss dynamic reconfiguration in sub-section 6.2.

4.4 Using Context-Reflective Connectors

It is interesting to note that in the buffer architecture versions, presented in the previous sub-sections, it was unnecessary to define the data type of the buffered items. In fact, the only requirement for the presented configurations to work correctly is that the data type of the Item parameter, associated with the

Consumer's and the Producer's `Put` and `Get` ports, be identical. This happens because the contextual-reflection capability provided by the deployed connectors. As described in section 3.1, guided by the configuration specification, the connectors can acquire from the Java environment the structural information needed to manipulate and invoke the method associated with each port-to-port binding.

Currently, we are investigating the use of this automatic adaptation capability to provide generic connectors to encapsulate interaction-related design patterns, such as: chain of responsibility, visitor, memento, mediator and observer [4]. Besides increasing design reuse, this allows us to automate code generation for supporting the specified pattern in different application architecture contexts. Figure 5 helps to illustrate the context-reflective capability: the standard observer design pattern, as defined in [10], is implemented through a generic connector used to mediate the interactions of a Tic-Tac-Toe game architecture. In this example, after each move, the connector gets the new game status (invoking the game method `GetStatus`) and forwards it to the display modules, using a multicast connector. In fact, this basic architecture can be adapted automatically to support several other board games having similar architectures. For this adaptation it would be sufficient to replace the application specific classes: `TTTplayer`, `TTTgame` and `TTTdisplay`.

A kind of context-reflective connector is also proposed in [27] in order to support architectural evolution. However, these connectors are designed to bind components using a specific architectural style (called C2), which imposes a particular structure for the application system. The connector's main responsibilities are the routing and broadcast of messages; the messages can be filtered internally by the connector, according to some specific policies. In addition, the proposed implementation does not support dynamic configuration changes.

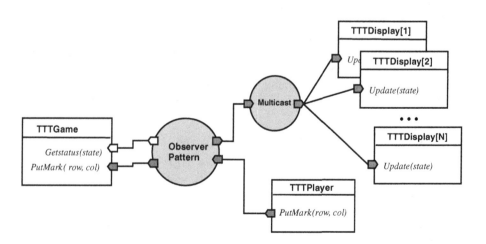

Fig. 5. A context-reflective connector.

5   Related Proposals

In this section, we discuss two approaches directly related to our proposal. A more extensive discussion is available in [32].

5.1   Reflection

Reflection is a paradigm, generally associated with object-oriented languages, with great potential to help to achieve separation of concerns. In practice, method interception (and redirection) is the primitive mechanism available to allow the use of reflection by programmers. By intercepting a method invocation, defined to have a reflex, the programmer can introduce some additional code (defined at a meta-level and sometimes called meta-code or meta-object) to introduce or add specific properties to the program. In fact, in many cases, this is equivalent to introducing a connector to glue together two or more module ports; the specific connector is specified in the configuration programming domain. For example, in a client/server application connectors can be used to fulfill requirements such as: call logging and tracing, persistence, data compression and encryption, access control, real-time and fault-tolerance.

One of our initial research goals was to compare the configuration programming and computational reflection approaches for application system customization. To begin with, we used the reflection technique to implement fault tolerance support in CORBA using the set of server replication policies presented in [7], which was originally implemented in Open C++ [6]. As a result, we obtained a set of meta-objects that encapsulate the fault tolerance support mechanisms for the chosen server replication policies [8]. Then, we verified that the fault tolerance code developed for the meta-objects can be used, without basic changes, to implement a generic connector that supports the same set of server replication policies presented in [7]. Using this special connector we were able automatically to add replication-based fault tolerance policies to CORBA-based client-server architectures [22]. This fault tolerance experiment showed that, at the programming level, configuration requires about the same effort as computational reflection and, as a benefit, the implementation is independent of special programming languages and compilers. We were also able to reproduce, through configuration and connectors, other programming examples presented in the literature to illustrate the use of reflection-based and other related proposals, e.g., [3,11].

5.2   Aspect-Oriented Programming

Aspect-Oriented Programming (AOP) is a new MLP paradigm being proposed to cater for separation of concerns [20] and [21], which in this context are considered as aspects of an application. According to the first AOP proposal, the implementation of a system in a particular programming language consists of: (i.i) a component language with which to program the components, (i.ii) one or more aspect programming languages with which to program the aspects or concerns, (ii) an aspect weaver for the set of languages, (iii.i) a component program, that implements the (functional) components using the component language, and (iii.ii) one or more aspect programs that implement the aspects using the aspect languages.

The weaver acts as a special compiler that combines the functional and aspect codes to implement a single running program. Analyzing the AOP literature, two types of code transformation provided by the weavers can be identified. The first, that does not appear to happen very frequently, consists of optimizations, guided by special directives specified at the aspect program level, that lead to more performance-efficient programs. The authors argue that, in this class of applications, the program analysis and understanding involved is so significant that compilers cannot be relied upon to do the required optimizations reliably; this would happen because the (meta and base) code join points cannot be treated separately [18]. We think that such kinds of optimizations are in most cases orthogonal to the overall system architecture. They can be dealt, at module or subsystem level, using special tools, without hindering the overall system composition. In ADL/CP terms, the aspect language program, its weaver and also the run-time environment support could be attached to specific modules or subsystems through related annotations, made at the configuration programming level. In [23] we suggest the use of such kind of annotation to select the data coherency protocol to be used to support module interactions in a distributed-shared memory (DSM) context.

The second code transformation style, which appears to be more common, is used when the code join points can be treated separately, and in essence is similar to that performed by reflective language compilers. In fact, as pointed out in [21] "reflection seems to be a sufficient mechanism for AOP, but many regard it as too powerful: anything can be done with it, including AOP". In this context, an advantage of AOP would be its ability to discipline the use of reflection by using special aspect programming languages. The Java based language, AspectJ, is a step in this direction, providing a construct: advise, that is used to specify the methods that are to be logically intercepted and the associated meta-level code to be executed [13]. In fact, the *advise* role is similar to that performed by bind constructs in ADL/CP based proposals, and this can be a bridge between the two approaches.

In our project, we were able to reproduce an application of the observer pattern presented in [13], coded in AspectJ, using connectors to specify and concentrate the code required to implement the mentioned pattern [32]. Regardless of the case with AOP, we did not have to use any special aspect programming language, besides some constructs that are almost standardized in most contemporary ADL/CP proposals. Yet, as regards the implementation of the observer pattern in AspectJ, we do not have to break module encapsulation in order to introduce special methods, method calls and data structures into the basic application modules. It should be pointed out that our solution assumes that the observed module provides a method to expose its internal state. However, this programming style requirement is very reasonable in context of the specific application.

6   Related Issues

In this section we discuss issues that are common to the MLP and ADL/CP approaches and try to relate these issues to our proposal.

6.1   Composition of Concerns

As pointed by other researchers, composition of concerns/aspects is an open research issue; e.g. [28,35]. We have to find appropriate syntactic mechanisms to structure the meta-level architecture and also find well-defined semantic rules to transfer control and data among meta-level components. In addition, techniques to reason about the composite meta-level architecture have yet to be developed. In this area, the ADL/CP approach already provides clear concepts and mechanisms for module and connector composition. In particular, we can benefit and take advantage of the techniques and formalisms being proposed to reason and verify correctness properties of software architectures, e.g., [1,2,24].

In our proposal meta-level code is associated with connectors, that can be composite components and thus can have any convenient internal structure. In order to improve flexibility for meta-level programming, R-RIO provides a special *transfer* programming construct, which is designed to pass control and data through composite connector structures. The implementation of this construct propagates the reference of the base-level module, which called the method that started the reification process, among the connectors through which that method execution traverses. This allows control to come back to the original module after traversing an arbitrary configuration of meta-level objects. The use of transfer also caters for efficiency in some configurations of connectors (e.g. pipelines), allowing us to bypass all (or some) of them, on the way back, before returning control to the invoking module. Extra fine performance optimizations are possible using configuration analysis techniques to unite together the code for individual connectors into a single piece of code, thus avoiding overheads related to method invocation, data transfer, context changes, etc.

Another issue for composite connectors is how the components of a composite meta-level architecture gain control over a base-level module, for example to access and modify its state. When there is no internal concurrency, either at the meta or base level, there are solutions that are orthogonal to specific run-time support environments. For example, in a state checkpoint application, special methods (supplied at the base level) can be used to get and update the application state to be preserved. However, in the presence of concurrency at either (base or meta) level, synchronization and race conditions appear and more refined mechanisms may be required. In some cases it is possible to identify *a priori* particular interaction styles between the two levels, e.g., as happens in a distributed transaction support framework. General purpose solutions are presented [11] and [28]; however they either restrict the meta-base level interaction relationship or rely on special features, which impose, changes in the basic support environment (Java virtual machine), hindering portability.

6.2   Dynamic Architectures

The architecture of some applications may have to be modified or extended during operation in order to cater for either planned or evolutionary (or unplanned) change. In this regard, the ADL/CP approach provides the capability of describing and managing system composition and structure explicitly and independently of application programming concerns, thus helping to attain separation of concerns in the configuration programming domain. On the other hand, most MLP based approaches do not either allow or offer clear concepts and mechanisms for supporting dynamic adaptation leading to ad-hoc solutions in this domain of concern.

In our proposal, for planned reconfigurations, we achieve explicit separation of reconfiguration actions through a special ADL construct that is used to specify the name and scope of configuration management scripts. The execution of these configuration management scripts can be externally triggered by invoking a standard configurator method. Other researchers propose extended ADLs with the capability of expressing configuration management policies explicitly, e.g. [5,16]. In [5] a scheme, called architectural reflection, is presented, in which reconfiguration activities have both their decision-making policy and the module/connector structure required for changes specified separately at a meta-configuration level, which is defined by special ADL constructs. Reconfiguration activities are triggered by the activation of rules (also specified through special ADL constructs) based on state and events related to the base level architecture computations. Although state and event-based internal reconfiguration triggering rules could have been added to CBabel (R-RIO's ADL), we opted for keeping our ADL concise, introducing decision-making concerns explicitly where necessary.

In fact, R-RIO supports a pragmatic version of the concepts proposed in [5] and could be used as a basis for a more canonical implementation of those concepts. Our approach conforms to the idea of providing skeleton ADLs to which to add the particular details of concern when necessary [17]. For instance, in a fault-tolerance experiment, based on server replication, we used a group communication service to implement special connectors in order to support diverse fault-tolerance styles [22]. The used group communication service already provides most of the information and mechanisms required for triggering and executing consistent reconfiguration activities [33]. Hence, we opted for implementing the reconfiguration decision-making code as a meta-component of the fault-tolerance support composite connector. For recovery after failures, the configuration changes, explicitly specified by a separate script at the ADL level, are triggered by invocations made from the fault-tolerance connectors. In this way, we separate both concerns and leave the configuration management functions explicitly encapsulated into a component.

R-RIO also supports unplanned configuration changes that can be performed through an interactive configuration interface, which is provided by the configuration management service. The change commands invoked through the configuration interface are reflected in the internal representation of the currently running architecture. After a sequence of configuration change commands, the resulting running configuration can be automatically converted to the corresponding textual specification in CBabel. It is feasible to analyze and validate an intended final architecture before imposing the actual changes in the current configuration. We have also experimented with a graphical interface that allows managing the evolution of software configurations by graphical means [23].

Other schemes for adaptive programming, such as that used in the Darts system [29], offer a limited set of adaptive policies, and the implementation mechanism for switching among these policies is embedded in the support environment. The programmer is restricted to adapting the running software configuration through directives called from application modules during system operation. Configuration programming provides flexibility and does not forbid the use of dynamic configuration support provided by current operating systems projects, such as Darts.

It is interesting to note that code fusion techniques, like those implemented by AOP weavers, can mix the basic functional and specific (meta) code pieces together, in order to compose the running application code. As a result, the run-time granularity of the reconfigurable code units is at least increased, which makes it difficult to support the dynamic evolution requirements of some applications; this was also pointed out in [26].

6.3 Implementation Flexibility

Our ADL includes an Interface Definition Language (IDL), used to specify the component's interfaces, and has a syntax compatible with CORBA IDL. In principle, the adoption of a standard IDL would help us to use in an application system architecture components implemented in different programming languages, provided they have in common a CORBA support environment. We have carried out independent configuration programming experiments using Java and CORBA support environments [19] and [22]. The Java implementation provides interoperability and component portability in standard Java environments. While not fully developed, the CORBA implementation promises to support interoperability for components written in different programming languages. It is feasible to construct automatically connector types which serve as bridges between these two environments (as well as between other support environments like Microsoft's DCOM); the information required is readily available using the Java Structural Reflection Interface and CORBA interface repositories. These adaptation bridges could also be obtained using conversion libraries provided by CORBA and Java products. The general availability of these bridge connectors would allow interoperability among modules being supported in different environments. Like others researchers we think that interoperability is essential to support current software engineering requirements [34].

6.4 Comments on Reuse

ADL/CP and MLP approaches provide clear concepts and powerful tools to compose and deal with evolving software architectures. However, either in ADL/CP or MLP environments, the immediate reuse of independently designed modules and connectors (or meta-objects) may not be possible. In some cases, in order to choose or design a connector for a given module application context, the designer has to know how the concerned modules interact and even some of the internal details of these modules.

Two examples illustrate this point: (i) in the architecture presented in sub-section 4.4 the game modules have to follow a particular design style to take advantage of the observer pattern connector mediating capability; (ii) connectors, used for communication in distributed systems, are generally considered "almost" orthogonal to the applications. However, when we look at the exception handling issue things get blurred. The mechanical side of exception propagation and handling can be standardized and automated. However, the complete treatment of an exception may require the intervention of the application programmer through specific coding, sometimes disseminated into several modules in the architecture. This has to be planned when designing the application, and requires appropriate module internal and external architectures. To summarize, there are limits on what can be solved independently at the meta-level. Perhaps, as observed by Saltzer, the treatment of end-to-end issues is inherently an application dependent concern [30]. Much more research is necessary to augment reuse in these cases.

7   Conclusions

This paper has shown that there is an immediate correspondence between some key concepts of Configuration and Meta-Level Programming. Its main result is that the integration of both approaches in a single configuration programming framework can assist in putting into practice meta-level programming in order to achieve separation of concerns and improving software reuse. Meta-level components can be mapped into connectors and application customization can be achieved by specifying these connectors to compose architectures through configuration programming. The static and dynamic configuration capability of modules and connectors simplify architecture composition and evolution through the execution of planned and unplanned architectural changes. In particular, the availability of context-reflective connectors may enable the synthesis of highly dynamic architectures as those made possible in the WWW environment.

The ADL description of a system is itself a specification and one can take advantage of formalisms already available for refining and proving properties of software architectures. With relatively little effort, a concise ADL can be used as a basis to express different concerns best suited for developing applications in a given domain. For instance, starting from our basic ADL, we are investigating how to attach to components descriptions of QoS (Quality of Service) specifications (behavioral contracts), similar as those proposed in [9]. This allows two new interesting and complementary capabilities: (i) verify beforehand if functionally compatible modules will obey QoS interaction contracts in a distributed system architecture; (ii) to assemble composite connectors, which may include the configuration of specific support components, required to meet the specified QoS contracts, as suggested in [14]. The latter capability may help to resolve most of the resource dependencies of an application in an automatic fashion, with little or no external human intervention.

Currently, we are developing R-RIO, which integrates ADL/CP and MLP approaches in a single, conceptual and practical, configuration programming environment. This experiment should help us to clarify many issues that this work does not directly address. A preliminary version of R-RIO is available for research use; see `http://www.ic.uff.br/~rrio` for details.

Acknowledgments. This work has been partially supported by the Brazilian research funding agencies CNPq, Finep and Faperj. Alexandre Sztajnberg is supported in part by a grant from CAPES - Brazil, proc. BEX 1014/99-4. We would like to thank our colleague Michael Stanton for his valuable suggestions for the improvement of the text, and also the anonymous referees for their constructive remarks.

References

1. Robert Allen and David Garlan. A Formal Basis for Architectural Connection. *ACM Transactions on Software Engineering and Methodology*, July 1997.
2. Mark Astley and Gul A. Agha. Customization and Composition of Distributed Objects: Middleware Abstractions for Policy Management. *ACM Software Engineering Notes*, 23(6):1–9, 1998.
3. Lodewijk Bergmans. *Composing Concurrent Objects - Applying Composition Filters for the Development And Reuse of Concurrent Object-Oriented Programming*. PhD thesis, Department of Computer Science, University of Twente, The Netherlands, 1994.
4. S. T. Carvalho. Integrating Design Patterns in Software Architectures. Research report, IC/UFF, Brazil, 1999. In Portuguese.
5. Walter Cazzola, Andrea Savigni, Andrea Sosio, and Francesco Tisato. Architectural Reflection: Concepts, Design, and Evaluation. Technical Report RI-DSI 234-99, DSI, University degli Studi di Milano, May 1999. Available at `http://www.disi.unige.it/person/CazzolaW/references.html`.
6. Shigeru Chiba. A Meta-Object Protocol for C++. In *Proceedings of the 10th Annual Conference on Object-Oriented Programming Systems, Languages, and Applications (OOPSLA'95)*, volume 30 of *Sigplan Notices*, pages 285–299, Austin, Texas, USA, October 1995. ACM.
7. Jean-Charles Fabre, Vincent Nicomette, Tanguy Pérennou, Robert J. Stroud, and Zhixue Wu. Implementing Fault Tolerant Applications Using Reflective Object-Oriented Programming. In *Proceedings of FTCS-25 "Silver Jubilee"*, Pasadena, CA USA, June 1995. IEEE.
8. Joni Fraga, Carlos A. Maziero, Lau Cheuk Lung, and Orlando G. Loques. Implementing Replicated Services in Open Systems Using a Reflective Approach. In *Proceedings of the Third International Symposium on Autonomous Decentralized Systems*, pages 273–280, Berlin, Germany, 1997.
9. Svend Frølund and Jari Koistinen. Quality-of-Service Specification in Distributed Object Systems. *Distributed Systems Engineering Journal*, 5:179–202, 1998.

10. Eric Gamma, Richard Helm, Ralph Johnson, and Richard Vlissides. *Design Patterns: Elements of Reusable Object-Oriented Software*. Addison-Wesley. Reading, MA, 1994.

11. Michael Gölm. Design and Implementation of a Meta Architecture for Java. Master's thesis, University of Erlangen-Nurnberg, Germany, January 1997.

12. Richard Helm, Ian Holland, and Dipayan Gangopadhyay. Contracts: Specifying Behavioral Compositions in Object-Oriented Systems. In *Proceedings of OOPSLA'90*, pages 303–311, October 1990.

13. Gregor Kiczales and Cristina Videira Lopes. Aspect-Oriented Programming with AspectJ. Xerox Parc http://www.parc.xerox.com/aop, 1998.

14. Fabio Kon and Roy H. Campbell. Supporting Automatic Configuration of Component-Based Distributed Systems. In *Proceedings of the 5th USENIX Conference on Object-Oriented Technologies and Systems*, San Diego, CA, USA, 1999.

15. Jeff Kramer and Jeff Magee. The Evolving Philosophers Problem: Dynamic Change Management. *IEEE Transactions on Software Engineering*, 16(11):1293–1306, 1991.

16. Jeff Kramer and Jeff Magee. Dynamic Structure in Software Architectures. In *Proceedings of the Fourth ACM Sigsoft Symposium On Foundations of Software Engineering*, California, USA, October 1996.

17. Jeff Kramer and Jeff Magee. Exposing the Skeleton in the Coordination Closet. In *Proceedings of Coordination'97*, Berlin, Germany, 1997.

18. John Lamping. The Interaction of Components and Aspects. In Cristina Videira Lopes, Kim Mens, Bedir Tekinerdogan, and Gregor Kiczales, editors, *Proceedings of ECOOP Aspect-Oriented Programming Workshop*, page June, Finland, 1997.

19. Marcelo Lobosco. R-RIO: A Java Environment for Supporting Evolving Distributed Systems. M.sc. dissertation, IC/UFF, Brazil, 1999.

20. Cristina Videira Lopes. *D: A Language Framework for Distributed Programming*. PhD thesis, College of Computer Science, Northeastern University, November 1997.

21. Cristina Videira Lopes, Kim Mens, Bedir Tekinerdogan, and Gregor Kiczales. Proceedings of ECOOP Aspect-Oriented Programming Workshop. Finland, June 1997.

22. Orlando Loques, Rodrigo A. Botafogo, and Julius Leite. A Configuration Approach for Distributed Object-Oriented System Customization. In *Proceedings of the Third International IEEE Workshop on Object-Oriented Real-Time Dependable Systems*, pages 185–189, Newport Beach, USA, 1997.

23. Orlando Loques, Julius Leite, and Vinicio E. Carrera. Parallel-Programming Environment. *IEEE Concurrency*, 6(1):47–56, 1998.

24. David C. Luckham, Larry M. Augustin, John J. Kenney, James Veera, Doug Bryan, and Walter Mann. Specification and Analysis of System Architecture Using Rapide. *IEEE Transactions on Software Engineering*, SE-21:336–355, April 1995. Special Issue on Software Architecture.

25. V. V. Malucelli. Babel - Building Applications by Evolution. M.sc dissertation (in portuguese), DEE / PUC-RJ, Rio de Janeiro, Brazil, 1996.

26. Frank Matthijs, Wouter Joosen, Bart Vanhaute, Bert Robben, and Pierre Verbaeten. Aspects Should Not Die. In Cristina Videira Lopes, Kim Mens, Bedir Tekinerdogan, and Gregor Kiczales, editors, *Proceedings of ECOOP Aspect-Oriented Programming Workshop*, page June, Finland, 1997.

27. Nenad Medvidovic. *Architecture-Based Specification-Time Software Evolution*. PhD thesis, University of California, Irvine, 1999.

28. Alexandre Oliva and Luiz Eduardo Buzato. Composition of Meta-Objects in Guaraná. In Shigeru Chiba and Jean-Charles Fabre, editors, *Proceedings of OOPSLA Workshop on Reflective Programming in C++ and Java*, pages 86–90, Vancouver, Canada, November 1998.

29. Pierre-Guillaume Raverdy, Robert Le Van Gong, and Rodger Lea. DART: A Reflective Middleware for Adaptive Application. In Shigeru Chiba and Jean-Charles Fabre, editors, *Proceedings of OOPSLA Workshop on Reflective Programming in C++ and Java*, pages 37–45, Vancouver, Canada, November 1998.

30. Jerome H. Saltzer, David P. Reed, and David D. Clark. End-to-End Arguments in System Design. In *Proceedings of 2nd Int'l Conference on Distributed Computing Systems*, pages 509–512, Paris, France, April 1981.

31. Mary Shaw, Robert DeLine, Daniel V. Klein, Theodore L. Ross, David M. Young, and Gregory Zelesnik. Abstractions for Software Architecture and Tools to Support Them. *Transaction on Software Engineering*, 21(4):314–335, 1995.

32. Alexandre Sztajnberg. *Flexibility and Separation of Concerns in Distributed Systems*. PhD thesis, COPPE/UFRJ, Rio de Janeiro, Brazil, 1999.

33. Robbert van Renesse, Kenneth P. Birman, and Silvano Maffeis. Horus: A Flexible Group Communication System. *Communications of the ACM*, 39(4):76–83, April 1996.

34. Peter Wegner. Interoperability. *ACM Computing Surveys*, 28(1):285–287, 1996.

35. Ian Welch and Robert J. Stroud. Dalang - A Reflective Java Extension. In Shigeru Chiba and Jean-Charles Fabre, editors, *Proceedings of OOPSLA Workshop on Reflective Programming in C++ and Java*, pages 11–15, Vancouver, Canada, November 1998.

CARP@ – A Reflection Based Tool for Observing Jini Services

Michael Fahrmair, Chris Salzmann, and Maurice Schoenmakers

Technische Universität München
Institut für Informatik
D-80290 München, Germany
{fahrmair | salzmann | schoenma}@in.tum.de

Abstract Jini[TM] offers the basic technology to develop distributed systems where the participating clients, services and their interactions can adapt dynamically to a changing environment.[1] To monitor the internal processes in such a system a reflection mechanism is necessary. However, the existing reflection mechanisms in Java emerged to be too weak to supply enough information for a suitable management of such a system. Therefore these mechanisms had to be extended by a reflective meta level upon Jini. The tool CARP@ (implemented itself as Jini system) is designed to visualize, analyze and control dynamic and distributed Jini systems. This is done by developing a meta architecture upon a Jini system that reflects the running Jini system.
This paper describes the meta architecture, the tool to monitor it and reports the gained experiences together with their implied consequences.

Keywords: Dynamic Systems, Reflection, Distributed Systems, Jini, Tool Support

1 Introduction

The areas and complexity of applications where computer systems are used is growing constantly. More and more devices are controlled by computers, and with a spreading Internet more and more computers are interconnected. The advantage is an ubiquitous available network. This leads to a demand for benefits of the emerging new possibilities. The problem is that the network of communicating components tends to become more dynamic and less controllable. Whereas conventional distributed systems were built upon *static* middleware like CORBA [9] or DCOM [11] (i.e. the concrete wiring between the components was set up by the programmer), new *dynamic* middleware like Sun's Jini [33,2] offers a more flexible way of self-organizing distributed systems. Here the system itself takes care of the concrete wiring, since the components spontaneously find, link and cooperate together during runtime.

---

[1] Jini and all Jini-based marks are trademarks or registered trademarks of Sun Microsystems, Inc. in the U.S. and other countries.

W. Cazzola et al. (Eds.): Reflection and Software Engineering, LNCS 1826, pp. 209–227, 2000.

These dynamic systems are characterized by the following two properties:

- The systems are *distributed*: A system consists of multiple active participants that are interacting to perform a certain task. This interaction is achieved by communication between them. As a consequence the system has to cope with a distributed management of resources.

- The systems are *dynamic*: The architecture, i.e. the presence of the components, their arrangement and their interconnections, but also the roles they take (as e.g. *client* or *server*) are changing during the runtime of the system. Due to the need for a high availability of systems it is often no longer possible to stop or interrupt them for a reconfiguration.

Jini is the first product that claims to exhibit those dynamic features. It offers interfaces and mechanisms for components to announce their own abilities, to look for services of other components and use these in a dynamic network of interacting components.

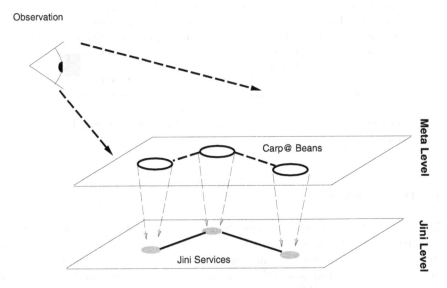

Fig. 1. Observing a Jini system via its CARP@ meta level.

Using Jini, it is now possible to develop dynamic, distributed systems in a comfortable way. But a lot of the interaction going on in a Jini system is hidden. A user for example, is not able to see any of the complex interaction of self connecting services (The interaction is roughly sketched in figure 3). Observable from outside are only two services that find each other and communicate or do not. On the one hand, it is of course desirable to keep things transparent if a developer wants to focus on the intended application he is creating. But on the other hand, it should be possible to watch and analyze these hidden interactions if something goes wrong (for debugging) or is inefficient. Without any tools it is not possible to see who is using a particular service. Especially when wireless spontaneous network technologies like Bluetooth [4] are used in future, it will be difficult to track down who is using a service and therefore hard to collect the necessary information for billing etc.

The tool CARP@ (pronounced *Carpet*) [6] was developed to watch and visualize a network consisting of several Jini components, together with the possibility to manage such a system, both at runtime. The ability to retrieve necessary information is gained by introducing a reflective meta level architecture. In this paper, we present CARP@, its reflective architecture and the results gained. The project was performed in a one semester period with a dozen of graduate students and the authors.

Reflection is known as a technique where a system can reason about itself [30] [22]. Therefore a description of the system itself, a meta description, is created at runtime. This process is called *reification*[16]. The system itself is unaware of the existence of the meta description. Furthermore this description is linked to the system in such a way that any change that is performed on the description is *reflected* to changes of system and vice-versa.

This is exactly what we wanted to achieve by the the CARP@ tool. However using the normal introspection as used in Java turned out to be not enough. Since Java offers a detailed reflection mechanism in the `java.lang.reflection` package [13], the dynamically discovered services of a Jini system can publish their interfaces via reflection and therefore interact with previously unknown objects. However to visualize the full interaction between Jini clients and services, the internal mechanisms and procedures in the system have to be accessible via reflection as well.

Another problem we faced, is that at runtime only collections of objects and remote references exist. In our opinion this information is to fine grained to extract a meaningful overview about the interconnected services of a complex system. What is needed more is an architectural overview on a higher level of abstraction. The classical reflection is thus extended here to an architectural level like in [7] and is furthermore extracted at runtime using the dynamic middleware, as this middleware makes the architectural design explicit in the implemented system.

The real goal lies in the ability to alternate the systems architecture by changing the architectural description of the system. To reach this goal probably other runtime classes must be used instead of the current Jini ones, because these are not able to perform all changes. For example an object migration at runtime from one location to another [32].

So the reification process includes two steps. First it uses normal reflection techniques to create a representation of the runtime objects as they actually appear. Next, it realizes a dynamic mapping of collections of these runtime objects to combine them to an architectural model with communicating service units. The model the user works with is thus not the meta model of the Java language, instead it is an implementation independent architectural model of communicating services.

Our paper is structured as follows: In the following subsection we give a brief description of Jini. In the second major section we analyze dynamic distributed systems in general and describe an implementation independent meta model to describe these systems. This model is then mapped to Jini systems in section 2.2. In the third section we describe our tool CARP@, including the design, the implementation of the meta model mapping, and the usage of the tool itself. We then close with an outlook on future work in the last section.

1.1   Jini: A Platform for Dynamic Services

Jini is a specification of a framework [3,12] , developed by Sun, that builds upon Java 1.2 and exists so far as a reference implementation that is based on RMI (see figure 2) [19]. Jini offers mechanisms to dynamically discover, link and invoke distributed objects. Since RMI also offers code migration, Jini is therefore able to discover objects dynamically, migrate them and execute them. Besides some internal mechanisms in the Java language, which won't be covered in this paper, it exists basically of a set of standardized interfaces and procedures, that handle the dynamic discovering, binding and introspection.

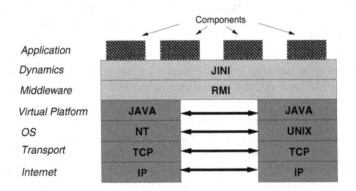

Fig. 2. The layers of a Jini system.

The following example illustrates a simple Jini scenario: in figure 3 a printer service is contacting the local lookup service. After sending its service description – "print service, color, 600 dpi" – the lookup service enrolls it into its local service directory. Now a camera service is contacting the lookup service and asks for a printing service. The lookup service returns the service proxy containing a reference to the printing service which is then used by the camera to print its pictures. Note that the different service components are completely independently developed, and the wiring is done completely dynamically by the system.

The most complex part of Jini is the discovering of new components. Each Jini component – a so called Jini *service* – contacts the local *lookup services* after entering a new subnet. A lookup service is, similar to the CORBA naming service, a unique component that holds a directory of the available services. After contacting a lookup service, it sends its service description to the lookup service that is enrolling the new service into its directory, according to the service description.

To participate in a Jini system, a component only needs to implement a few Jini interfaces. The wiring of the corresponding components is done on the fly by the system itself. Therefore it is possible that two components (previously unknown to each other) can dynamically build up a connection and interact, only via a preparatory agreement on the interfaces of the services needed. However, in this paper we do not cover this, but the internal meta-level of CARP@ and its reflection mechanisms.

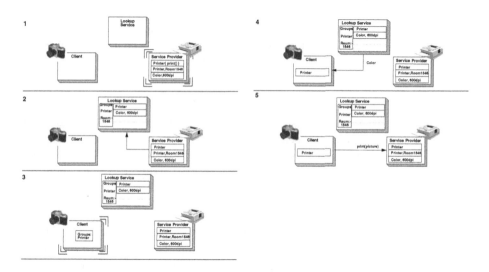

Fig. 3. The lookup scenario of a Jini service.

2   Dynamic Distributed Systems – Abstractions and Techniques

The type of systems we are dealing with in this paper are *dynamic distributed systems*. A well known abstraction of any kind of distributed systems is the existence of *components* and *connectors* [29], where a relation between these two sets assigns the components to connectors and therefore determines which components are able to communicate and how this is performed.

In ordinary distributed systems, e.g. a CORBA object system, this relation or *wiring* between components, is fixed, which means the relation is defined once at design time and expected to be constant during runtime. In dynamic distributed systems the wiring as well as the set of components is *not fixed*, in contrast they are expected to change frequently. This means that the communication structure between the components as well as the set of components itself is dynamically changing at runtime – some may come and some may go. The actual communication structure at runtime is thus unknown at design time.

There are numerous techniques provided by companies (SUN, Microsoft etc.) that offer middleware to develop systems with these characteristics. Jini, developed by Sun is besides its competitors like Microsoft's "Universal Plug and Play" (UPnP) [31] and Salutation [26] one of the most promising candidates.

However to understand an existing dynamic system, it is easier to have a more general implementation independent view on it without too many technical details. Therefore we define a model that captures the main characteristics of a dynamic system.

In this section we first give an implementation independent abstraction of dynamic systems and later on a mapping to Jini systems, which we also used for our tool.

2.1   Modeling Dynamic Distributed Systems in General

In this section we present a small model to describe dynamic distributed systems. The goal is to have a condensed description that allows us to express the configuration of a system in a very convenient way. Based on this model a designer or administrator may easily understand the system structure. When there is a consistent mapping then the system can be customized by performing changes on an abstract level.

This model is an abstract description and can be used independently of a concrete implementation like Jini. Each element in system implementations based on Jini, UPnP [31] or Salutation [26] may be mapped to elements of this model. But in the scope of this paper we will only look for a model to describe Jini related systems.

The model we have chosen to represent the service system in general is not based on classes and references but is an architectural model based on the idea of *components* and *connectors* [29,27] as used in the area of architecture description languages ADL's [23] like Darwin [24], Wright [1] or more recently also in the Catalysis approach [10].

Components encapsulate functional units and the connectors specify how these components are glued together. In general specific contracts or protocols are attached to connectors. These protocols describe the permissible messages and how the components will exchange them via the connectors. In our context a distributed system is modeled in a data flow oriented way , similar to other abstractions of distributed systems for example ROOM [28] and Dynamic Focus[18]. The latter is a formal model that is based on denotational semantics and streams.

Our model exists of *components*, *locations*, *ports* and *channels*. Components in our model are identifiable running units that perform some kind of computation. From an abstract point of view, dynamic systems consist mainly of service components, or services, which are components on the conceptual *system level* view and may differ from components on the *implementation level* (e.g. one service component may be implemented by a set of implementation components).

A service component usually provides thematically grouped functionality on the application level, whereas an implementation component provides a technical solution and even may register as more than one service component. So one can see services as logical components in contrast to the physical components that actually implement them.

Services of course need to be able to communicate with other services in some way in order to perform more complex tasks. Communication can be performed in many different ways. In short communication can be targeted or untargeted, synchronous or asynchronous. For targeted communication one might also distinguish between 1:1 and 1:n communication. Targeted communication also requires a service to 'know' its communication partner. This is accomplished in our model by introducing different types of so called *channels* as connectors between services.

As we want to describe distributed systems, there is also a need to specify a service *location*, that represents a platform (e.g. a JVM) on which the service is executed.

Bringing in dynamics we need further elements to describe our system in an abstract implementation independent way. Foremost services can come and go, which introduces no new problems as long as we just want to describe an actual appearance of our system. Next, the implementation of existing services can change transparently during runtime which is also no problem, because we only describe our system implementation independent, by distinguishing between service components and implementation components.

In a dynamic system in principle, but also in consequence of new services appearing or services leaving the system during runtime in an unspecified way, communication links (channels) must be established or cut during runtime, so there should be a possibility to find the right communication partner during runtime. This problem is solved by adding some kind of type information and selection criteria.

Type information of services is added by the new element *port*. Ports are points where a service component provides or requires a service interface. Ports are wired together by channels. Services can have multiple types for accepting communication i.e. messages from other services.

These ports are called *inPorts* and further specified according to the kind of communication they can handle:

– *interfaceInPorts* for single target communication
– *eventInPorts* for multi target communication

As broadcast communication does not require target information there are no channels for broadcasting and therefore no ports respectively.

The channels are directed which means that there has to be an equivalent to inPorts on the other end of the channel. This kind of port is called *outPort* and its existence (without a channel) indicates, that the service this kind of port is attached to 'knows' a certain type-information of other services and is able to communicate with them. An outPort with a channel attached to it indicates, that at the moment this service holds a target reference of another existing service of a given type and is ready to communicate or already communicating with this other service.

Like inPorts, outPorts are named according to the kind of communication they are used for (*interfaceOutPorts* and *eventOutPorts*).

Services without any interfaceInPort and with at least one interfaceOutPort are called *clients*. The interfaceOutPort indicates that a client may use a service. Services can have additional specification information which goes beyond type information that allows to further distinguish between services of the same type and therefore the same external interfaces. This additional service information is called *properties*. Properties can be everything from additional system structure information, like groups up to detailed functional and non functional specification of a service, e.g. vendor, language, security certificates, extra abilities like printing color and so on. Actual communication is done by sending *messages* over a channel.

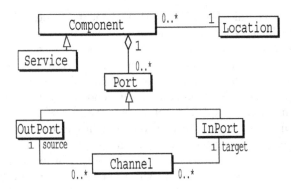

Fig. 4. A simplified meta model to describe the architectural elements.

Figure 4 shows a simplified UML class diagram [14,25,5] of the meta model that describes this architectural model. A model on an architectural level allows the use of related sets of class instances as single components and hides all the detailed auxiliary classes and objects that are typically used in Java to implement listeners, events and so on. Another advantage is that connectors, here represented by channels, are more abstract items than simple remote references. So by means of channels we can describe any kind of communication, like method calls, distributed events or even buffered event queues.

Figure 5 shows a graphical example for a snapshot of a system described in terms of the abstract model. The camera is a device or *location* that contains a *client*, called service browser. The service browser has found a printer service that is located on the printer device. The service browser created a *channel* using an UI *interfaceInPort* and sent the *message* "create GUI". The created printer GUI also established a channel to printer service and sent a "Print" message using a the more specific `Printer` *interfaceInPort*. Looking at the figure it becomes clear where clients and services are located, what participants are communicating with each other and what type of messages are used on each channel.

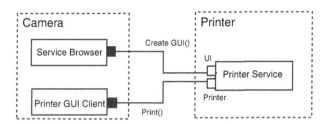

Fig. 5. An example for two clients using a service via different interfaces.

2.2   Modeling Jini Systems

Of course we want to extract and visualize real systems, so a concrete mapping between our abstract system model and the middleware technique that is used (e.g. Jini, UPnP, Salutation) is needed. For the purpose of this paper we stick with Jini, although it is also possible to map the abstraction on any other of the mentioned products.

A *service* component in Jini is the component for which a service proxy is registered at a lookup service. Looking back at our example from section 1.1 and figure 3 this would correspond to the printer service.

Each public interface of the registered service proxy represents an a single *interfaceInPort*. In our example this could be the interfaceInport `printer` that represents a public interface called e.g. `PrintingServiceInterface` with a method like `public void print(PrintData pd)`.

Clients are service components that do not actually register themselves to provide interfaces but instead are able to hold at least one reference to another service interfaceInPort.

Clients of services in Jini get in contact with services via the lookup service. After downloading a service proxy they cast the reference to a known interface type. Each used interface type represents a single *interfaceOutPort*. A *channel* exists as soon as the reference to a service is not null.

Again looking at our example, the camera software component would be a client with one interfaceOutPort called e.g. `PrintingServiceInterface` which means, that the camera component has got a reference like `PrintingService-Interface printer` and is able to invoke the method `print`. As soon as the client has found an instance of the required interface with the help of the lookup service and downloaded the necessary proxy object, a channel between in- and outPort `PrintServiceInterface` exists.

EventInPorts are implementations of `RemoteEventListener` interfaces and *eventOutPorts* are containers holding remote references to these listeners. In our example, the camera client could implement a listener interface to receive 'out of paper' messages which would add an eventInPort to the client. The print service of course would have to hold references to possible message receivers of this event in a container, for example a `Vector` which would result in an additional eventOutPort attached to this service.

The *location* of a service is the network address of the machine were the component is located that registered the service object or represents the client. In the example this would be the IP-address of the VM host that runs the print service respectively the camera client.

Messages are all method calls that correspond to the interface determined by the inPort, in our example calls to `print` or `outOfPaper`.

Properties can be directly mapped to Jini's attributes. Jini attributes are grouped in so called entries. In the printer example 'color, 600dpi' or 'room 1546' would be entries that further describe the ability and location of the print service and can be used to distinguish between multiple services that all implement the same interface `PrintingServiceInterface`.

Table 1 summarizes the mapping between the Jini middleware implementation and our abstract model described in section 2.1.

Table 1. Mapping to abstract model for Jini.

Abstraction	Jini
Service	Component registered in lookup service
Client	Component with reference to service
InterfaceInPort	Implemented `Interface` of service
EventInPort	Implemented `RemoteListener` of service or client
InterfaceOutPort	Reference to a service-interface
EventOutPort	Container of references to `RemoteListener`
Channel	Not null port reference
Message	Method call
Location	IP-address of VM-host
Property	Jini attributes, groups

3   Carp@ - A Tool to Visualize Dynamic Distributed Systems

In this section, we describe the prototype implementation (section 3.1) of the tool Carp@, which might be of interest, because the prototype was implemented as a dynamic distributed system itself.

Carp@ is a tool to observe, administer and manage a dynamic network of Jini components with all their communication relationships at runtime. In a dynamic ad hoc networking environment, the concrete architecture evolves during runtime. Decisions like choosing an implementation for a component or deciding a communication structure are not done at design time but at runtime. Therefore in our opinion there exists an increased need to extract an architecture description at runtime. This description can then be used to decide about the effect of changes. See the previous section for a detailed description of the abstract system model being used.

Carp@ goes beyond showing simple Jini-services like other browsers do and shows additional important information (like locations, channels and messages) that is not available otherwise, but is needed to understand the interaction in a Jini system. All this information is gathered by Carp@ at runtime mainly by reflection. How this is done is described in more detail in section 3.2. Finally we describe briefly the general usage of the tool (section 3.3).

3.1   System Architecture

The Carp@-system itself has been designed as a dynamic system using Jini services as its main components, so that it is possible both to manage Carp@ with itself and to extend it during runtime. An example snapshot template of the dynamic architecture is shown in figure 6 with service dependencies from top to bottom.

The meta-level contains all Carp@ services being involved with gathering, manipulation and storage of information about the observed application system. The Carp@ core system consists of two services assigned to this level, the report-service and the meta-model-service. The report-service gathers basic information pieces, both by querying special meta-level objects, called carpat beans (see figure 6 and Section 3.2) and standard Jini-services, about the observed application ranging from very simple ones, like name and attributes of its services up to complex system structure information like exchanged messages, communication channels or interface ports. All these pieces are stored in the meta-model service that contains a Carp@-internal model of the observed application system (see the meta architecture in section 2.1) built up from the gathered information. This model might be just displayed by a simple view-service (following the MVC-principle [17]) assigned to Carp@'s application layer or used to actually manage the observed system by using an extensive console application which might furthermore use specialized management services to actually control the observed application system's services e.g. by setting their attributes, changing their names or doing some configuration (figure 6).

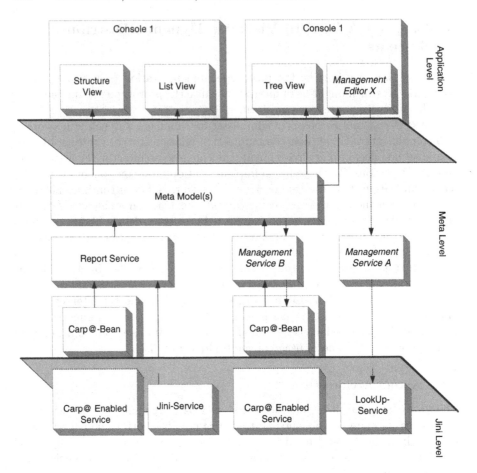

Fig. 6. The model collects and propagates data gained by reflection to the user interface views.

3.2 Getting the System Model of a Jini System by Reflection

Having a mapping (see section 2.2) between Jini elements and our abstract system model (as described in section 2.1) that we want to visualize is not enough. Because we are in a dynamic environment, things can change in not predefined ways which means that we have to gather most of the necessary information at runtime to constantly 'feed' our system model.

The basic technique of CARP@ is to find out as much as possible about the system by reflection and other system describing sources. We believe that before a system can be changed at runtime, the first step is to understand and to observe it at runtime. An administrator can then manipulate the system through the model he retrieved by introspection (shown in figure 6). These changes on the meta level are then reflected in the system's runtime behavior.

However, normal Jini-services, clients and standard reflection techniques in Java cannot yet deliver the additional information that is required to observe locations, channels and e.g. memory usage. Therefore CARP@ contains a special component model, called *carpat beans*. These bean components have to be created by the programmer and extract as much interaction as possible through reflection. To make a Jini service or client fully observable by CARP@, the programmer also has to notify them about changes that cannot be detected by standard reflection. So in short some simple programming guidelines have to be fulfilled by the programmer to get full observation possibilities.

Figure 7 illustrates the techniques used to create the architectural description of the system. The carpat beans use the standard Java reflection techniques and maintain additional information, like keeping track of used services. All gained information is then transformed and interpreted as changes in terms of the meta model. To make method calls observable as well as to track the transfer of mobile objects like service proxies we used code instrumentation. This instrumentation is done until now on the source code level but will in future be performed on the fly on the class file before the class is loaded. This way also services for which no source code is available can be observed. Byte code instrumentation requires reflection techniques based on class files unlike the standard Java reflection that can be performed only on loaded class files.

Special runtime classes deliver information like the location of a component or they keep track of the called methods. This can be used to measure the number of calls or to create message sequence diagrams [25,5].

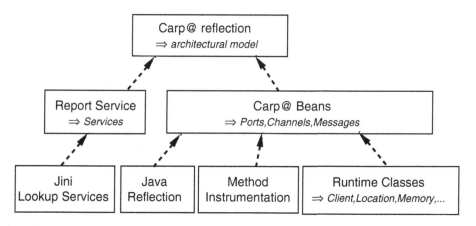

Fig. 7. Different techniques used to create an architectural description on the meta level.

In the following paragraphs we now examine in detail, which information can be retrieved by standard Java reflection mechanisms, which can be obtained by additional Jini reflection and which cannot be gained by both of them.

Components

Components i.e. Jini services or clients are of course the most complex part of an dynamic system to manage, so a lot of information has to be reflected from different sources:

- Location cannot be discovered by standard reflection (see the paragraph about locations below)
- Groups & attributes can be discovered with Jini by querying the lookup service entries.
- Operation information (like consumed memory) cannot be retrieved in a device independent way at the moment.
- Ports, channels and messages are detected by CARP@-reflection

To gather all necessary information about service components, a CARP@ bean has to be created for each new service. The service has to implement an additional CARP@ bean access-interface and aggregate the created bean.

```
    public class Service implements CarpatBeanInterface, ...
private ServiceCarpatBeanable carpatBeanService;
private com.sun.jini.lookup.JoinManager joinManager = null;
    ...
```

The CARP@-bean itself is a Jini service and registers at nearby lookup-services so it is possible to observe Jini clients that do not usually register themselves and therefore could not be detected otherwise.

Remember that although for now the programmer has to do this code instrumentation on the source code level, in future it will be performed automatically on the class file before the class is loaded.

Locations

As said before (section 2.2), locations are mapped to network addresses, in this case IP addresses. At the moment there is no method to discover locations directly by Java or Jini reflection, but there are indirect methods to get at least the IP-address of a virtual machine (VM) if there are active objects running on it, nevertheless it is not possible to detect locations where no service is executed.

Further information about locations like for example device descriptions, physical location information or operation information like used and free memory, workload etc. also cannot be gathered by standard Java or Jini reflection without further effort. Some of it could be retrieved via attribute descriptions of running Jini services, which might contain information about the location a service is running in. Other information can only be retrieved by special reflection services that bridge locally or network wide available information from e.g. network management systems or device dependent drivers into the Jini infrastructure.

InPorts

InPorts are in general, as described in section 2.2, implemented interfaces. The necessary information can be gathered by standard Java reflection.

OutPorts

OutPort detection works similar to the detection of inPorts, but cannot be done with standard Java reflection, because the attributes in question might be located in inner classes. Therefore the CARP@ bean has to be notified by calling

`public void newInterfaceOutPort(Object obj, Class portClass)` or
`public void removeInterfaceOutPort(Object obj, Class portClass)`
respectively.

Channels and Messages

Contrary to static information like implemented interfaces, channels and messages are dynamic information in that channels are only valid as long the field corresponding to the channels outPort is not null and method calls of course could only be observed as long as the called method has not finished.

Channels could be detected by standard Java reflection by polling the eligible outPort representing fields , but apart from being not very accurate in an distributed environment this would moreover generate a lot of network traffic and would therefore be quite a performance bottleneck.

So it seems to be better to introduce new reflection mechanisms by generating an event each time the reference to another service is set. Same thing applies to messages because there is no standard or Jini reflection mechanism to trace method calls. Both is done by calling the corresponding CARP@-bean methods `newChannel` and `removeChannel`, respectively `messageCallSent`, `messageCallReceived` and `messageCallExecuted` whenever a remote reference is set or a method called. Method-calls are tracked with three different instrumentations to gather all necessary information for recording message sequence charts.

Summary

Summarizing all the facts one can see that with standard Java reflection it is only possible to get static information about our dynamic system, whereas Jini does only have dynamic reflection capabilities as far as the retrievable information is used by standard Jini middleware infrastructure components itself, like names of groups and attributes, but no further dynamic information about application systems.

3.3   Using CARP@

CARP@ is quite easy to use. In a running Jini system the user can start the model service. It will investigate and collect data about all services, that are found in all reachable lookup services. The model is constantly updated at runtime.

To see the information about the Jini system that is collected in the model service, the user starts the graphical user interface client and can browse through the system as figure 8 shows. Multiple clients may exist and are notified constantly about changes while the structure of the Jini system evolves.

The user interface allows the user to browse through the system to watch all relevant data and to open up different alternative views.

The most intuitive view is the *structure view*. It shows a graphical representation of the collaboration in a Jini system in a ROOM [28] like notation. While the Jini system is running, all the views are constantly updated and show the

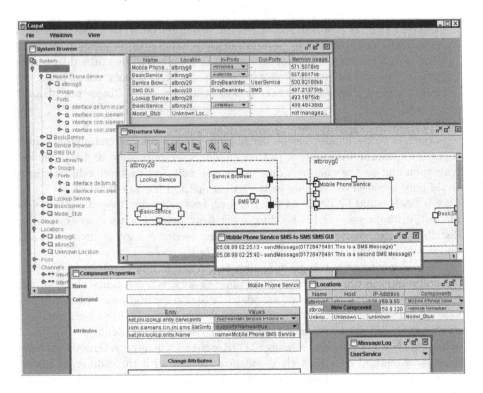

Fig. 8. The CARP@ system running.

current situation. When a new Jini service participates in the system (for example because somebody started it in the network watched by CARP@) it simply pops up as a box. When a Jini service disappears, for example because the service leaves the network, it will be shown grayed and will finally be removed. The graphical layout is automatically performed but can be manually influenced.

Besides the graphical representation in the structure view, CARP@ shows detailed information in various lists. Here the user can see not only the memory consumed by a location, but also conventional Jini information. For example there is a group list, that shows the groups, where a service joins at. Jini attributes, that describe the services, are also visualized.

With CARP@ the user can of course not only show all this information, but can also *administer* the Jini system by adding, changing and removing Jini groups and attributes.

Besides simple administration CARP@ has *management functionality* like starting or stopping Jini components on remote locations, which is very comfortable when more complex test scenarios have to be set up or when the performance with multiple clients has to be tested. Furthermore the ability of forcing a component to migrate to a certain location is in work. This feature is provided for testing purposes concerning the best deployment of Jini components over the network.

Besides illustration of system internals we used the tool so far for debugging purposes. Especially for a self-adapting system like Jini it is essential, that under certain conditions the system designer is able to comprehend the internal actions. But also for purposes of billing the reflective model of CARP@ is useful: especially in an ad-hoc environment the use of services should be logged, which is easy with a reflective model.

4   Conclusion and Future Work

In this paper we presented CARP@, a management tool for dynamic Jini systems. We used CARP@ in a Jini project and the observation abilities were found very useful for the design and testing phase of dynamic systems.

It is still somewhat unclear how an exact mapping between the implementation components and the service components should be defined. So where should be the boundary around a collection of small objects like a service objects and several different listener objects to view them as one single component or connector? The model and its mapping could also be extended to contain different standard connector types. For example the use of Javaspaces as buffered asynchronous channels [15].

Another open issue is the definition of system situations where it is "save" to modify the configuration of a system. How should constrains be defined and enforced that define that it is save to perform a change? Examples of the configuration changes would be changing the location of a service, exchanging a service implementation or changing the wiring between components on the fly at runtime. More generalized solutions to these problems would be more satisfying.

CARP@ is now available in its first beta version [6]. Future work includes the creation of additional views like message sequence charts [21] to visualize the message trace for dedicated parts of a Jini system. Other work will include more specific administrative views for lookup services and Java spaces. The management of Jini systems, like migration of services at runtime, and their definition within Sun's new management platform Jiro [20], will be other areas to investigate. Furthermore the similarities and dissimilarities between Jini and other dynamic middleware like Salutation [26] and UPnP [31] should be investigated and the abstractions including the reflective architectural meta model should be adapted.

However, making a Jini service or client fully observable by inserting code at the source code level is too restrictive. Currently we are working on an integration of a class file transformer that instruments the code at runtime on a bytecode level. Tools like JOIE [8] and new Java JDK 1.3 reflection techniques will be used for this. The advantage is that also components where no source code is available can be observed completely. The byte code transformation is done with reflective techniques based on the meta information contained in the class file. Because the code must be changed before it is loaded, normal Java reflection can not be used. But before observability can be achieved completely automatically the mapping mentioned above must be defined.

Acknowledgments. We would like to thank Max Breitling and Wolfgang Schwerin for valuable comments and the whole CARP@ team for a lot of overtime work.

References

1. Robert Allen and David Garlan. A Formal Basis for Architectural Connection. *ACM Transactions on Software Engineering and Methodology*, July 1997.
2. Ken Arnold. The Jini Architecture: Dynamic Services in a Flexible Network. In *Proceedings of the 36th ACM/IEEE Conference on Design Automation*, 1999.
3. Ken Arnold, Bryan O'Sullivan, Robert W. Scheifler, Jim Waldo, and Ann Wollrath. *The Jini^{TM} Specification*. Addison-Wesley, 1999.
4. Specification of the Bluetooth System v1.0A. http://www.bluetooth.com/, July 1999.
5. Grady Booch, James Rumbaugh, and Ivar Jacobson. *The Unified Modeling Language User Guide*. Object Technology Series. Addison-Wesley, Reading, Massachussetts 01867, 3 edition, February 1999.
6. CARP@ Homepage. http://www4.in.tum.de/~carpat/.
7. Walter Cazzola, Andrea Savigni, Andrea Sosio, and Francesco Tisato. Architectural Reflection: Concepts, Design, and Evaluation. Technical Report RI-DSI 234-99, DSI, University degli Studi di Milano, May 1999. Available at http://www.disi.unige.it/person/CazzolaW/references.html.
8. Geoff A. Cohen, Jeffrey S. Chase, and David L. Kaminsky. Automatic Program Transformation with JOIE. In *Proceedings of USENIX Annual technical Symposium 98*, 1998.
9. CORBA Homepage. http://www.omg.org/corba/.
10. Desmond F. D'Souza and Alan Cameron Wills. *Objects, Components, and Frameworks with UML – The Catalysis Approach*. Addison Wesley, Reading, Mass., 1999.
11. Guy Eddon and Henry Eddon. *Inside Distributed COM*. Microsoft Press, 1998.
12. W. Keith Edwards. *Core Jini*. Prentice Hall, 1999.
13. David Flanagan. *JAVA in a Nutshell*. O'Reilly & Associates, Inc., 1996.
14. Martin Fowler and Kendall Scott. *UML Distilled*. Addison Wesley, New York, 1997.
15. Eric Freeman, Susanne Hupfer, and Ken Arnold. *JavaSpaces^{TM} Principles, Patterns, and Practice*. Addison Wesley, 1999.
16. Daniel Friedman and Mitchell Wand. Reification: Reflection Without Metaphysics. In *Proceedings of ACM Conference on Lisp and Functional Programming*, Austin, Texas, USA, 1984. ACM.
17. Eric Gamma, Richard Helm, Ralph Johnson, and Richard Vlissides. *Design Patterns: Elements of Reusable Object-Oriented Software*. Addison-Wesley. Reading, MA, 1994.
18. Ursula Hinkel and Katharina Spies. Anleitung zur Spezifikation von Mobilen, Dynamischen FOCUS-Netzen. Technical Report TUM-I9639, Munich University of Technology, 1996. German.

19. Jini 1.0. http://developer.java.sun.com/developer/products/jini/, November 1999.
20. Federated Management Architecture Specification Version 1.0. http://www.jiro.com, November 1999.
21. Ingolf Krüger. Towards the Methodical Usage of Message Sequence Charts. In Katharina Spies and Bernhard Schätz, editors, *Formale Beschreibungstechniken für verteilte Systeme. FBT99*, 9. GI/ITG Fachgespräch, pages 123–134. Herbert Utz Verlag, June 1999.
22. Pattie Maes. Concepts and Experiments in Computational Reflection. In *Proceedings of the Conference on Object-Orientated Programming Systems, Languages and Applications (OOPSLA'87)*, 1987.
23. Neno Medvidovic. A Classification and Comparison Framework for Software Architecture Description Languages. Technical Report UCI-ICS-97-02, Department of Information and Computer Science, University of California, Irvine, feb 1996.
24. Matthias Radestock and Susan Eisenbach. Formalizing System Structure. In *Int. Workshop on Software Specification and Design*, pages 95–104. IEEE Computer Society Press, 1996.
25. James Rumbaugh, Ivar Jacobson, and Grady Booch. *The Unified Modeling Language Reference Manual*. Addison Wesley, Reading, Mass., 1999.
26. Salutation Architecture Specification V2.0c. http://www.salutation.org/, June 1999.
27. Chris Salzmann and Maurice Schoenmakers. Dynamics and Mobility in Software Architecture. In Jan Bosch, editor, *Proceedings of NOSA 99 – Second Nordic Workshop on Software Architecture*, 1999.
28. Bran Selic, Garth Gullekson, and Paul T. Ward. *Real–Time Object Oriented Modeling*. Wiley & Sons, 1994.
29. Mary Shaw and David Garlan. *Software Architecture – Perspectives on an Emerging Discipline*. Prentice Hall, 1996.
30. Brian C. Smith. Reflection and Semantics in a Procedural Language, 1982.
31. Universal Plug and Play – Device Architecture Reference Specification Version 0.90. http://www.upnp.org/, November 1999.
32. Voyager Overview. http://www.objectspace.com/, 1999.
33. Jim Waldo. The Jini Architecture for Network-Centric Computing. *Communications of the ACM (CAM)*, 1999.

Author Index

Lecture Notes in Computer Science

For information about Vols. 1–1760
please contact your bookseller or Springer-Verlag

Vol. 1803: S. Cagnoni et al. (Eds.), Real-World Applications and Evolutionary Computing. Proceedings, 2000. XII, 396 pages. 2000.

Vol. 1805: T. Terano, H. Liu, A.L.P. Chen (Eds.), Knowledge Discovery and Data Mining. Proceedings, 2000. XIV, 460 pages. 2000. (Subseries LNAI).

Vol. 1806: W. van der Aalst, J. Desel, A. Oberweis (Eds.), Business Process Management. VIII, 391 pages. 2000.

Vol. 1807: B. Preneel (Ed.), Advances in Cryptology – EUROCRYPT 2000. Proceedings, 2000. XVIII, 608 pages. 2000.

Vol. 1810: R.López de Mántaras, E. Plaza (Eds.), Machine Learning: ECML 2000. Proceedings, 2000. XII, 460 pages. 2000. (Subseries LNAI).

Vol. 1811: S.W. Lee, H.. Bülthoff, T. Poggio (Eds.), Biologically Motivated Computer Vision. Proceedings, 2000. XIV, 656 pages. 2000.

Vol. 1813: P.L. Lanzi, W. Stolzmann, S.W. Wilson (Eds.), Learning Classifier Systems. X, 349 pages. 2000. (Subseries LNAI).

Vol. 1815: G. Pujolle, H. Perros, S. Fdida, U. Körner, I. Stavrakakis (Eds.), Networking 2000 – Broadband Communications, High Performance Networking, and Performance of Communication Networks. Proceedings, 2000. XX, 981 pages. 2000.

Vol. 1816: T. Rus (Ed.), Algebraic Methodology and Software Technology. Proceedings, 2000. XI, 545 pages. 2000.

Vol. 1817: A. Bossi (Ed.), Logic-Based Program Synthesis and Transformation. Proceedings, 1999. VIII, 313 pages. 2000.

Vol. 1818: C.G. Omidyar (Ed.), Mobile and Wireless Communications Networks. Proceedings, 2000. VIII, 187 pages. 2000.

Vol. 1819: W. Jonker (Ed.), Databases in Telecommunications. Proceedings, 1999. X, 208 pages. 2000.

Vol. 1821: R. Loganantharaj, G. Palm, M. Ali (Eds.), Intelligent Problem Solving. Proceedings, 2000. XVII, 751 pages. 2000. (Subseries LNAI).

Vol. 1822: H.H. Hamilton, Advances in Artificial Intelligence. Proceedings, 2000. XII, 450 pages. 2000. (Subseries LNAI).

Vol. 1823: M. Bubak, H. Afsarmanesh, R. Williams, B. Hertzberger (Eds.), High Performance Computing and Networking. Proceedings, 2000. XVIII, 719 pages. 2000.

Vol. 1824: J. Palsberg (Ed.), Static Analysis. Proceedings, 2000. VIII, 433 pages. 2000.

Vol. 1825: M. Nielsen, D. Simpson (Eds.), Application and Theory of Petri Nets 2000. Proceedings, 2000. XI, 485 pages. 2000.

Vol. 1826: W. Cazzola, R.J. Stroud, F. Tisato (Eds.), Reflection and Software Engineering. X, 229 pages. 2000.

Vol. 1830: P. Kropf, G. Babin, J. Plaice, H. Unger (Eds.), Distributed Communities on the Web. Proceedings, 2000. X, 203 pages. 2000.

Vol. 1831: D. McAllester (Ed.), Automated Deduction – CADE-17. Proceedings, 2000. XIII, 519 pages. 2000. (Subseries LNAI).

Vol. 1832: B. Lings, K. Jeffery (Eds.), Advances in Databases. Proceedings, 2000. X, 227 pages. 2000.

Vol. 1833: L. Bachmair (Ed.), Rewriting Techniques and Applications. Proceedings, 2000. X, 275 pages. 2000.

Vol. 1834: J.-C. Heudin (Ed.), Virtual Worlds. Proceedings, 2000. XI, 314 pages. 2000. (Subseries LNAI).

Vol. 1835: D. N. Christodoulakis (Ed.), Natural Language Processing – NLP 2000. Proceedings, 2000. XII, 438 pages. 2000. (Subseries LNAI).

Vol. 1837: R. Backhouse, J. Nuno Oliveira (Eds.), Mathematics of Program Construction. Proceedings, 2000. IX, 257 pages. 2000.

Vol. 1838: W. Bosma (Ed.), Algorithmic Number Theory. Proceedings, 2000. IX, 615 pages. 2000.

Vol. 1839: G. Gauthier, C. Frasson, K. VanLehn (Eds.), Intelligent Tutoring Systems. Proceedings, 2000. XIX, 675 pages. 2000.

Vol. 1840: F. Bomarius, M. Oivo (Eds.), Product Focused Software Process Improvement. Proceedings, 2000. XI, 426 pages. 2000.

Vol. 1841: E. Dawson, A. Clark, C. Boyd (Eds.), Information Security and Privacy. Proceedings, 2000. XII, 488 pages. 2000.

Vol. 1842: D. Vernon (Ed.), Computer Vision – ECCV 2000. Part I. Proceedings, 2000. XVIII, 953 pages. 2000.

Vol. 1843: D. Vernon (Ed.), Computer Vision – ECCV 2000. Part II. Proceedings, 2000. XVIII, 881 pages. 2000.

Vol. 1844: W.B. Frakes (Ed.), Software Reuse: Advances in Software Reusability. Proceedings, 2000. XI, 450 pages. 2000.

Vol. 1845: H.B. Keller, E. Plöderer (Eds.), Reliable Software Technologies Ada-Europe 2000. Proceedings, 2000. XIII, 304 pages. 2000.

Vol. 1846: H. Lu, A. Zhou (Eds.), Web-Age Information Management. Proceedings, 2000. XIII, 462 pages. 2000.

Vol. 1847: R. Dyckhoff (Ed.), Automated Reasoning with Analytic Tableaux and Related Methods. Proceedings, 2000. X, 441 pages. 2000. (Subseries LNAI).

Vol. 1848: R. Giancarlo, D. Sankoff (Eds.), Combinatorial Pattern Matching. Proceedings, 2000. XI, 423 pages. 2000.

Vol. 1849: C. Freksa, W. Brauer, C. Habel, K.F. Wender (Eds.), Spatial Cognition II. XI, 420 pages. 2000. (Subseries LNAI).

Vol. 1850: E. Bertino (Ed.), ECOOP 2000 – Object-Oriented Programming. Proceedings, 2000. XIII, 493 pages. 2000.

Vol. 1851: M.M. Halldórsson (Ed.), Algorithm Theory – SWAT 2000. Proceedings, 2000. XI, 564 pages. 2000.

Vol. 1853: U. Montanari, J.D.P. Rolim, E. Welzl (Eds.), Automata, Languages and Programming. Proceedings, 2000. XVI, 941 pages. 2000.

Vol. 1855: E.A. Emerson, A.P. Sistla (Eds.), Computer Aided Verification. Proceedings, 2000. X, 582 pages. 2000.

Vol. 1857: J. Kittler, F. Roli (Eds.), Multiple Classifier Systems. Proceedings, 2000. XII, 404 pages. 2000.

Vol. 1860: M. Klusch, L. Kerschberg (Eds.), Cooperative Information Agents IV. Proceedings, 2000. XI, 285 pages. 2000. (Subseries LNAI).